Richard Gill

Free Trade

An Inquiry into the Nature of its Operation

Richard Gill

Free Trade
An Inquiry into the Nature of its Operation

ISBN/EAN: 9783337063627

Printed in Europe, USA, Canada, Australia, Japan

Cover: Foto ©Suzi / pixelio.de

More available books at **www.hansebooks.com**

FREE TRADE

AN INQUIRY INTO THE NATURE OF ITS OPERATION

BY

RICHARD GILL

WILLIAM BLACKWOOD AND SONS
EDINBURGH AND LONDON
MDCCCLXXXVII

All Rights reserved

PREFACE.

THE present study of the free-trade question was projected with the ultimate view of exposing what the writer still considers to be a very popular delusion. For the prosperity which attended the early operation of the free-trade principle (after a short interval of depression, the terminal period of a natural depression which commenced during the protective system, and encroached upon the first operation of free trade) was then believed very generally, and is supposed now, but in a less degree, to be due to the immediate and benign efficacy of the new principle. To prove the falsity of this inference is the burden of this present treatise. In it there is displayed, and without any prejudice to the requirements of party systems or of hypothesis, the real working of the principle of free trade. From its perusal it will be evident, if the original data are allowed to be true, that prosperity did not succeed free trade as a "direct," but as an "indirect," consequence.

This being so, it will at once be perceived that much of the existing depression in trade is dependent on the partial and unequal action of free trade, and hence that the cause of much, but not all, of the suffering of the poorer classes is derived not from causes which are more or less under their own control, but from the adverse operation of a stern and unyielding principle upon which they cannot possibly possess any direct influence.

R. G.

St Bartholomew's Hospital,
April 1887.

CONTENTS.

CHAPTER I.

THE PROGRESS OF OUR COMMERCE ANTECEDENT TO THE INTRODUCTION OF THE FREE-TRADE PRINCIPLE, ... 1

CHAPTER II.

THE COURSE OF EVENTS WHICH LED UP TO THE INTRODUCTION OF FREE TRADE INTO OUR COMMERCIAL POLICY, ... 40

CHAPTER III.

THE POSITION OF SIR ROBERT PEEL, . 87

CHAPTER IV.

THE PRIMARY AND BENEFICIAL ACTION OF THE FREE-TRADE PRINCIPLE: TO WHAT IT WAS DUE, . 155

CHAPTER V.

CRITICISM OF THE INDIRECT AND DIRECT OPERATIONS OF FREE TRADE, ... 177

CHAPTER VI.

THE DESCRIPTION OF THE DIRECT EFFECTS OF FREE TRADE, ... 224

CHAPTER VII.

THE ATTITUDE OF PARTIES IN THE STATE RESPECTING THE PROGRESS OF OUR COMMERCE, AND THE PRINCIPLES WHICH PRESIDE OVER IT, . . 291

FREE TRADE.

CHAPTER I.

THE PROGRESS OF OUR COMMERCE ANTECEDENT TO THE INTRODUCTION OF THE FREE-TRADE PRINCIPLE.

1. *General view of the course of our trade.*—If we take a retrospective survey of the progress of our trade, we shall find that, under the protective system, the line of advance was broken at intervals by the occurrence of depression; and that, at the period when the principle of free trade was introduced into our commercial code, the various trades and industries were suffering from a recurrence of distress.

But we must observe, in particular, that at this epoch in our commercial policy this arrest in the progress of our trade, judging from experience, was of a temporary character only, and that during the agitation which marked the advocacy of free trade, the country was in a state of disturbance from causes entirely unconnected with it. And we shall perceive, later on, how this feeling on the part of the public was utilised by the free-traders, and diverted from its former narrowed channel into the ocean of a much more vital question.

It will be of advantage to make a cursory observation of some of the more important changes that took place in the progress of our commerce up to the time of the application of the free-trade principle.

By far the most important alteration was the imposition in 1815 of the Corn Laws, a legislative procedure which was initiated by the efforts of those whose interests were associated with the welfare of agriculture.

It was soon determined that the corn-produce of this country tended to be constant, and that, if it fluctuated at all, it was prone to incline towards the direction of decrease. But the population increasing constantly at a certain rate, it thus came to be recognised that this island, now no longer self-supporting with respect to corn, must depend in a gradually increasing larger measure upon foreign sources for the complement of its annual supply.

This difference between Great Britain and other countries was, from a legislative point of view, a fundamental one. There was, however, this to be said in our favour, that if our ability to grow enough corn, owing to the limitation of space, gradually diminished relatively to an increasing population, what we lost in the corn-markets of the foreigner we perhaps more than gained in our export trade, which continued in a flourishing condition.

As the constant untaxed foreign importation of corn would tend to interfere with its cultivation in this country, those who were concerned in its production, together with the owners of the soil, being then powerful enough, demanded that the same protection be allowed the produce of the land as was afforded to our other industries; and such a demand was recognised as being the logical consequence of our established commercial policy, which had for its object the protection of the native industries of the country, which had slowly grown up and been fed by the talent and genius of our countrymen: the ultimate result of which was to place the nation in the most favourable position for supplying its own wants.

This was the corner-stone of the political economy of the protectionists; and where we lost in the importation of certain articles, the chief of which was corn, the balance was more than maintained by the exportation of our manufactured goods, which was slowly but certainly increasing.

The central idea of the policy was—there can be no question about it—a purely selfish one. It was to nourish as far as possible the industries of the country, in order to employ to the fullest extent the labour of its inhabitants.

By this means the system of protection sought to maintain the universal and equable employment of the nation; and with the aid of material prosperity to afford the majority of the people the means leading to content and happiness.

In spite of notions of free trade which then were prevalent, the agricultural and landed interests gained the day. And the Corn Laws, which were in the course of the next thirty years to become the source of so much anxiety, and to offer the main ground of contention between the rival parties in the State, became the laws of the land. The selfish element predominated in the breasts of our ancestors; and free trade had yet to burst through the powerful fence of self-interest.

The next period of import—passing by the occasions when our system was adjusted, on the basis of reciprocity, to alterations in the commercial systems of other nations, which tended to the disadvantage of our trade—was in 1826, when an Order in Council was made to permit the importation of foreign corn, free of duty, on the discretion of the Government.

Thus a means was devised by which the dire consequences of a local scarcity of corn from bad harvests might be counteracted with the greatest efficiency. In 1827 Mr Canning proposed his sliding scale; but this was rejected, as not providing that amount of protection which it was the original intention of the Corn Laws to secure. And in the following year another scale, constructed by Lord Glenelg and Mr Charles Grant, was brought before the Commons, but it met with the same fate as its immediate predecessor. The position of the agriculturists and the landowners was firm and resolute. It was felt that to admit a modification in the existing Corn Laws would be to accelerate the plans of those who, using such a relaxation as a false argument, would endeavour to effect their total repeal.

In 1830 the duty on sugar was reduced by three shillings the hundredweight; and at the same time the customs duties on colonial spirits were diminished by the amount of sixpence per gallon. This reduction took place consequently on a similar remission in the excise duty on home-made spirits. There was some discussion in the House that the colonial spirits should not be affected to the same favourable degree as those home-made. But the distinction between the colonial and home-made was gradually receding. The differences between the mother country and her colonies were not of the same nature as these between the United Kingdom and foreign nations; the element of kinship appeared to remove all those inequalities which remained in the case of the foreigner.

It was in 1839 when Mr Villiers made his celebrated statement in Parliament that universal free trade was possible before the year 1824.

If this was an argument that free trade should be advocated with the greatest zeal, then it is certain that the ardent pleader in the hypothetical justice of his cause completely forgot the grounds on which parallel cases may be constructed.

If free trade was possible before 1824 to all nations of importance, surely the circumstances relating to that possibility, having undergone such changes in the interval as to forbid any resemblance being drawn between the conditions of 1839 and those of 1824, would altogether preclude the assumption of any safe and reliable inference.

In the following year the duties on imported articles were increased "to the extent of five per cent on all raw materials, upon articles of food, upon everything which constituted the import trade of the country." Such an addition was imposed by the Whig Chancellor of the Exchequer, with a view to remove the deficit of the Budget, a deficit which was becoming an annual phenomenon.

The measure, however, did not meet with success. And considering the impoverished state of the country at the time, the trade depression, commencing in 1837, being still in progress, was it likely?

It is curious to observe how this fact was made use of by Sir Robert Peel when he introduced his Bill to reduce, with the final view of their abolition, all import duties, as well as to secure the admission of articles up to the time prohibited. Sir Robert, when he advanced his argument for the reduction of these duties in some cases, and their entire remission in others, stated his conviction that they could not possibly be regarded as a stable source of the revenue of the country; because an attempt had been made by his predecessor to increase the produce of import duties by additional imposts, and had failed.

But Sir Robert Peel did not advance the special reason of this failure. He did not associate this failure on the part of the country with its inability to afford the additional burden which the requirements of the Exchequer had been compelled—and it was a rash compulsion—to place upon it. Take the instance when the country was in a state of prosperity, and the demands of the Exchequer were increasing. In such a case, would not the anticipation of the financier have been realised?

But the assessed taxes answered to the addition imposed upon them. Hence Sir Robert Peel's conclusion: that from this particular example, and when the circumstances of the country were exceptional and unfavourable to indirect taxation, the country was better able generally to bear direct taxation than the burden of an addition to its import duties.

From this general inference, drawn from a particular phenomenon, Sir Robert Peel originated the idea of reimposing the income-tax; the result of which procedure would enable him to effect the complete abolition of all customs duties, and to remove the obstacles which prohibition erected in the extending course of our trade.

In 1841, when Sir Robert Peel was questioned as to his intention regarding the Corn Laws, he accused the noble leader of the Opposition—after referring in a sarcastic manner to the reduction of the import duty on timber as the only means of having conferred any benefit upon the commerce of the country—with having deserted the interests of the country, if he considered that the present Corn Laws required any modification which he had not attempted to effect in them. His party had just emerged from the sphere of power; and if he thought that the Corn Laws had any material share in the causation of the national distress, why had he not proposed some change?

But the fact was that the previous Ministry was not sufficiently powerful to bring about the change they thought desirable: which was that the ordinary Corn Laws be replaced by a fixed duty. And this Sir Robert Peel well knew.

In the following year, however, Sir Robert proposed a sliding-scale, which succeeded in obtaining the assent of both the Houses of Parliament.

But this measure, probably devised to soothe the anxieties of both parties, was regarded by the protectionists as directly tending to deprive them of their customary rights—and as foreshadowing the ultimate repeal of the Corn Laws; and by the free-traders, as not sufficiently meeting the difficulties under which the country was suffering.

But the fears of the protectionists were not allayed; nor were the hopes of the free-traders fulfilled! And thus, by a policy which was intended to diminish opposite feelings, Sir Robert Peel failed in satisfying either party in the State.

The periods of depression which marked the reign of protection varied much in intensity; but they all agreed, in the opinion of Sir Robert Peel, in being the natural result of a low state of interest, and an apparent prosperity of our trades and industries. Such a state of things tended to the excessive advance of money at a minimum cost, and to the indulgence of a wild, and as it was sometimes described, an insane, speculation. But however depressed the trade markets became by this procedure, they subsequently recovered; and if the depression which was hanging over our commerce at the time when Sir Robert Peel acceded to power, was similar in nature to that which had preceded it, the probability was that, after speculation had run its course, the markets would regain their former buoyancy, and the prosperity of the nation be again ensured.

But did this period of depression, which began in 1837, and was still prevailing when Sir Robert Peel referred to the distress of the country in the opening session of the Parliament of 1842, so differ in its causation from those which had previously occurred, and were well within the recollection of many who heard him, as to call for some new legislative treatment, specially applicable to the altered conditions of depression?

Not in the judgment of the Prime Minister: the main source of depression had been at work, and much of its pernicious consequences was still evident. To undue speculation Sir Robert ascribed the origin of the nation's troubles; but in addition to this, the chief cause, other collateral influences had combined their effects with those of the former one to prolong and intensify the distress. But Sir Robert Peel avowed that he had witnessed depression as bad as, or even worse than, the particular one under discussion; and asserted that a sudden revival followed the severest which had come under his observation. He expressly stated his conviction that, in spite of the agitation of the Anti-Corn-Law Leaguers, the operation of the present Corn Laws had no material share in effecting the present ills of the country. The wars in India and China, and strained relations with the nations of Europe, acted "concurrently and simultaneously" with internal causes to bring about the existing distress of the people. But what was the prospect? Sir Robert looked with the greatest confidence to the native energies of his country; and predicted that the progress of natural causes would surmount the obstacle which now obstructed the path of trade prosperity!

The opinion of the highest authority on domestic affairs, as to the causation of the depression of 1837-

1842, was that it differed in no essential feature from those of other periods of depression. What entered to create a slight amount of disagreement between the effects of its combined cause and those of preceding occasions, was that amount of distress, producing the interruption of the ordinary commercial transactions, which follows the conduct of wars in foreign countries, and the presence of unfriendly sentiments towards neighbouring nations. But this was not the opinion of a numerous section, mainly of the manufacturing part of the community, which promulgated the purely abstract doctrine "of buying in the cheapest market and selling in the dearest," and which therefore advocated the principle of free trade.

The distress of the nation, arising from the depressed state of the markets, was ascribed to the vicious influence of the system of protection, which kept out of the country a sufficient amount of raw materials to supply labour for all; and which, by preventing a corresponding increase of the capital of the country, by diminishing a possible enlarged export trade, interfered directly with the natural growth of our commercial industries. The attribute of *natural* was given to the rapid and almost feverish activity of trade by the free-traders; it was reserved by the protectionists for the uniformly gradual and equable advancement of our industries.

But especially were the Corn Laws attacked, as being directly the cause of the high price of bread, and as bearing with undue severity upon those who toil for their daily subsistence.

It was the doctrine of the free-traders that all raw materials should be admitted into this country duty free; and that as corn was the first and the most important of raw materials, the disability under which its admission laboured should be removed.

Great stress, therefore, was laid by the free-traders upon the supposed injustice with which the protective principle bore upon the labouring classes. The application of the free-trade system would reduce the price of bread, and thus would react advantageously for the large manufacturers; and in the eyes of the visionaries, who regarded the principle in the abstract, as if its immediate efficacy would obtain eternally, the first seed was sown for the future and permanent prosperity of the sons of toil.

As long, therefore, as the commerce of the country continued in a flourishing condition under the system of protection, while yet there was no income-tax, and the growth of our trades and industries slowly but equably advanced according to the law which relates to the production of strength and stability, there was no real ground for any alteration in a system under the benign influence of which the nation had overcome the greatest disasters that could befall it—had even attained the successful accomplishment of the most terrible wars.

During prosperity, and while contentment was spread over the land, theoretic legislation had no sound opportunity of improving her claims. But though the times were unfavourable to its development, the spirit of free trade was kept alive mainly in the persons of those who—and some occupied a share in the administration of the country's affairs, and were well read in the hypotheses of Adam Smith—advocated her cause, not unconditionally, as many who subsequently supported the principle imputed to them, but conditionally upon the expectation that free trade should fairly operate throughout the commerce of the world.

Herein lay the difficulty which involved the greater freedom of their action. They could only effect this fair action of a principle, undoubtedly, if rightly employed, potent for good, by a concurrence with similar sentiments on the part of external nations.

Here was an object which, universally pursued, would be attended with general good in the opinion of the free-traders; but the partial attainment of which might be associated with disasters.

But if such an opinion were practically entertained—and there is ground to suppose it was, from the assertion of the Hon. Charles Villiers—the protectionist feeling of the country, which regarded the slow fruits of certainty more favourably than the splendid results of a doubtful experiment, was too powerful to permit of so desirable — from the disinterested point of view — an alteration in international commercial systems, for the influence of agriculture was then in the ascendant.

It is natural thus to suppose that, with such a display of antagonistic feeling, the free-traders would await a lucky moment, when they might advance, with some prospect of success, their truths upon the notice of the nation. Such a time would be supplied by a recurrence of depression; and a new framework of its causation, and the method of its operation, were at hand. The chances, too, of their success would be increased by a continuance and aggravation, it might be, of distress produced by collateral causes, to the proper action of which they would close their eyes.

How difficult it is to convince the public that, while in a state of prosperity, they are pursuing a pernicious policy! But how easy, when a nation is in distress, owing to the operation of natural causes, and when their sufferings may be increased by the occurrence of wars in various parts of the world—how easy it is to point to false causes as the fountains of all their ills!

Then is the lucky moment, when the popular ear may be charmed by whispering into it the means of revenge. It is a dreadful fact to convey, but it is lightly done. The people have been deceived, and there is only one deliverer. Free trade will dissipate the sufferings of the nation.

The paths of plenty and content are opened up. In a moment of passion the people follow the way. Her false leaders depict the grandeur of the objects at the end of the journey, as well to divert attention from off the obstacles which surround their progress as to enliven those who fall by the way in their eager excitement to catch a glimpse of a state of prosperity which exists only in the imagination of their enthusiastic minds.

A people becomes absorbed in the contemplation of false promises. The true causation of distress is deserted: anything to be relieved of our present sufferings, says the spendthrift and reckless, while the thrifty sees in this state of depression the foundations of past expectations and the adequacy of his means to counteract their vicious tendency put to the test.

Thus a favourable opportunity presenting, the free-traders proceeded to the development of new forces; and as they gained the spurious adhesion of their countrymen, so did they gradually become a recognised, though a false, power in the State.

As the free-trade doctrine advanced, so the cause of protection began to wane; and Hypothesis, having at length, but with much patience, overcome the difficulties in which she had been previously involved, now in the ascendant, occupies the position which Experience, for so long a time and with such benefit to the country at large, used to hold.

A change in the balance of our commercial system was on the point of occurring, in which the solid merits of Protection and Experience would be outweighed by the evanescent prosperity which a vain Hypothesis conferred! In 1842 there commenced the gradual introduction of the new system, at the hands of the Minister who had stated the causes of the national distress, and predicted a happy issue of it. The principle upon which Sir Robert Peel acted was to reduce duties of a prohibitory nature gradually, until prohibition was finally abolished.

The articles which came within the sphere of this alteration were the raw materials used in manufacture and certain articles of subsistence. Salted meat was admitted free, fresh meat subjected to a small duty, and live cattle introduced for the first time into this country and without duty. The reason which Sir Robert Peel gave for admitting live cattle duty free was that the growth of the population of this country and the growth of its cattle no longer held their relative proportions. The production of cattle had been decreasing.

The price of meat was thereby being raised; and to supply the deficiency, and to tend to lower the prices, he permitted the admission of foreign cattle.

The remission of taxation continued during the next and following years, and by the commencement of 1845 the effects of the previous depression had nearly disappeared. This gradual improvement in trade had been observed by Sir Robert Peel; and he subsequently alludes to it as being due to the change which he effected in our commercial code. But in the years 1846 and 1847 there again appeared symptoms of aggravated distress; and loud was the clamour, in its first progress, for the removal of its hypothetical cause on the part of the free-traders.

What was the position of Sir Robert Peel with reference to this recurrence of distress? While the operation of free trade was nearly unrestricted, he asserted, in answer to those who laid the blame of distress upon the action of the new principle, that "free trade was not the cause of this distress, but the mitigation of evils and distress then prevalent."

The railway mania of 1845 and 1846, by locking up the capital of the country, and by diverting from the commercial world those resources which ought to have stimulated the circulation of trade and promoted the wages of labour, together with the general deficiency of harvests all over Europe, sufficiently account for this period of depression occurring during the early development of the principle of free trade.

And when the effects of these had passed off, commerce and trade generally began to assume a very lively condition; and in 1848 our exports amounted to £133,000,000, as compared with £59,000,000 in 1847 and £49,000,000 in 1841.

The unfavourable harvests all over the Continent serves to explain the relatively small amount of exported goods during 1847. But after 1848, the excitement of the markets was such that the demands upon them could scarcely be supplied.

It is easy, therefore, to trace the rapid rise which the principle of free trade effected in our commercial and manufacturing systems, when this was left free to act upon surrounding conditions favourable to its development, and no longer trammelled by the influence of adverse forces.

And the immediate consequences were just what the advocates of free trade predicted. Labour was plentiful; wages were high; bread was cheap.

There was only one class of the community left deserted, while the rest of the nation enjoyed the blessings of a temporary prosperity — a prosperity which, so far as the social development of the labourer was concerned, was the harbinger of coming dangers. The agricultural class had been abandoned for the presumed welfare of the country: the part had been sacrificed for the whole.

The repeal of the Corn Laws, so it was said at the time, had sealed the fate of agriculture in this country, and of every one dependent upon it; nor was this surprising, when it was openly proclaimed that England was essentially a manufacturing country, and that agriculture had come to occupy a subordinate place in her industries.

But despite the efforts of the protectionists to stand

by agriculture in her hour of need, the farmers of this country were, by the adverse action of free trade, the first to feel its untoward effects, for they were left at once to the mercy of foreign competition.

So long as the principle of free trade was unhindered by some of its own effects, and so long as we retained entire possession over neutral markets, the wealth of this country continued rapidly to increase, and the prosperity of labour to flow.

But even these times of prosperity are characterised by the natural recurrence of trade-depression.

And when surrounding nations are developing their internal resources, and are beginning to enter those fields of industry which had been entirely our own; when competition arises, and the foreigner is enabled to supply the customary articles at a cheaper rate; then, when the equilibrium in external commercial relations, disturbed by the application of a new principle, has been established by the activity and enterprise of surrounding nations, will the scale descend against the prospects of free trade, and our commerce begin to decline!

And when such unfavourable conditions as these exist, what benefit does the free-trader derive from importing raw materials, free of duty, when the congested state of the markets cannot be relieved?

For it is obvious that the markets will become congested when, the supplies remaining constant or increasing, the demands upon them diminish.

And what direct loss does this free-trade country sustain by her articles being subjected to a tariff in foreign ports?

The loss is the amount of duty which our merchants pay upon the admission of their manufactured goods into foreign countries, and which may be applied, and is sometimes, for the purpose of assisting a growing industry there by means of a bounty, in order that the foreign merchant may be enabled to undersell the free-trade merchant, and thus directly protect the labour of his own countrymen.

But the free-trade merchant throws the whole of his loss upon labour.

What, then, is it that suffers by means of this inequality, between free trade and protection ?

It is labour, and free-trade labour too.

Sir Robert Peel states in one of his speeches that "a constant, injurious, and exhausting process is going forward." This was before the introduction of free trade. It seems as if this exhausting process had reached its culmination in the present day, for with so unequal a method of competing with the trade of the foreigner, we may, in truth, be accused of courting our own failure, and increasing our own distress!

2. *The course of our trade under the system of protection is graphically depicted on the opposite page.*

3. *Conclusions to be drawn therefrom.*—Sir Robert Peel clearly indicated the special feature of our growing trade when he compared its slow but certain advance under the policy of protection with its sudden rise when that practical system was rudely interrupted by the introduction of the principle of free trade.

There was the slowly but surely increasing growth of

FREE TRADE.

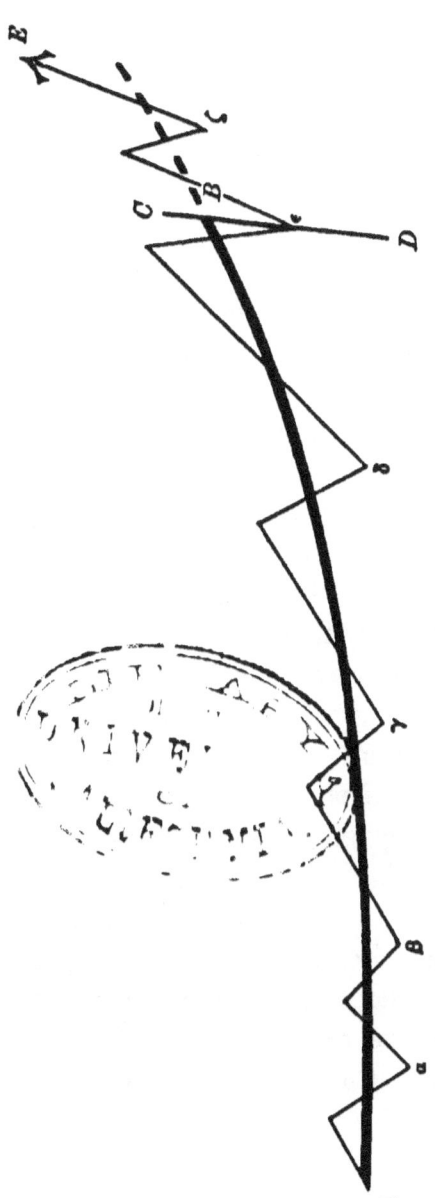

AB = the curve of the equable advance of our trade under system of protection, broken at CD = the epoch of the introduction of the free-trade principle. This is shown by gradually increasing exports: thus — 1827-32, 37 millions; 1832-37, 43 millions; 1837-42, 49 millions. (These are the averages for each year, taken from Sir Robert Peel's figures.)

$a, \beta, \gamma, \delta, \epsilon,$ and ζ mark periods of depression which assume a paroxysmal or recurrent character. All these periods had in common two factors according to Sir Robert Peel—(1) A low state of interest; and (2) A comparative state of commercial prosperity preceding them. Each had special causes: thus, in 1816 it was in convertible paper-money; in 1819, the restoration to the metallic standard; in 1826, the abuse of the unlimited discretion which the bank had of the issue of notes, "a condition favourable to wild and insane speculation."

ζ = the period of depression during the early operation of the free-trade principle.

The dotted line denotes the trade increase due to natural growth.

E = the stimulation to trade markets by application of artificial principle of free trade by Legislature.

the native industries of the country—a growth which had a certain relation to the gradually increasing number of its inhabitants.

Did it occur to Sir Robert Peel to discover this intimate relation, and to foretell the consequences which might possibly attend its disturbance?

Thus, suppose the case of a period of depression like unto the one then prevalent throughout the country. There would be a certain distress ensuing under protection; but if under free trade, England being isolated in her general commercial policy, a larger amount would ensue, by reason of a slowly but constantly exhausting drain upon the resources of the country. For when our markets were contracted, the foreign duty on our manufactured articles would be the more felt by us. Under such circumstances, and as labour is the final source which bears this loss, would not the ill be thereby greatly augmented in the case of a population which is gradually increasing while the means of occupation were becoming more and more restricted, and, it may happen to be, altogether destroyed?

What, it may well be asked, was the particular motive which impelled Sir Robert, under the comparatively favourable circumstances of our trade during that period of depression, to make an alteration in its equable advance, the ultimate consequences of which he could not certainly portray?

Did he prognosticate the operation of the free-trade principle in the possible case when this country alone should remain a free-trader?

The fact remains that in spite of our exports increasing while depression continued to reign in the markets, Sir Robert Peel was induced to alter the principle of our commercial code.

There can be no doubt that he utilised the hypothetical truths of the free-traders in order that he might place the national finances on a more solid foundation than they had lately been; and also that he might dry up the springs of an agitation that was likely to become prejudical to the national interests.

Remembering the statement which he made over and over again, that the operation of the Corn Laws had no material share in the causation of the ills of the country, the question inevitably arises—

Did Sir Robert Peel, pursuing a policy of expediency, make use of the free-trade principle to tide over a national crisis, the magnitude of which he exaggerated, and the purpose of which he appears to have ignored? or, Did he really believe in the eternal and unconditional efficacy of this free-trade principle, whose action was to be attended with prosperity to the nation at all times, and no matter what were the varying characters of the external conditions which affected the sphere of its influence?

4. *The basis of the protective system.*—The grounds upon which the founders of our commercial system protected the native industries of the country were those simply of self-interest. In every commercial bargain the tendency always exists for both the contracting parties to be gainers by the result: thus a species of mutual reciprocity is established.

From the earliest times, when England began to

export her manufactured goods, her intercourse with foreign nations was constructed on the lines which govern such intercourse between individual and individual. This idea of the growth of our commercial policy was entertained by Sir Robert Peel, and he gave expression to it in the House of Commons.

Gain, therefore, is the mutual end of each international treaty, as it is in the case of every individual bargain. And each party seeks to be, relatively, the greater gainer of the two. Thus it was when Mr Pitt displayed his reasons for endeavouring to effect a commercial treaty with France in 1785. This is the vital principle which underlies the conduct of all commerce and trade. To neglect it is to shut our eyes, as practical men, to a motive from which we can never become freed. For the motive of self-interest is predominant throughout the commercial world.

There are many proofs of the jealousy with which former legislators regarded the relationship of our trade connections.

Even when it was proposed to admit Ireland to the advantages which our extensive foreign and colonial trade offered, the opposition with which it was met, and especially in the northern provinces of the kingdom, was bitter and vindictive. In 1780, when Lord North was at the head of the Government, measures were taken to introduce Ireland to a share in our colonial trade. To these the shipowners were particularly antagonistic, quite irrespective of their tendency towards a just and enlarged policy of the nation; but none were more hostile to them than the shipowners of Liverpool. These gentlemen declared that if Ireland were allowed to participate in our colonial trade, " the town of Liverpool would inevitably be reduced to its original insignificance."

And so in 1785, when Mr Pitt endeavoured to seal more closely the union between the two kingdoms by means of a single commercial code, the opposition with which his Bill was met, both on this and the other side of the water, was such as to increase rather than allay the ill-feeling which the sister islands, perhaps naturally, entertained for one another.

After much discussion, carried on with much heat and temper, and after his first Bill was rejected by the Irish Parliament then sitting in Dublin — for there were many who regarded this enlarged policy as a means of aggrandising the trade interests of Great Britain at the expense of Ireland, and some who held that the smaller nation ought by right to be protected from the grasping tendencies of a larger and more flourishing community—the second Bill of Mr Pitt, to cement the commercial union between Great Britain and Ireland, was passed by both Parliaments and became law. And Great Britain and Ireland thus came to be, with some slight exceptional articles, free-traders, with respect to their mutual commercial policy.

But so strong was the influence of the East India interest, and such the peculiar support by which the Company's trade was secured, that it was impossible, at this time, to do more than to afford a slight relaxation of their stringent regulations in favour of Ireland. For it was the object of Mr Pitt to place Ireland exactly on the same level of commercial advantages as Great Britain. But this happy issue did not take place till the year of the Union, 1800, when Mr Pitt's effort was crowned with success, and Ireland became as free a participator, nominally, in the East India trade as Great Britain was.

It is of importance to discern the motive which impelled Mr Pitt to this course of action.

The foundation of it was to remove all grounds of complaint on the part of Ireland, and to afford her every facility for developing prosperity in her commercial progress.

By increasing the ordinary trade between the sister kingdoms, and by the removal of inequalities, a larger intercourse between the inhabitants of the two isles would result, with the supposed beneficent intent of allaying any sources of irritation which might remain, and of dissipating all opportunity of discord and hostility between the different races of the Anglo-Saxon and the Celt.

This advantageous result of international treaties was still further enlarged upon by the same Minister, when, in bringing forward the outline of a commercial treaty with France, which he abundantly proved would react with enormous benefit in our favour, he asserted that the increased development of this intercourse between different nations, of opposite manners and habits of life, was the principal means of disarming unworthy suspicion and the spirit of hostility.

Why, then, did not Mr Pitt advocate, universally, the principle of free trade?

Why did he remain content with having effected its partial operation between Great Britain and Ireland?

And when he introduced free trade into the commercial relations of the United Kingdom, why did he not extend this supposed benefit to mankind at large— to all the other nations of the world ?

The action of Mr Pitt is to be regarded as a means to an end. His policy with reference to Ireland is clear and distinct. The commercial union was but the antecedent to a legislative union, which the far-seeing statesman anticipated was necessary for the tranquillity and safety of both kingdoms.

Ireland was a weak point in the British empire, and might become the centre of attack by a neighbouring foe, as happened not long afterwards, when France became a republic. It was of paramount importance to weld the different parts of the British empire into one solid whole, and the simplest and surest method Mr Pitt followed, when he aimed at gaining the confidence and goodwill of the Irish people. The union was to be founded on similarity of hopes and international friendship, as against that kind of false union which is effected by the aid of arms.

What, therefore, Ireland was to gain by those concessions, which were regarded as being nothing short of ruinous to the interests of this country, the whole empire was to gain by the additional strength which would accrue to it, from the causes of disaffection and sedition being banished from a small part of it for ever! This was the position of Mr Pitt when he struggled for that intimate union between the two kingdoms, as tending to the increased security of both.

When, therefore, he enunciated the doctrine of free trade between Great Britain and Ireland, his motive was self-evident. But what motive had he to introduce the principle of free trade into the commercial code of the United Kingdom?

Where was the similarity in relationship between the United Kingdom and any other country, and Great Britain and Ireland? Where the security, that if a change in commercial relations were effected by one people, it would be followed by another?

Mr Pitt's policy brought the commercial codes of the kingdoms of Great Britain and Ireland under the controlling action of a single force. It is obvious that such a result, however much it may be desired by philanthropists, is impossible where treaties are entered upon by foreign countries, for the security of the action of a single force is no longer attainable.

Nowhere, in any of his commercial speeches, does Mr Pitt notice even the possibility of such altered state of affairs.

But what was his intention with reference to those treaties which he attempted to conclude, and succeeded in some instances, with foreign nations? Gain to his country. Thus, in the commercial treaty which he proposed to France, he demonstrated completely how we should be the largest gainers. France was a much larger kingdom than our own; our exported articles of manufacture were of much greater use than their imported wines; our field of operation in France would be conterminous with the limits of the country; the stimulus given to our manufactures would spread its effects through the greater part of this country, and affect, proportionately, a very large part of its inhabitants; while the reaction upon the vineyards of France would be limited to a comparatively small space, and benefit only a very small number of its population.

And these were the means by which he asserted in Parliament that the hostile spirit of nations was to be destroyed!

But it has been announced by the upholders of the free-trade doctrine that Mr Pitt's sentiments and policy, when reduced to a common term, form a link in the chain of reasoning, the terminal element of which is the establishment of the efficacy of the free-trade principle. And the grounds upon which such a precarious adhesion is maintained are—1, the introduction of free trade between this country and Ireland, as anticipating the subsequent and general development of international free trade; and 2, the enormous benefits which would accrue from a more extended and constant commercial intercourse between nations, inasmuch as it would tend to consume their energies in the direction of peaceful pursuits, and to restrain, by such a means, a natural and warlike disposition, as shown by the important results Mr Pitt deduced from the increase of international commercial treaties.

Those, however, who care to analyse the motives which prompt men to action, will conclude that, whatever may have been Mr Pitt's hypothetical sentiments concerning free trade, his practice is based upon the foundations of past experience and present security.

But the free-traders, stretching this point, infer that while Mr Pitt regarded the desirability of this end, he must of necessity have admitted that free trade, by stimulating international intercourse, would gain the end in a more rapid manner than our commercial system under protection; and therefore that, from a logical point of view, Mr Pitt was a free-trader.

There is an error, however, which underlies this chain of reasoning, and which reflects not a little upon the soundness of judgment which this illustrious statesman is made, in this so arbitrary a fashion, to display. It consists in the assumption that free trade is the only cause which can effect the end in view, instead of being one of several causes, and then only acting beneficially when surrounding circumstances are favourable.

What about the certainty of free trade being capable of consummating that gigantic object which alone can satisfy the desire of the man of peace, of labour, and of thought?

There was evidence enough at the commencement, and surrounding circumstances remaining in a favourable condition, that the application of free trade to our commercial system would bring about such an alteration in our ordinary commercial relations with the rest of the universe, as to make the majority of mankind forget, for a while, why there should be any cause of enmity between them.

But regard the remote consequences of the introduction of the new principle, the many obstacles that may possibly attend its course, and imagine that ultimate result, when subsequent events are framed, on the part of external Powers, to act adversely to its growth and development, and therefore to the appearance of that "peace on earth" which is the outcome of philanthropic legislation so called.

What if surrounding nations might refuse to follow the lead which this country gives, in the progress of civilisation, to overthrow the barbarous custom of warfare; but, at the same time, to react, for a given period, towards the improvement of its own wealth and the increase of its own resources?

In such a possible state of future affairs, how would the free-trade principle diminish the spirit of international enmity, which is but the exaggeration of the spirit of individual rivalry?

The sources of discord and hostility have not been destroyed by this measure—nay, rather, they are inflamed and increased—for the supreme temporary ascendancy such a policy would acquire for this nation would be regarded with the fierce eyes of envy by those who would look upon the adoption of such a departure from the natural course of commercial growth as opposed to their own individual, slow but constantly increasing, development.

What hatred, then, would be engendered in the breasts of those who were affected adversely by the partial operation of the free-trade principle, by the experience of their commercial progress arrested, and their trade in part destroyed!

It is not possible, therefore, that neighbouring nations should become more intimately connected, especially when so arbitrary a policy is enacted directly against the individual interests of each.

And what would result? The experience of an injustice sharpens rivalry; energies are developed and extended until the effects of that injustice are effaced; and during the interval, hatred and hostility are nourished with the thoughts of future vengeance!

Such a possibility must have occurred to the fertile

imagination of Mr Pitt. Is it the object of a wise legislator to increase the chances of raising up afresh and maintaining the spirit of international hostility?

The error above alluded to, which pervades the arguments of the free-traders, is concealed in the assumption that, of the two ways of promoting the commerce of nations, free trade operating partially is the most rapid and the most certain.

It is obvious that when these two so widely different means are regarded, not only must their immediate results, whether beneficial or adverse from the ideal point of view, be contrasted, but their future consequences as well. And who could contemplate the course of the free-trade principle, acting with restriction and therefore inefficiently, without calling up the disasters that would surely attend its path?

Free trade might indeed, for the time, appear to the eye of the prejudiced to be invested with the especial function of spreading peace over the earth. But upon what do they build? Upon the insecure expectation that the operation of their principle shall become universal. Such do not apprehend the germs of future dangers which the united action of the free-trade principle scatters in its course towards decline.

Many during the time that the free-trade doctrine was discussed must have weighed the relative merits of the systems of free trade and protection in effecting the closer intimacy between the nations of the world, and intending to remove the bane of international enmity.

And in the discussion the question must have arisen, whether or not the great object of mind—the diffusion of peace throughout the world—would be more certainly effected by a slow but sure process,—a process which, however gradual it might be in its development, tended to diminish the subsequent occurrence of evils, —or by the sudden interruption of the former means adapted to this end, the immediate effects of which, for the time, might flatter the hopes and exalt the vanity of those who believed—and believed, how falsely and how dangerously!—that so large a measure as the pacification of the world could be effected by such precarious means in so short a space of time.

Besides, the simple fact, perhaps not understood by all, could hardly have escaped the observation of those who, directly concerned in the management of their country's affairs, remarked the inequality which characterised the various stages of the civilisations of surrounding nations and the different periods of their commercial growth.

With such a difference between contemporary levels, how could those nations on a lower level be expected to regard those on a higher with aught but jealousy and envy?

This source of international inequality was present during the reign of protection, and is a natural cause of hostility.

If free trade was introduced, even universally, would these different levels be reduced to one and the same level in a comparatively short time? If not, an interval would elapse; and, in this interval, the same jealousy, which before existed under protection, would continue during the operation of free trade.

Does free trade, then, abolish all the sources of jealousy and enmity in the world?

The protectionists had this in their favour, that they followed the simple beauty of the curve in the development of their commercial progress. They took the course prescribed by nature. The evils which they recognised as existing in the system of protection—and what system is devoid of evils?—would gradually be removed in course of time. What they most of all dreaded was the introduction of a new principle, the action of which was violent, and whose results were involved in the obscurity of uncertainty. In a word, they preferred the present safe guidance of experience to the dangerous drifting of a hypothetical policy!

The action of Mr Pitt is sufficient proof that he doubted the certainty of this method of free trade when foreign nations are concerned; and his continuance of a system which had grown up with the wants of the commercial part of our community, goes to show that the desirable object of universal peace was to be best attained by the slow and equable advance of our trade and commerce, and by the maintenance of the principle by which they were then regulated.

Nor was Canning, the favourite pupil of Pitt, any more the advocate of the abstract principle of free trade than was his master.

Canning was the disciple of progress and reform, but only when these were associated with the material well-being of the nation. He was perhaps the most brilliant exponent of a tendency which was making fast efforts in his day towards liberalisation in our foreign and domestic policy. But no matter what the nature of his dealings with foreign Powers, they were all founded upon the basis of mutual reciprocity. When the Spanish colonies revolted, and while Spain was assuming a threatening aspect towards this country, Mr Canning, then the Foreign Secretary, took the advantage of recognising the independence of the new republics, to weaken the position of Spain in Europe. " I called the new world into existence to redress the balance of the old." And so with reference to the sliding-scale which he proposed in 1827. While admitting the justice of the Corn Laws, as the very means of advancing the cultivation of the soil, his liberal spirit urged him to relax in some degree their stringency. And so in the case of Mr Huskisson's policy: whatever may have been the true nature of his sentiments, the actions of that politician were founded purely on reciprocity. Thus when, in 1816, the United States, in following our example and protecting her native industries, acted in a manner prejudicial to our commercial interests in that country, it was deemed advisable that the hitherto stringent regulations of our system should be relaxed; but the change was based upon the event of good accruing to both peoples.

And so in 1824, when Prussia followed suit, the same relaxation was advantageously given; and afterwards to Sweden, Norway, and other countries.

Mr Huskisson has been held up to public notice by the free-traders as having entertained decided views with regard to the efficacy of their principle. But the influence of even so high an authority on the subject of commercial affairs is a little weakened by the fact that he was not a consistent upholder of the doctrine; and we have the evidence of Sir Robert Peel, when defending his own position in 1846, that Mr

C

Huskisson had wavered considerably in his attitude towards the subject of the Corn Laws; and that he had more than once changed his mind on the beneficial operation of these measures; and even when he was supposed to have arrived at a final conclusion, that he had changed his views again.

But, whatever his true position with reference to the principle by which our trade should be regulated, no one can deny that any legislator, however ardent an advocate he may have been of progress and reform, conceived, at the time, that this abstract principle of free trade would not act in any other manner except for the interests of the nation at large.

Much may have been pleaded that the adaptation of the free-trade principle would lead to the pacification of the world. But the believers in the doctrine could not shut their eyes to the plain fact that free trade, even though operating partially, in their own opinion would work to the advantage of the nation, however much they may have lauded its efficacy in other channels. What was nearest the heart of these enthusiastic pleaders was the gain which would accrue from its application to our commercial code.

But selfishness ever wishes to be concealed, and so free trade was praised, not because it would certainly increase the wealth and add to the prosperity of the country, but because of its other and more special virtues, and in particular, its civilising influence upon mankind at large.

It is not difficult to show that, whatever may have been the original intention of the founder and the early promoters of the doctrine of free trade, the motives of those who most of all agitated for its introduction, were peculiarly narrow ones. For who were the chief supporters of the Anti-Corn-Law League? The manufacturers of the northern counties.

And upon what grounds, so far as this country's welfare was concerned, did they advance the efficacy of the free-trade principle? Upon the grounds that its application would stimulate trade and commerce; that it would thereby cheapen bread and raise wages; and that it would increase their profits, and so tend to their own aggrandisement.

What they claimed, in a moment of general forgetfulness of its wider influence, as the first-fruits of the principle, was the improvement of the social condition of the labouring mass: they forgot to mention the means thus afforded to them of indefinitely increasing their own riches!

Thus, apart from the notions of some theorising politicians, the free-trade principle was really advocated upon and carried by self-interest. And self-interest of what nature? Was it that self-interest which regarded more the future, and was satisfied with the abandonment of certain privileges, if this nation was to enjoy an increase in her prosperity in common with the other nations of the world? or was it that kind of self-interest which is concentrated in the proper advancement of the welfare of one's own country, as opposed to that of surrounding kingdoms?

It was neither of these; the selfish interest which won the cause of free trade in this land was the selfish interest of class. A portion of the community separated itself from the rest, and identified its welfare with the welfare of the whole nation. In this alone is the peculiar selfishness of free-trade politics exhibited.

The difference between the motives upon which protection was based and by which free trade was introduced is nothing. For they both spring directly from self-interest. Where the difference appears is in the intention with which they were severally put into practice.

Protection had for its sole object the proper advance and welfare of all the classes of the community; its sphere, therefore, was general: while that of free trade was partial from the very first, for it regarded only the immediate prospects of the manufacturing interest at the expense of the agricultural; nor did it secure, even in the faintest degree, the ultimate prosperity of the former.

The difference in the actions of the two principles is worthy of remark. There was abundant evidence of the safety and security provided by the policy of protection. Its course could be proved by the latest statistics to be sufficiently certain. For the surrounding conditions remained in a similar state. But when free trade was introduced, it must have appeared obvious to all, even to the most sanguine of the free-traders, that the relations which our commerce had before with external nations must become disordered. And who could with certainty trace the ultimate course which these altered conditions might take?

But certainty was deserted for uncertainty: rights which had existed since the earliest days of our commercial growth were abandoned; and the possibility of the reckless sacrifice of the future commercial prosperity of the country was for the first time introduced by a Minister, for the mere sake of tiding over, with the hollow object of giving the public affairs a more stable appearance, the then depressed state of the nation.

Whatever grounds, then, philanthropic legislation may obtain from the sentiments which many illustrious statesmen of this country are supposed to have entertained with reference to the subject of free trade, it is certain that the policy of these same statesmen, with the single exception of Sir Robert Peel, pursued the paths of experience. And it is curious to observe that, while those who were free-traders hypothetically, acted on the policy of protection, some who subsequently were powerful advocates of the value of the new principle, had previously and freely expressed their sentiments in favour of protection — a contrast of opinion all the more extraordinary as occurring within so short a period of time.

For what was the opinion of Lord John Russell in 1822? "Let but the foreigner once compete with the agriculture of this country, and she is destroyed."

What peculiar influence was that which led the noble lord, from countenancing the ordinary operation of the Corn Laws, to incline to the opinion that a "fixed duty" was the proper means of satisfying the conditions of the times in 1842? And what alteration occurred in the circumstances in which he found himself placed in 1845, to justify him in abandoning the notion of a fixed duty and in advocating the free admission of corn?

Had the time arrived when even Lord John Russell could no longer conceal his true sentiments on the vexed question of the day?

The opinion of Sir Robert Peel is well known, and was delivered on many occasions in Parliament before the actual period of the repeal of the Corn Laws.

" Existing rights were to be maintained, and the cultivation of the land protected."

What was the directing force which effected so unseemly a contradiction in his ultimate position ? The critical state of public affairs, based upon the supposed injustice of the Corn Laws, but really deriving its origin from a widely different source.

Sir Robert Peel exaggerated the magnitude of the agitation with which he had to deal. He failed to perceive the foundations upon which it was constructed, and he entirely misapprehended its tendency.

To conclude. It can scarcely with justice be inferred that, however ardent an advocate of reform, Mr Canning was a free-trader, simply because he introduced a sliding-scale to prevent the excessive action (as he supposed it then to be) of the existing Corn Laws. If Mr Canning supposed this action to be excessive, justice would impel him to restrict their operation by a new system, within the limits which the Corn Laws were originally intended to possess. To reduce the action of a principle from an unjust to a proper extent, is not an argument to abolish the principle altogether. Is it difficult to imagine that a principle may be sound in structure, but that its operation may exceed what it was at first intended to effect ? So much regarding Mr Canning's position as a free-trader. Let us proceed to the inference to be drawn from Mr Pitt's policy affecting Ireland.

It is obvious that the conditions existing between England and Ireland, at the time that free trade was applied to the commerce of the two nations, totally differed from those which obtained between the United Kingdom and any of the surrounding nations.

Can any sound conclusion be derived from such a hypothetical parallel as that which results from supposing that the conditions which existed between the United Kingdom and a foreign Power were similar to those which had existed between England and Ireland before their legislatures were incorporated into one Parliament?

CHAPTER II.

THE COURSE OF EVENTS WHICH LED UP TO THE INTRODUCTION OF FREE TRADE INTO OUR COMMERCIAL POLICY.

5. *The free-trade agitation.*—While the prospect of greater gain impelled the manufacturers to promote the advancement of the free-trade principle, the reasons of those who had steadily opposed the new system were gradually overcome by the economic doctrine of the free-traders, "of buying in the cheapest market and selling in the dearest." This Sir Robert Peel himself subsequently admitted; and Sir James Graham, in his place in Parliament, asserted that it was impossible any longer to withstand belief in the economic principles of the free-traders, and that all men of sense were already agreed as to their general truth.

The subject against which the free-traders specially levelled their arguments was the protection which was still afforded to the cultivation of the soil. Their object was to demolish completely the grounds upon which the protective system was based, and to overwhelm the uniform phalanx of the protectionists, who were thus driven to preside over the welfare of agriculture.

Corn was still subjected to a duty on admission into our ports. They advanced, therefore, their fundamental proposition, that, as "corn was the chief and most important of raw materials," it should be admitted into the country duty free. And while the free-trade principle was in partial operation, and when live cattle were freely imported, so eager were they for the near fulfilment of their designs, that they censured the logic of the Minister who allowed the free importation of live animals, but taxed the food upon which they were fed. They pictured in glowing colours the prosperity which would attend the unrestricted development of their favourite principle; and in order to arouse an enthusiasm among the labouring classes, assumed a spurious connection between trade depression and the Corn Laws. In a word, the goal of free-trade aspiration was the repeal of the Corn Laws.

Opposed to this assault upon an important branch of national industries, the agricultural interest withstood any further alteration in the Corn Laws than what was enacted by the sliding-scale of 1842; and commenced to upbraid a Minister who had been borne to power by virtue of their influence. Still Sir Robert Peel reiterated that the operation of the Corn Laws was not the cause of the country's depression; and while endeavouring to conciliate the popular agitation, which was already being displayed in favour of their repeal, by large remissions of taxation, he struggled to retain the support of his old party.

At this time the opinion of Lord John Russell, which,

like most others, underwent the usual course of vacillation during this critical period, was in favour of a fixed duty.

Thus the leaders of the rival parties in the State held views respecting this important question which were antagonistic to what is represented as the true expression of public opinion of those days.

But one argument, as fallacious as most of the rest, was urged by the free-traders as likely to have influence upon those of philanthropic tendencies, and whose desire it was to mitigate the hard condition of the working classes. It was this: that corn was maintained at a high price, with the single purpose of increasing rent. This statement had particular effect on Sir Robert Peel, and he animadverted upon it in Parliament, as exhibiting a source of mischief which was likely to end in the ruin of labour. There can be no doubt, from his subsequent action to his tenants in 1846, that he was firmly convinced of its truth.

It is quite possible that on certain occasions the price of corn might be affected by this natural phenomenon. But it is clear that such occasions are quite exceptional; nevertheless, from these particular and easily explicable data, the free-traders drew the general conclusion, and fenced it round with the sentiment of injustice.

And Sir Robert Peel, thus regarding the assertion in an unlimited sense, instead of referring it to those periods when, to pursue that line of action which takes place in every other branch of industry, the prices are raised by the farmers to meet the demands which are made upon them, fell into the trap.

At any rate, the conflict between the manufacturing and agricultural interests was nearing a bitter termination. And it reached its climax when the free-trade rhetoricians boasted that England no longer was an agricultural country; as if this were a sufficient argument, while agriculture was still in a flourishing condition, why wrong should be done to tens of thousands of the inhabitants of the country. But the protectionists had some hopes, though they were meagre ones; for while the favours shown to free trade were gradually increasing, Sir Robert Peel, whatever his inmost sentiments may have been, was still out of doors the upholder of those existing rights which attached to the soil.

But to expose the fluctuating nature of opinion during the free-trade agitation, the labouring classes at first were taught to believe that the tyranny of their masters was the cause of all their sufferings. The action of the workmen in the south of Lancashire shows the animosity which prevailed on one side. These men had been cajoled by specious demagogues into the belief that they would never succeed in obtaining their rights unless the Chartist demands were forced from an unwilling Parliament. It was not without some difficulty as to the nature of the means to be employed, that the leaders of the free-trade movement eventually gained over the adhesion of the working classes to the merits of their cause, by pointing to the free-trade principle as containing the germ of that contentment for which they were clamouring.

But when master and man had come at last to combine their efforts, then the importance of the anti-corn movement rapidly increased; and the conclusion became irresistible, that the Anti-Corn-Law League was a power in the State. And so indefatigable were the exertions of the promoters of free trade, that the farmers were at last converted to a belief in the new principle; for their rent would be diminished thereby, and a diminution of rent would be associated with an increase in profit. As a natural consequence of the latter desirable result, the agricultural labourers' wages would be raised. The means, however, which the free-traders practised in some instances cannot be described as being very far removed from the imputation of being dishonest. Thus the evidence of one agricultural labourer, "I be protected and I be starving," was circulated far and wide, with the obvious intention of associating in the minds of the ignorant labourers their starving condition with the system of protection, which had been wisely framed for their general benefit. In the face of the experience of past periods of depression, such a false association was not worthy of the merest consideration. Was the present depression anything different from previous ones? Sir Robert Peel said not; but the free-traders, in their eager anxiety to advance what they held to be a righteous principle, condescended to the practice of a lower standard of morality in their endeavour to win the support of the lowest classes of the community.

With what truth might the statement have been advanced if they could have shown that, as depression was a natural phenomenon, and free trade in no way able to counteract its occurrence without protection, the chances of the labourers starving would thereby have been considerably diminished?

Has subsequent experience proved that these chances

have been decreased under the "benign" influence of the principle of free trade?

The time when the Anti-Corn-Law League became a powerful instrument in the State was when Mr Cobden succeeded in removing its headquarters from Manchester to London. Thus, from being a provincial movement, identified with the interests of the manufacturers, and therefore regarded with suspicion by those who held the welfare of their country at heart, it began to assume a metropolitan character: it now no longer was confined within its former narrow boundaries; its object was brought before the notice of the whole nation, and its cause was pleaded, and pleaded eloquently, by Mr Cobden in the House of Commons.

It is a subject of remark that the Anti-Corn-Law Leaguers made no progress beyond their own contracted sphere, till the advocates of the repeal of the Corn Laws transferred the base of their operations to the metropolis.

It is true that the Hon. Mr Pelham Villiers had brought forward his annual motion for the abolition of the corn-tax for some years previously to the time when Mr Cobden took the helm of the repeal agitation into his hands. But this annual motion was preferred, simply to be rejected; and it subsequently came to be regarded as an annual farce.

Still, the position of the Hon. Mr Villiers respecting the abolition of the Corn Laws may be said to have been, what cannot be remarked of Mr Cobden, of the kind called disinterested. Mr Villiers advocated the cause of free trade on purely abstract grounds; he stood aloof at first from all appearance of agitation, but eventually, when the Leaguers sought his assistance, he gave it willingly.

On the other hand, Cobden was a cotton-spinner, and would become materially benefited by the introduction of the free-trade principle. He was essentially the champion of the manufacturing interests; and inasmuch as these were taken to be representative of the entire nation, he was naturally regarded as the organ of popular opinion. There can be no question, when Mr Cobden's position is considered with reference to only one portion of time, and that the period of prosperity which was assumed, and assumed on good grounds, to be the immediate effect of the operation of the free-trade principle, that it is entirely a genuine one. What he knew very well would take place, was that all the trade markets would be violently stimulated; that the merchants would, in consequence, increase the field of labour, and that therefore the condition of the working man would be greatly improved. But antecedent to the prosperity of the labourer must be the prosperity of the master. And where Mr Cobden's short-sighted policy comes within the measure of the severest censure is, that he made no ultimate provision for the prosperity of the working man when the prosperity of the merchant was unattainable. Besides, by this action, when the condition of commercial affairs might, from many natural causes, fall into the deepest depression, would the labourer be placed in any more favourable position than he was under the existing system of protection? Would he not rather suffer the more, from the simple fact that his labour was no longer protected? And compare under such distressing circumstances the relative positions of the merchant and his labourer. The farmer, by the happy turn events took, would be enabled to amass a relatively large fortune; the hardships of duties would not bear upon him, however much they might affect his successors; but the labouring man—in what particular would his lot be softened? It is not the general character of the working man to save much of his weekly earnings: what, then, can he console himself with but the memory of brighter times? And what directly brought these bright times about? An Act of Parliament. Thus is he led unconsciously to put his faith in the power of the Legislature to bring back that prosperity which he once enjoyed. Thus is he liable to be entrapped by the false promises of the designing rhetor, who aims at becoming popular by the precarious method of advancing the cause of the people.

Did Mr Cobden or any of his colleagues frame any means to counteract the influence of free trade, supposing this to become in the course of time pernicious?

The peculiar feature of the oratory of the free-traders was that their allusions were altogether limited to the immediate effect of their favourite principle. They looked not ahead; no complications were enumerated as likely, under certain conditions, to affect its progress injuriously; the remote effects of free trade were allowed by the free-traders to take care of themselves.

But the nature of parliamentary opinion was entirely adverse to the cause of free trade. The landed interest, which had raised Peel to power, was represented by a large majority, and this was naturally in favour of protection to the cultivation of the soil; and there were strong reasons why the landlords should take this course, for there were many burdens upon the land.

Out of doors, therefore, there was a violent movement in the direction of free trade. The meetings which were held in its favour were always attended with uproar, and oftentimes terminated by assault. The blessings the new principle was to bring in its train and the prosperity which was to attend the country were so zealously, if ignorantly, portrayed to the ravished senses of the mob, that the enthusiasm of the sketch was caught by the bosom of the people, which swelled with indignation at the thought that the hateful Corn Laws prevented them from entering the promised land of peace and plenty and happiness.

But indoors, protection was nominally, if not safely, guarded, until there appeared a contingency which entirely convulsed the judgment of men as to the exact remedy which should be called forth to meet its dreaded effects. The famine in Ireland, which had been predicted, was looming in the distance!

6. *Character of the times and attitude of Sir Robert Peel.*—What was the exact nature of the influence of this contingency upon the judgment of Sir Robert Peel it is impossible to ascertain. But it seems most probable that Sir Robert seized the possibility of a famine, in order that he might, with the appearance of less inconsistency, and as if by a natural consequence forced to a separation from the protectionist party, proceed with the work of reforming the tariff. That he was aware of the efficacy of the free-trade principle to elevate the condition of the masses, is evident from

the defence which he put forward after his second desertion from the Conservative party. But it is equally certain that he did not accurately ascertain the method by which the prosperity of the labourer was to be effected; nor did he regard the future progress of those conditions which then reacted favourably to the operation of the free-trade principle. He appears to have been content, like so many of the thinkers of the time, with the prospect of the successful results of the new system: the relations of this period of success to what immediately preceded it, and to that adverse state of affairs which might possibly, and under certain circumstances would assuredly, follow, were unconsidered; and thus the even and smooth course of the whole and continued progress of the working man was forsaken for the contemplation of a particular part of it, which, inasmuch as it was bound up with the characters of plenty and content, acted as a blind to the imagination of future evils and distress. He looked to posterity, he said, and to the present labouring classes for having effected much that would react towards the interests of labour. Present interests, he might have added; and continued in a parenthesis, the future interests of labour are enshrouded in uncertainty! But he forgot to admit that he had introduced an element of discord in the mutual harmony of internal relations, which could have none other effect than that of a pernicious precedent to subsequent generations. For in all large undertakings, it is customary to look to the prosperity of each individual part in the welfare of the whole.

How then could the welfare of the nation have been considered when legislation resulted, when the conflict between Manufacture and her elder sister Agriculture was being decided, in the virtual destruction of the prospects of the latter?

And if the masters, by reason of a certain temporary depression of their trade, cannot afford a greater supply of labour, if even they are forced to reduce the wages of the producers when the demand for their produce is restricted, are not these natural phenomena with which, at any time, it is hazardous to deal? For such interference should imply the control over all those elements which affect the processes of demand and supply. Is such control possessed by the Legislature? And the results of such action of interference, by being partial and artificial, terminate in the interruption of the normal line of progress. What direction will the course of our trade finally take, when the initial consequences of such interruption have been allowed to subside?

Thus, by interfering with the relative conditions of the manufacturing and agricultural interests, Sir Robert Peel offered an unfortunate example. His father, the first Sir Robert, is well known to have had a lively dread of legislative interference of any kind in the economy of our trade. But the wisdom of the father, however crude it may appear now, was not perceived in the action of the son. For, supposing depression to occur during the operation of the free-trade principle, the labouring classes, having the actions of 1846 and previous years before them, would incline to the Legislature for the means of its removal, instead of patiently abiding the results of a natural phenomenon. By such an example are the working classes taught to look upon the goodwill and a false omnipotence of Parliament, when their attention should be diverted to the clemency of their masters. Thus are they led to suppose that their masters have not a peculiar and proper interest in their wellbeing and contentment!

How such a belief in the omnipotence of Parliament, where Parliament is powerless, tends to the destruction of the spirit of independence and the decay of individual energies, it is not necessary to describe.

This view of the explanation of Sir Robert Peel's desertion from the Conservative party is strengthened by a knowledge of his cautious behaviour. For there was time enough for even a cautious legislator to arrive at a sound conclusion in the interval between the period at which the famine was predicted and its actual occurrence.

It is impossible to suppose that Sir Robert Peel was taken unawares, and that his action partook of the ingredients of alarm and impulse. On the contrary, there was every opportunity for him to weigh the relative values of the various opinions which were before him, and of the extent to which those opinions were held by the country at large. And, perhaps a consideration as important as any other during this perilous time, Sir Robert had to balance the chances of his continuing in power, supposing that he acted in a manner likely to withdraw the support of the larger part of his followers. It is even in no small degree probable that Sir Robert Peel, considering the helplessness of the Whigs, with whom free trade had become identified, to effect the great reform of the tariff, fell into the expectation that the inevitable division in his camp would leave him with a sufficient force, when united with the assistance of the Whig party, to conduct the Government of the country till the dissolution, which was close impending; and then, after such an important service in the cause of labour, he might hope to be raised to power again, and this time effectively, upon the shoulders of the people.

But there was this obstacle in the way. Sir Robert had been led by the light of reason to acknowledge the truth of the new doctrine. And to defer its operation on account of resistance which must at some time be met, and, if possible, overcome, seemed to him to be in direct opposition to his own conscientious scruples, and adverse to the interests of the State.

As there was no near and certain expectation that Lord John Russell would be powerful enough to bring about this desirable reform, and as he had already given up the idea of a fixed duty in a letter which he sent from Edinburgh to his London constituents, where he declared himself in favour of total repeal, what little support the Prime Minister had up to this time received from the partial opposition of Lord John, and which enabled him to temporise, was now gone, and Sir Robert Peel was left alone to take upon himself the whole of the responsibility of the projected reform in the tariff.

But though fully preoccupied with the management of the measure he had decided to espouse, the occasion must have arisen when his isolated state brought back to the powerful memory of Sir Robert Peel the similar condition of that party which he had, and not once only, been guilty of so ruthlessly abandoning!

With his previous antecedents, therefore, as expressed in certain articles of his speeches, Sir Robert Peel had no other course left open to him but to bring forward, and "strain every sinew to carry," the repeal of the Corn Laws.

But before he commenced the struggle openly, it was regarded as necessary that he should go through the formality of resigning, as if to proclaim to his countrymen that he had not, except as a matter of compulsion, undertaken the measure of his adversary, lest he might be accused of snatching the glory of its adoption, which properly belonged to another. But although Lord John Russell was requested to form an administration, he was unable to do so, and Sir Robert reassumed the reins of power.

Thus, with the support of the people apparently, and with the protectionists only in Parliament to oppose—and what was the nature of the opposition of the chief to his former followers?—Sir Robert Peel proceeded to consummate the work of reform which he had begun in 1842.

When in that year he remitted the import duties of certain articles, and removed the prohibition which weighed upon others, did he then anticipate that he would be compelled to pursue the logical conclusion, as it was falsely supposed to be, of the doctrine upon which he acted, in the repeal of the Corn Laws within so short a time?

Though, from the tenor of his remarks, however obscured he desired these to be, the inference becomes irresistible that Sir Robert was convinced that the tax upon corn must follow the rest of import duties, and become abolished, it seems that circumstances had constrained him to perform more rapidly what he had projected should be gradually induced. But the contingency of the famine intervening, and the attitude of the Whigs causing the intolerable isolation of his position, he grasped at the exaggerated importance this might afford him, to assist him out of the peculiarities of his situation.

The efforts of certain orators at this time were not without a much larger share of success than was really their due. The cry of a tax upon the people's food was issued from every platform which could boast a speaker; and some few whose logical capacity appeared to mark them out as superior to their brothers, denounced the Minister who yielded in one direction while he resisted in another. These orators of the free-trade school hurled forth their sarcastic criticism upon the man who repealed the duty on fresh meat while he continued the tax on corn. For what was the difference between the two cases? Are they not parallel? And if remission is admitted in the one instance, on what grounds was it refused in the other?

Why, then, should the Prime Minister endeavour to avoid the logical conclusion of his initial action?

Such was their style. But the arguments of the free-traders were not possessed of the soundness which, ignorantly or from prejudice, they attributed to them.

They did not perceive that the action of Sir Robert Peel in remitting the duties on fresh meat and allowing the free admission of live cattle was based upon a cogent and irresistible fact—the fact that the production of cattle in this country was unequal to the wants of the community. The population of this country was increasing more rapidly than the production of its cattle, hence it was necessary that the deficiency should be attracted from foreign sources—and what animosity was evinced lest France should be the fortunate medium of the supply! Fear, however, from this possibility was dissipated when Sir Robert Peel showed that France was a cattle-importing nation.

But in the case of the admission of corn duty free, what serious influence would such a policy exert upon the industry of the agricultural element of the country? There could be no possibility of such a serious disturbance in the instance of fresh meat and live cattle, the more especially when these were needed, and their free admission was likely to be followed by a fall in price. Where was the analogy between such an action and that of repealing the duty on corn, which had for so long been admitted on the payment of a tax, except in the calm and interested reasoning of the manufacturer, who viewed the abolition of the Corn Laws as a means of increasing the depths of his pocket; or in the wild imagination of the enthusiast, who fancied he saw in this extraordinary interruption in the normal progress of our commercial affairs the germ of the continued prosperity of the country?

The ground of action in the first instance was self-interest. Is it possible that the measures of 1842 and of subsequent years would have been enacted without the certainty of gain accruing to the nation? An inordinate and unwholesome gain!

In the case of corn, however, where was the difference? The difference lay altogether in the ·extent of the influence by which the total remission of the duties upon the taxed articles would affect the cultivation of the soil and the production of cattle respectively.

Now in the case of meat and cattle, it is obvious that the admission of a small amount to meet a deficiency would have no appreciable lasting effect upon the production of cattle in this country. What was required represented but a small proportion of the total demand of the population. Nor was the amount thus admitted, though it might gradually increase year by year, likely to depress in the near future the production of cattle by the inhabitants of the country.

But in the instance of corn, the amount to be admitted free of duty represented a very large proportion of the whole of the corn that was consumed by the inhabitants of this island. And would this proportion between home-grown and imported corn remain more or less constant as years rolled by? By no means. The ratio would gradually change, for the annual importation of corn must necessarily increase, by reason of the fact that the produce of this land is limited by its area of arable soil. Setting aside, for the moment, the economic maxim that the productivity of the soil tends to decrease until it reaches a point where its cultivation is no longer remunerative, it is evident that the remission of the duty upon imported corn was of enormous importance upon the cultivation of home-grown corn, for it directly tended to reduce the price of corn to a level where its cultivation would no longer be profitable to the speculative farmer. Thus an industry which was already the subject of a natural impediment, would be still further subjected to the influence of an artificial one; and Agriculture, and those consequently who were interested in her welfare, having been up to the present protected by those time-honoured rights which had grown out of her wants, would now, when the Corn Laws were abolished, be at the mercy of a foreign competition, in which it was certain that the force of greater strength would win. The outcomes, therefore, of these two supposed parallel cases were totally dissimilar; the one may have been needed, but the other certainly was not justified in the peculiar circumstances of the times.

As matter of fact there was no real parallel between the opposite cases of fresh meat and corn: what parallel was drawn was constructed with the design of strengthening the merits of the free-trade cause. It was a parallel only on the surface. The two cases differed completely when the details came to be considered.

But the free-trader was content to argue, that because fresh meat was admitted duty free, so should corn enter our ports without the imposition of a customs duty. Of this nature was the reasoning of the free-trader. So long as he believed the principle was true in the abstract (surrounded as the abstract is with all kinds of contingencies), he was bound to follow it to its furthest limits, even when these were bordering upon the region of disaster. And he did this without reference to external conditions, and the possible changes in those conditions—whether new ones would arise—any of the present ones disappear; and what would be the probable nature of their fluctuation, and consequently their influence, upon the progress of the free-trade principle.

But who were the men who advanced the free-trade doctrine, and without whose influence and assistance the operation of the free-trade principle would never have come into play? The manufacturers, and in particular the Manchester Chamber of Commerce.

And upon what main grounds did they promulgate the doctrine of free trade? Upon the grounds, simply, of self-interest, and self-interest of the narrowest kind— the self-interest of class.

The manufacturers saw in the immediate future of free trade, if not for a long, at any rate for a definite length of time, a brilliant period for the manufacturing industries of the country. And, at the same time, they were convinced that their own fortunes would rise with the early growth and development of the free-trade principle.

Their anticipations, therefore, were possible in the near future, if free trade was to reign in the commercial world of Great Britain and Ireland, even though neighbouring nations might still continue the system of protection. And the haste with which they urged on the cause of free trade is rather indicative of the alarm which their selfish disposition was prone to originate, when they conceived that the means of their enrichment might possibly be retarded, or perhaps dissipated for ever.

But in the case of the selfish disposition of the protectionists, who were advocating at the time exactly what the manufacturers were clamouring for in the future, self-interest was ignored. And the manufacturers elected to sacrifice the interests of the weaker for those of the larger part of the community, and thus struck the fatal blow at the agricultural prospects of their country!

7. *Criticism of the economic doctrine of the free-traders.*—That "you should buy in a cheap market and sell in a dear one" sounds all very well when there are cheap and accessible markets in which to buy, and dear and accessible markets in which to sell.

It must occur to all, that as the nature of surrounding circumstances varies, so, too, must the result of those changes vary with them.

The doctrine above enunciated would be sound enough, and one upon which to act, if it could be relied on beforehand—

1. Will the markets in which we buy remain cheap? and
2. Will the markets in which we sell continue dear?

Whether the future operation of their principle was taken into consideration by the free-traders need not be discussed. The approach of present prosperity always obscures the prospect of future disasters to those whose fortunes are about to take this happy turn. And when is prosperity thus commenced ever considered to be apt to vanish? There is some extenuation in the case of those merchants who blindly followed in the path of an abstract principle, for they would not detect the treacherous nature of the materials upon which it is built. They believed that free trade was going to be the cause of the prosperity for which they longed; and when they experienced it, the association of free trade and prosperity was strongly riveted in their minds. But they did not trace the true succession of phenomena. And they consequently fell into the error of ascribing to the cause itself what was but due to the transient operation of one of its effects. But every one worthy of the name of political economist must indeed have taken this prospective action of a "cause" into account, lest after the principle of free trade had been in operation for any length of time its ultimate effect, instead of being beneficial to the body of the trade and commercial interests of the country, should become injurious, and not only injurious but directly opposed to its healthy and prosperous growth.

The free-traders saw only the present and immediate advantages to be reaped from the application of their favourite principle. It was to dissipate the sources of depression (and it succeeded in removing some of these, but this lasted only for a time); it was to make England more prosperous than she had ever been before (but did the free-traders anticipate that this prosperous action would be inevitably followed by an equal reaction in an opposite direction?); and it was to be the means of pacifying the world! As if the disappearance of one source of international hostility was sufficient to effect, of itself, the destruction of all the rest!

But if the enthusiastic promoters of the new doctrine were thus passionately blinded to the possible future operation of the free-trade principle, it was not the part of the Legislature, thus unwittingly, and constrained even by the false representations of a "power in the State," to afford the country even the possible chance of running into the depths of a far deeper depression and more sorrowful state of affairs, because directly leading to decline, than it was ever plunged into before.

The future consequences of this principle, broadly in

all the possible, and more narrowly in the more probable, conditions by which surrounding circumstances, induced by the action of foreign nations, might affect our commercial progress, should have been exposed by the wise legislators of the time; and some of these actually were felt by the legislators of the party which was now opposed to Sir Robert Peel and his Whig supporters. But the very essence of their gravity was met from the ministerial benches by an appeal to the present.

Look at the labourers' wages, they have risen in some instances as much as 20 or 25 per cent; at the bullion in the Bank of England, it has been increased by five millions; and at the prosperity of the kingdom generally, as shown by the rapidly increasing exports and imports,—and then state, has the free-trade principle acted adversely? There was no answer to these facts, so obviously true. But the protectionist might well have replied—Will these conditions, leading to the commercial prosperity of the nation, continue similar to what they are at present? And if not, when shall we expect a break in this transitory sunshine of prosperity, and how will it be effected?

But the ultimate possible results of the application of the free-trade principle to our commercial system required a powerful imagination to unfold the different courses surrounding nations might take, and to deduce the effect in each particular and possible line of action upon the progress, or otherwise, of our commercial growth.

However philanthropic some visionaries may assume the free-trade principle to be in its results, it is in accordance with common-sense, that a nation is not bound to follow any particular doctrine, or to continue in it when once it has been put into practice, provided there is the possibility of the doctrine acting adversely to its interests.

If, then, the doctrine of free trade, in the abstract, had the benign nature that was so wildly lavished upon it by those who pleaded for its adoption, there must have been strong grounds for surrounding nations to have regarded it with no less envious eyes than ourselves, and to have entered the race for the prize of leading the van of civilisation. But the fact that there was no struggle for such a supremacy proves rather that the action of the free-trade manufacturers of Manchester, who were, in the first instance, so loath to transfer the centre of their base to the metropolis, was perhaps a little more individual and a little more selfish than they were willing to own.

Why did the free-trade manufacturers advance the principle of free trade? Because they perceived that the then particular condition of the country was favourable to its action.

But did it occur to them to inquire, Will the action of the principle always be favourable, and will surrounding conditions always remain similar to what they were at the time of its initial operation?

There was no such anticipation exhibited; and the whole nation was cajoled into the belief that a principle was favourable in its operation always, because it reacted during its early stages in the favour of the working man!

Thus the Manchester manufacturers tended to sacrifice, not only the future interests (and ought these ever to have been subjected to uncertainty and insecurity?) of the labourer, but they pawned as well the prospects and the grandeur of their descendants. They were to prosper for a time, out of all proportion to the requirements of commerce and the good of the State. In short, they forsook the future, and lived for the present alone! The only tribute that can be paid to their narrow policy is that many of them made large fortunes by the advantage, which they afforded generally to the circle of merchants, of a disturbance in the relations of international commerce, which resulted momentarily, by reason of the favourable nature of surrounding circumstances, in the gigantic development of their trade.

But has the action of these manufacturing enterprises terminated in securing for our goods dear markets abroad, and for ourselves any cheaper markets at home than we experienced before the introduction of the free-trade principle?

Have the labouring classes, who were to be so materially benefited for all time, been really the subjects of a piece of philanthropic agitation? or, in other words, are the labouring classes now, after a period of operation of the free-trade principle extending over forty years, in a better position to supply the demands of their daily wants than they were under the more certain and securer system of protection? Are they so favourably treated that they can save more, and thus erect a barrier against the occurrence of hard times? It is for the experience of the present generation to determine this most significant question.

The observation of labour during the past years

shows that while the field of the working man has been gradually contracting, his weekly wage has also at the same time been slowly decreasing. And it is of importance to notice that this general shrinkage and deterioration of labour is due, not so much to the want of capital—an absence of which formed the chief source of the depression before free trade was introduced—but to the fact that there are no markets to induce men of wealth to continue their customary enterprises on the certainty of a profitable interest accruing to the capital which they put into circulation. The feature of the present depression is for the manufacturer to make even the smallest profit for the time and money which he expends in the extension of his trade.

But at the time of the introduction of the free-trade principle, when the taxes were removed from the food of the people, and the latter placed in a more advantageous situation for saving and exercising the attribute of thrift, an income-tax was laid upon all incomes above £150 a-year, amounting to 3 per cent. What was remitted to the labourer, therefore, was burdened upon the manufacturers, and these, from the largeness of their profits, could even cheerfully afford to pay the necessities of the new tax. The logical conclusion of such a domestic policy is obvious: it was to place the labouring man in a relatively more comfortable position, inasmuch as he has now cheaper food and (it was expected, and it had happened during the initial period of the operation of the principle) a proportionate wage even during times of depression, because wages, like similar elements, are maintained at their level till they are forced to reduction; but throughout this period, and while profits are becoming more and more contracted, the manufacturer has to refund to the State an income-tax which is all the harder to bear, because the source which previously supplied it is slowly drying up.

When the present deplorable condition of the working man is considered along with the decline in the prospects of manufacture, what beneficial effect—as both these phenomena can be directly traced up to the adverse action of the free-trade principle—has been derived by this redistribution of the burdens of the people, and by lessening, for the time being, pressure upon the working classes, which is now reappearing with redoubled force?

The primary effect of what must be undoubtedly regarded as a philanthropic piece of legislation has come slowly, and almost imperceptibly, to be nullified, owing to the ability of the labouring man to increase his expenditure in another direction, now that he has a surplus consequent on the reduction in the price of bread. And it is capable of easy demonstration that the improvement of his fortunes would lead to a more luxurious habit of living; and, first, the nature of his dwelling would be changed. He would become accommodated with a better lodging, for which he will have to pay, owing to the inevitable presence of the law of competition, a constantly increasing rent.

Thus the principle of fluctuation remains, though it has been diverted from its former channel—indirectly from the produce of the land, directly to the land itself!

After censuring the aristocracy for grinding down the wages of the labourer to the point of starvation, by means of the unwarrantable assumption that increase in the price of corn goes directly to increase rent—the manufacturer, nevertheless, managed to consume, during the transient period of prosperity of the free-trade principle, the main profits of the work of the labouring classes—there was no need to announce to the manufacturers that their action tended in a direction far worse than that of reducing wages to the level of starvation, for the immediate effect of the change was an addition of 20 and 25 per cent to the wages of labour.

The result was advantageous to all parties except the landowner, the subject of blame and reproach; but did the labouring man get a higher proportion of the total profits of his labour, even when his wages were increased by a fourth, under the new condition of things, than under the old, when profits were, of course, relatively much smaller in amount?

Was there any great degree of virtue, then, in this alteration which the manufacturers effected in the condition of the working classes? For who were by far the larger gainers by the change? The manufacturers themselves; who now began to act just like the landowners whose conduct they had so severely reprobated but a short time since. The tyranny of the aristocracy and starvation wages must first of all be associated in the minds of the ignorant; a proper degree of enthusiasm must be worked up in the ignorant mob; the idea of injustice must be gradually unfolded; wrongs must be suffered which exist only in the excited imaginations of those who can feel, but who do not take the trouble to reason; and the manufacturers must pose as the great deliverers of the people, and as having snatched them from the jaws of an insatiable exaction!

But is it true that the manufacturers saw in the measure of free trade the means of advancing their own aggrandisement and took advantage of it?

Where comes in the virtue, then, of their action? And what was the difference in attitude between the landowning portion of the community and the manufacturers towards the great producers of wealth?

For the moment the manufacturers had stepped over and taken the ground of the aristocracy; and what were the means they openly utilised to effect the change of position? The common one of showing that the present masters are unjust; and then, because human nature is unchangeable, having succeeded in dispossessing a hypothetical tyranny, of exactly following in the footsteps of those whom they had so unjustly and so arbitrarily maligned!

But the manufacturers succeeded in veiling the selfish motives by which they were inspired. Nor is it for the undiscerning crowd to distinguish between the apparent and the real—it follows even a false prophet.

And now, after the prosperity of the manufacturers has run its short and unnatural course, what is the result upon the present interests and future outlook of the labouring man? Profits are no longer possible to the master, wages consequently become scarce, and the working man who was to gain so much by the adhesion which he was persuaded to give in former times, is now left a prey to the fortunate owners of the land upon which his dwelling rests. Where now are his deliverers? And to what a sorry plight have ill-advised measures led him?

He has, at the present day, a higher rent to pay

relatively to what he was subjected before the year 1842, and the means open to him for acquiring his livelihood are becoming more and more precarious.

But this is not the only effect which the ambition of manufacture has succeeded in bringing about. For not only has this resulted in the aggravation of the distress of labour, after a transient period of prosperity; not only have the manufacturers rendered by their imprudent tamperings, what before was a bad, a far worse state of the labourer, but they have unconsciously, by their arbitrary proceeding, increased the burdens of their own descendants, by reason of the fact that, in the process of the formation of their own fortunes, the resources of other countries were called forth, energies were awakened, and so great an alteration induced at home and abroad in our commercial relations, that those markets which before were alone open to them, and at the mercy of their price, now have the advantage of buying their customary goods at a lower cost, because of the presence and gradual ascendancy of a foreign competition.

Thus, in the track of the free-trade principle there have been created new forces to counteract the evil tendency with which it operates against neighbouring nations; and as the final result of their endeavours, its former and beneficial action towards us gradually becomes diminished.

Before, the circumstances which affected its action were favourable, but now they are unfavourable. And these adverse conditions have been directly brought about by the successful efforts of foreign nations to undersell us in those markets which at one time were our monopoly, but which can scarcely be considered at the present time to be our own.

Again, at home, are the markets any the cheaper, relatively, to what they were before the accession of Sir Robert Peel to power in 1841? Taking into consideration the paroxysmal and restricted character of ordinary trade depression, this can hardly be advanced as true. In the extraordinary rise in our trade's activity, what was due to a natural advance is not usually discriminated and its precise amount ascertained. Even Sir Robert Peel ascribed the whole of the prosperity which attended the action of the free-trade principle, when this was freed from the effect of local and transient influences, to the virtues of the principle itself! But it is obviously of importance to analyse the elements of this "ascent," and to separate what was due to "natural causes" from that which resulted from an "artificial stimulation," applied at the hands of the Legislature. For there is ample evidence that before 1842 our trade was undergoing a uniform and progressive advance; and there is also evidence that during the whole of the period of the free-trade agitation the people were unhappily inflamed into a belief of the falsehood that the Corn Laws were depriving them of those comforts which they were extravagantly taught to believe should be by right their own.

Where is the evidence of that progressive factor in the present course of the trade of this country? Has the natural and certain growth of our commerce been strangled by that unnatural overgrowth which was capable only of a short, if active, existence?

And what is the evidence of the cumulative and progressive distress—a distress which is not partial nor limited, but is universally spread throughout the country, and affects every trade and diminishes all our commerce? Where are those dear markets of which the free-traders prophesied? They are things of the past! And where is that cheap bread at home which was brandished before the eyes of the populace to arouse them into a sense of false injustice? Bread can neither be cheap nor dear when there is no money with which to buy it! What recks it to the labouring man whatever may be the price of bread, so long as he has the certainty of employment and of his weekly wage? Is there, then, so very much difference between dear bread and cheap lodgings, and cheap bread and dear lodgings? The difference is apparent when, with dear bread and cheap lodgings, the labourer had the means of obtaining his daily subsistence; but now with cheap bread and perhaps no lodgings at all, the labourer is thrown upon the generosity of the philanthropic portion of the community.

The free-trade economists, who propounded the doctrine that you should buy in a cheap market and sell in a dear one, never imagined what might be the possible consequences of the immense alteration they were on the verge of effecting in the world of commerce. They seem to have acted as if the markets would continue respectively cheap and dear, and that the relationship which existed in these times would remain the same for ever.

What they should have contemplated first was, not the present advantage of the new system, but some of its possible future effects.

But, it must be reiterated, they proceeded in their measure without any regard to the future; the free-trade principle was contemplated by them in its present bearing alone!

There is another criticism of the free-trade doctrine, "of buying in a cheap and selling in a dear market," which displays the faulty analysis upon which its foundation is laid.

When the free-traders talked of buying in a cheap market, they referred to the raw goods which we were accustomed to import into the country for the purpose of converting, by British labour, into manufactured articles.

Could they ever have contemplated the possibility that the measure which was to make the foreign markets cheap for buying purposes was also to make our own markets the dearest relatively, and therefore to repel the merchant from home to foreign labour? The principle of free trade enabled us to admit raw material at a very cheap cost; but at the same time, it bore the germ of the future supply of our own markets with the manufactured goods of the foreigner. So that now, as the ultimate result of the free-trade doctrine being put into practice, we not only admit raw goods from foreign sources, but we admit manufactured articles as well, with how much injustice to British labour it is needless to dilate!

But it must be; this possibility escaped the contracted views of the free-trade economists, because it was not an immediate but a remote effect. For it is impossible to suppose that the free-traders thought that England would not maintain her complete monopoly of neutral markets.

The admission of manufactured articles! We shall then be able to export our raw materials; but this country is not so fortunately placed as to be able to export, to any large extent, the produce of the land. We have to rely, as the free-traders predicted, solely upon the exportation of our manufactured goods.

But if this exportation is interfered with, how then are we placed with reference to our neighbouring nation?

They have raw articles which they can freely export; they have, as well, their manufacturing industries, which are protected, and which are slowly growing and developing in strength; but this country, when its manufacture is injured, has nothing to fall back upon. And it is curious to observe that this injury to the exportation of manufactured goods is inflicted by the former actions of the manufacturers themselves!

Time only was required for the symptoms of the injury to become evident.

8. *What led to the repeal of the Corn Laws?*—There can be no doubt that the selfish motives of the manufacturers were freely utilised by Sir Robert Peel; and there can be as little doubt but that the same legislator was constrained to give too great an importance to the manufacturing interests of the country, to the neglect of another and equally important industry.

When Sir Robert Peel acceded to power in 1841, the first difficulty with which he had to grapple was the miserable state in which the condition of the finances had been left by the Whig Minister. The deficit of the year was $2\frac{1}{2}$ millions, and this, taken in connection with the fact that the deficit had become an annual phenomenon, was sufficient to prove that the sources from which the revenue was derived were becoming gradually but increasingly less and less productive. But it must be remembered that during the period 1837-41, there was a very considerable disturbance of the ordinary progress of trade, owing to the occurrence of one of those crises which are prone to attack the monetary world when circumstances are conducive. The prosperity of the country, therefore, was retarded; and the deficit in the several branches of the revenue is thus explained in those instances where the wellbeing of the people enables them to afford such luxuries, the consumption of which was then attended with profit to the State.

The problem, "How to meet the deficit?" was the first to occupy the attention of the new Premier. And the difficulties in which he was involved were expressed in the treatment of the Whig leader by the Prime Minister, when questioned as to the ultimate modification the Corn Laws were to undergo. Sir Robert Peel sarcastically replied that he had no further suggestion to offer with regard to the sliding-scale, which he had already framed; and that it was of the first importance to place the financial condition of the nation on a sound and flourishing basis.

Many things would occur at once to the mind of Sir Robert, but perhaps all did not receive the same care of individual attention. Then the late Whig Chancellor of the Exchequer had increased the import duties on all articles which constituted the import trade of the country, at the same time that he had raised the assessed taxes throughout the kingdom. By these means he had expected to balance income and expenditure; but the gain which he had anticipated from the increment to the import duties fell short of his prognostication, and thus he was left once more to face an inevitable deficit. And this in spite of the fact that his treatment of the assessed taxes fully responded to his expectations.

Simply on this instance, and while the country was deranged owing to the consequences of a trade convulsion, Sir Robert argued that the mode of levying the revenue by means of indirect taxation had reached its limit, and that if taxation was to be productive, resort must be had to the direct method.

Direct taxation! the opportunity afforded Sir Robert Peel the idea of proposing, but for a time only, the burden of an income-tax. It was obvious that such a tax would react adversely to the interests of the various professions; the great body of the manufacturers, however, who saw the sure means of being able to bear its weight with ease, and as they thought with security, offered no objections, and consequently the Premier put his "idea" into practice.

The immediate effect of the imposition of the income-tax was to distribute a part of the burdens of the country upon those whose incomes exceeded £150 per annum; and a portion of the produce of this tax was set aside for the purpose of relieving the labouring classes of some of those hardships beneath which they were supposed to be groaning.

And it may be remembered here, that Sir Robert had on a previous occasion, some years before, expressed his intention of not dealing with the produce of this hypothetical tax, to effect the remission on malt and other articles which are subject to excisable duties. Did it occur to Sir Robert Peel at that early date, 1835, that the remission of import duties was of paramount advantage to the nation?

At any rate, after the adjustment of the Corn Laws by means of the sliding-scale of 1842, by which the protectionists thought that the protection offered to agriculture was too little, while the free-traders proclaimed that it was too much, the Prime Minister introduced his scheme for placing the finances of the country on a sound foundation. An income-tax was to be levied on all incomes of £150 and upwards, to the extent of 3 per cent; it was to exist for a period of three years; and it was calculated to produce a little more than 7 millions per annum. But at the same time, and conjointly with the Income-Tax Bill, another Bill was introduced, with the express object of reforming the tariff. As these two Bills were taken together, there is evidently displayed the intimate connection which Sir Robert Peel had finally decided upon between the two measures. To counteract the annual deficit, an income-tax was proposed—a productive source of revenue. This would place in the hands of the Chancellor of the Exchequer a sufficient sum yearly for the next three years, which would be available for the discharge of the recent debts that had been incurred by the late Government. Still a large balance would remain. And this was intended to be applied to the remission of the import duties upon all raw materials admitted into the country. The introduction of the new system was, however, to take place gradually; and thus we find that in the first year, 1842, duties to the amount of £1,092,000 were remitted; in 1843, £411,000; and in 1844, £458,000.

In this way Sir Robert Peel was carrying into action the principle of an almost imperceptible introduction of change into the affairs of our commerce, which he subsequently enunciated in one of those speeches in Parliament in which he effectively proved that the operation of the Corn Laws was not responsible for the distress of the country; but that free trade, inasmuch as it was founded upon reasonable arguments, which his generation could not overcome, was admittedly the last course the commercial body could pursue, with respect to the subject of "corn."

Why, this introduction of the principle of free trade gave Sir Robert Peel a loophole, by means of which he might disembarrass himself from the disaster of an apparently constant and increasing annual deficit. The income-tax supplied him with the means of successfully conducting the financial concerns of the nation for three years.

Only for three years? Sir Robert must have had the prospect of good accruing from the partial action of the new principle. Else why was the time during which the income-tax was to bear, limited to three years?

Was this a means of accustoming the nation to the idea of a permanent income-tax, which would be met at the outset with so much opposition, even by the manufacturers? For even the manufacturers were somewhat jealous of the probability of this burden upon them either increasing in amount or becoming permanent, as is evident from their refusal to grant the Chancellor of the Exchequer in the next Administration an addition of 2 per cent to the income-tax, to meet a return of the deficit.

Or did Sir Robert Peel anticipate that, by the end of three years, if the action of the principle of free trade answered his expectations, he would really be in a situation to abolish the income-tax altogether, and that he would be able to draw a sufficient revenue, to replace it, from the favourable action of free trade? There are some grounds for the inference in the increased consumption which Sir Robert concluded would inevitably succeed the diminution or the entire remission of import duties. For in the instance of sugar, he showed afterwards that the reduction in the duties had been attended with the greatest advantage to the nation.

But during these three years, the free-trade principle was in partial operation; and at the end of it, therefore, he would be in a position to judge of the efficacy of its partial action, and thereby enabled to deduce the total effect of the unrestricted operation of the new principle.

But the results at the end of the first period of three years were not such as to permit of the removal of the tax upon incomes. In 1845, Sir Robert obtained from a willing Parliament the renewal of the income-tax for a further period of three years. This measure was the more readily passed because those who had most largely to bear the burden were mainly concerned in manufacture, and had already tasted of the initial and favourable action of free trade, and, in consequence, were cheerfully disposed to contribute a portion of their newly acquired profits.

But although the results were not sufficiently favourable to lead Sir Robert Peel to depend upon their stability and permanence, they were favourable enough to impel him to extend the operation of the principle. It was in this year 1845, when the country had recovered from the effects of the previous distress, that Sir Robert Peel expressed the absolute necessity of abolishing all duties of a prohibitory nature; and it is important to analyse the grounds which led him to a conclusion which was so violently opposed to the whole of his past career. At this time, then, Sir Robert Peel had only the statement of the Whig Chancellor and the experience of three years of the action of a principle whose subsequent course, it was unavoidable to deny, was altogether dependent upon the fluctuating nature of surrounding circumstances. Can the permanent action of a principle be deduced from the mere experience of a period of three years of its action, which was limited, and when the future conditions which would influence its operations were unknown?

But it appears that Sir Robert Peel had already made up his mind as to the final efficacy of the free-trade principle in the abstract, and that he was compelled to give, as his plausible grounds for becoming a convert to the belief in free trade, this observation of its partial action extending over three years, and as well, "other reasons which are derived from other sources." Thus was he to appear consistent in the public eye: the details of the experiment in free trade he afforded with a sparing hand. It mattered not whether the principle should have only been in action for three days; such an unimportant difference in one datum could have had no influence upon the conclusion which Sir Robert Peel drew from no evidence at all. For Sir Robert Peel, like all the free-traders, had made his conclusion first, and supported it by precarious arguments afterwards.

The problem which Sir Robert constructed was pitilessly incomplete. Is it possible so grand a conclusion can, with any degree of safety, be supported on such a slight foundation?

Thus, if Sir Robert Peel did base his inference upon experience, it was unwarrantable, for the most important factors in the experiment were then unknown to him; and it was experience, and experience of a very bitter kind ultimately, that alone could supply him with them. But it is in the highest degree probable that, as the principle Sir Robert Peel introduced was an abstract one, so the arguments for its application were likewise abstract and existed only in "idea." This free-trade system was an ideal system purely, the initial results of which were foretold as prosperous, but the ultimate action of which was ignored! But it was a likely remedy for the distresses of the times, and its merits should be tried; and perhaps Sir Robert, fastening upon this immediate prosperity which was certain to attend the action of the principle of free trade, saw in its introduction a means to regulate successfully the national finance, and at the same time to remove the cause of discontent, which was then associated with the prevalent distress, by an increased activity of the markets for a time. And then after that, when depression again reigns, some other means must be devised to meet the special difficulties of the case.

But although it is certain that Sir Robert Peel was brought to believe in the efficacy of the principle of free trade in the abstract, it is questionable how far the perilous condition, as it was described by the free-traders without grounds, of the country reacted on his judgment in favour of its adoption; and the conclusion must always remain a matter of doubt whether Sir Robert Peel really believed in the ultimate favourable issue of free trade, or whether he utilised it to extricate himself from a network of extraordinary difficulties.

It is strange that nowhere in his numerous speeches on the subjects of our trade and commercial relationship does Sir Robert draw any distinction between the duties on imported corn and the duties on other imported materials, whose production in this country was scarcely worthy of protection. Many a time he refers to the rectitude of the course which he had hitherto pursued in the maintenance of existing rights; but whether, during this eventful time, he merely referred to his past attitude, and concealed those arguments or diverted their real tendency, in the practice of which he was so able a master, which made him doubt the necessity of continuing such rights in the future, it is difficult to estimate.

When in his speeches a Minister and legislator continually asserts that neither himself nor his colleagues have any intention of amending the Corn Laws, but by his actions is placed in the unenviable position where they are carried, as he knew they would be, to their logical results of directly proceeding to their repeal, there must be some strong ground why he was able to assume an attitude which can only be described by an epithet of disapprobation. Sir Robert, as we have observed, did not recognise the want of parallel between the cases of meat and corn, but appears to have insidiously conveyed to the protectionists, through the means of a false logical conclusion, his ultimate intentions with regard to their policy.

And now, in addition to other difficulties, the disasters of party disruption began to loom in the near future of Sir Robert Peel's administration!

By such reforms as he had already effected in the tariff, he had given his party strong reasons to suppose that he was no longer so closely attached to its members or their principles as heretofore. And when, as he continued in the work of reform, the proof which he offered to the protectionists that he would leave the Corn Laws exactly where they stood by the alteration of 1842, was considered neither as sufficient nor trustworthy, the relationship between the centre and base of the Conservative party became subjected to a strain. Measures were anticipated; the old desertion was called up, and Sir Robert again received the aspersions of the majority of his former party—that party which had looked up to him for the most intimate support! The fact could no longer be kept concealed; the Prime Minister had come to have discordant views with the larger section of his party. And when Sir Robert Peel differed, he was, by a natural weakness, inclined to persevere in his own way. It was thus when Canning and Peel were colleagues in the Liverpool Administration; and again expressed when Peel refused office under his more successful rival. Was there in these differences of opinion merely differences of opinion or something more? Something in the nature of an unworthy dislike, or the ungenerous desire of occupying that position, and enjoying those honours which properly belonged to another of greater brilliancy and power?

The incident of this difference of opinion proves that the motive which actuated Sir Robert Peel in the course he took was a purely selfish one; and was not the same result to be expected from conditions which were more or less similar to those of the days of the Catholic Emancipation and the interval of hunting Canning to death?

Nor was the present crisis unassociated with the possibility of future glory, and this was what Sir Robert fully anticipated would attend the memory of the statesman who had emancipated labour from the burden under which she was then, as he supposed, suffering.

There is some proof of the animosity with which, perhaps, he retaliated toward the party of protection in the proceedings which were antecedent to the introduction of the Bill to repeal the Corn Laws. In connection with this particular instance, we must recall to mind the unsatisfactory state in which Ireland then was, where sedition and rebellion were doing their work.

The Irish Arms Bill was brought forward along with the Repeal (Corn Laws) Bill; but by some misunderstanding the protectionists were led into the error that the Arms Bill would be taken first, and that the Repeal would follow it. The contrary, however, happened to be the case; and the incident shows that Sir Robert Peel, contrary to the usage of conduct which prevailed between the leaders of the rival parties on important measures, ignored the action of his subordinate.

But what was the reason of so extraordinary a behaviour? The fact remains, that when Sir Robert Peel introduced the fatal Bill to repeal the Corn Laws somewhat earlier than had been generally expected, he found the protectionists wellnigh unprepared. They concluded that the Repeal Bill would come on after the Easter holidays; and in the meantime they set about the method of opposition on which they were determined. Thus the protectionists were taken at a disadvantage!

The Corn Laws were repealed! And this measure was brought about by the Minister who had been for such a long period of his public career, nominally at any rate, on the side of protection! By the suddenness of Sir Robert's action, the protectionists received a blow which entirely disconcerted them, and legislative protection to our trade and industries became buried in the limbo of the past!

In the pursuit of this policy, Sir Robert Peel, who had been the subject of perhaps the severest exposal it has befallen the lot of any public man in high station to experience, may have been brought to the reflection that mind is unstable, and the action of will vanishes. But he afforded himself the opportunity of comparing his attitude respecting the question of Emancipation, which concerned only a difference of mere opinion, and the matter of the repeal of the Corn Laws, which struck at the foundation of national prosperity!

But he had gained his point; he had acted according

to the might of his reasoning power, first fed by the fallacious doctrines of the interested political economy of his day, stimulated by the demands of a selfish trade, working its own unhealthy, because dangerous, development even at the expense of the whole nation, of which it formed a limb only; and lastly, strengthened by the clamours of an inflamed populace. For the present he had done well, according to his account, which appeared later on in his celebrated manifesto; but what evil had he been unconsciously maintaining up to the year 1842? Did such an admission on the part of the late Prime Minister reflect favourably upon the past endeavours of his stupendous intellect? He had been guilty, then, of a mistake: he had nourished this for the major part of his official existence, and it was only by a chance that his mind was opened, and he saw the truth! But such considerations would not blight the happy picture which he described around. He would not pause to examine whether the means which had led to his open conversion then had not already been within his grasp almost from the very day when he became a servant to the monarch of his country. He saw around him a grateful and prosperous people, and he looked for nothing but the regard of posterity and the smile of labour!

He, too, had fallen into the fatal error of staking all the interests and the glory of the nation on the present. The future, in the insidious embrace of the free-trade principle, was entirely neglected!

But when inconsistency is permitted to creep into the thoughts or the actions of man, the tendency ever remains, and may become exaggerated. The character possessing so obvious a defect is worthy of being repelled as exhibiting either one of two deformities, each equally repugnant. In the first instance, we have the picture of a man who is liable, from what we know of human nature, to hold certain opinions from certain consequences flowing from such; but change these consequences, as they may be really, by the appearance of new factors, or apparently by reason of the admission of some data which before had escaped the range of his knowledge, and then adhesion to these former opinions ceases.

There are two kinds of selfishness—the one of the pleasures of the senses; the other, of the product of the intellect, and from an inordinate degree of the latter it is difficult to exonerate Sir Robert Peel.

The other picture is that of a man who has no definite line of action, simply for the reason that he cannot foresee difficulties, by his inability to vary the possibilities of future results with the assistance of a powerful imagination. However great the memory may be, if imagination be not at hand, there is the tendency, ever waiting to be put into action, of being swayed from time to time by the opinion of others, which come to be more cogent, according to the varying importance of certain collateral and transient conditions. And it is not difficult to perceive that interruption to the normal course of natural progress under such circumstances is fraught with the direst consequences. For if change is to be when this event falls out, so will change have to be when that other occurs. Thus is sown the endless means of interminable change!

The life of a nation, as compared with the life of an individual, is vast indeed. And in the case of the ultimate and pernicious action of a principle upon its commercial development, the signs of decline will take a proportionately longer time to become evident to the political observer's eye.

CHAPTER III.

THE POSITION OF SIR ROBERT PEEL.

9. *Sir Robert Peel's defence.*—The reforms which Sir Robert Peel succeeded in effecting so arbitrarily in the commercial code of the country eventually left him isolated in the parliamentary arena. The great Conservative party, which he had done so much to develop and maintain, viewed in a state almost amounting to despair the leader who had thus deserted them in the moment of their triumph. A few faithful followers surrounded him after he had openly seceded from that *country* party whose boast it was no longer that they had raised him to power.
Up to this point it will be observed that the case against Sir Robert Peel has been laid chiefly on the grounds that he did not sufficiently analyse the prospective action of the free-trade principle, nor did he in any the least degree provide for its possible pernicious operation. For in what way did free trade act? As a stimulant, by increasing the circulation of our trade markets. But the effects of stimulation tend to pass off unless they are nourished. What else, then, did he leave to take the place of the free-trade principle when,

in the course of time, its power to stimulate had ceased to be? what was to replace its primary stimulant and beneficial effect?

It is impossible to believe that free trade, as a stimulant to the activity of the markets, can continue the same degree of potency with which it first set out. For it is evident that, out of its continued operation, consequences arise of a nature to paralyse its beneficial action.

Did Sir Robert Peel anticipate this operation of the free-trade principle when surrounding circumstances would tend, with a gradually increasing force, to impede that very effect, upon the presence of which its action for good depended?

It is true that a review of the position of the country at the time was not such as to inspire him with the highest hopes, although he fully predicted that the energies of his countrymen would be equal to the occasion of the then depression—and perhaps he had in mind the operation of free trade in the primary period of its action, for it was evident to all that Great Britain and Ireland were becoming year by year less and less capable of producing their former proportionate amount of corn. There was thus all the more reason why the Legislature should endeavour to attract the produce of foreign lands, to invite competition, and in this way to reduce the price; for if the gold of the country was to be drained inevitably away, it was to the interest of the nation that the outgoing capital should be the least possible.

But although the ultimate prospect of this country being a corn-producing one was reduced almost to a nothing—though it might have been anticipated that the time would arrive when we should have almost entirely to rely on foreign sources for a supply of corn—it does not seem, from an examination of the opinions expressed during this critical period, that the idea was entertained of the possibility of our being wholly supplied from our colonies.

To counteract the constant drain of gold thus induced, Sir Robert Peel relied upon the increasing exportation of our manufactured articles; and the ratio of the outgoing and incoming of gold with reference to these markets was greatly in our favour. But was this ratio to exist for ever? If we were to depend solely upon our manufactured articles for the money spent in the consumption of corn, was not this an argument rather that these manufacturers, the source of this wealth, should be efficiently protected? There could be no doubt of the actual existence of an evil at the time when Sir Robert Peel was called upon to put the legislative engine into work; but if this eminent politician was not sure of the ultimate as well as the immediate effects of the principle of free trade, he may with truth be condemned as having cured one evil by means of a larger source of misfortune to the country!

And this leads to the discussion of the morality of Sir Robert Peel's action, which may be called in question on very different grounds.

He must have been assured that, however firmly and however sincerely he was newly wedded to the doctrine of free trade, the party, of which he was the once trusted chief, was as sincerely and as steadfastly devoted to the principle under which the trade and commerce of the country had grown to its present vast magnitude. It was not as if the opinion of the majority of the Conservative party were of small moment, and not representative of very large and very important national interests. Sir Robert Peel knew as well as any other politician of the time that the party of protection, as it was called, represented by no means a powerless division of the community. What, then, was the chief source of his opposition to those interests which had up to the present time been associated with the prosperity of the country?

The answer Sir Robert Peel gives very distinctly and quite frankly. In the previous period of his political career he had been fighting the battles of the vanquished. He had followed in the paths of a natural progress, which was the outcome of a harmony between the various interests of the State. Existing rights he had regarded with a jealous eye; the agricultural interests of the country could not be disturbed without the infliction of injustice upon a large body of the community. The schemes of abstract politics he had rejected as opposed in the end to the welfare of the country; as being arbitrary, because limited to certain conditions in the nature; and as acting adversely to the interests of surrounding States.

This was his apology for having been blinded to the reality of a mistake of more than thirty years' standing. But Sir Robert was astute enough to apprehend the growth of forces, though he undoubtedly mistook their direction, and to mould himself to the condition of the times.

But now, after having confessed an error which covered by far the largest portion of his official career, he was persuaded by the light of reason that his former path had been in the wrong direction, and this notwithstanding the plain fact that he had had ample means of discovering his error. But the whole of his philosophy underwent a violent change; and his action proves that he sought political truths only in the foundations of abstract principles. Some extraordinary alteration must have attended the mental structure of the man who asserted, with the full conviction that he would be believed, the falsehood that "competition increases wages."

The plausible reasoning, however, of the free-traders overcame what remained of the solid judgment of the Prime Minister and Sir James Graham, the ablest, perhaps, of his colleagues. It likewise prevailed over the Duke of Wellington; and this is the more remarkable, as free trade was supposed to express the sentiment of the people. In the astounding benefits which the free-trade principle, in the hands of these enthusiasts, was to confer upon the country, Sir Robert Peel and his colleagues for a while lost the use of the faculty of anticipation. The immediate action of the principle was painted in the brightest colours; but the remote effects were unconsidered, were dim, therefore, and left for time to develop!

Impelled by a popular movement, of which he took advantage, and thus attracted to a hypothesis to which he had not given a sufficient critical attention, Sir Robert, with some obvious reluctance, which he evidences in many of his speeches, played over the part which had already become familiar to him. For the second time he abandoned his party; and, if for no other reason, he has justly earned his place in history as the only politician in whom this instance of double apostasy can be traced. In the Roman Catholic Relief Bill Sir Robert Peel's individual power was not sufficient to enable him to cast aside the trammels of party principles. He maintained his true opinion, therefore, in political silence: there was no course left open for him, if he were still to aspire to office, but deceit. In the Repeal (Corn Law) Bill, however, he was sufficiently powerful, he thought, to dispense with ordinary party obligation, and he effected this, supposing that, when in authority, the manly course to pursue was to expose his true opinions, "after he had carefully concealed them for a certain length of time." Such breaches of faith between a leader and his party are certainly not desirable; and is it in accordance with the foundation of representative government that so arbitrary an action on the part of a leader of the House of Commons should be possible? For, passing by the lesion of political faith which such conduct entails, it can only be characterised, when looked at from the view of subsequent apostasies to which the initial example gives rise, as a noxious precedent, which to know is to avoid.

What was the attitude of the protectionists? They were sound in their principles and sincere in their attachment to them. They attempted fairly, with the means at their disposal, to resist what they regarded as a violent, and eventually a destructive, innovation in the commercial system of the nation.

It is true that the feeling of the times was strained,

and oftentimes showed itself in undue excitement and outrage. But is the statesman always to be guided by the enthusiasm of a mob, and especially in the present case, where the earlier movements of the people were opposed to those of the leaders of the free-trade agitation, and where the labourers were finally gained over by the promise of future aggrandisement? Are all the interests of the country to be governed by those measures which relate to the success and unwholesome overgrowth of one only? Is the welfare and the livelihood of a relatively small part of the community to be sacrificed in order that the largest body may be placed in a position of comparative ease and comfort, and this, so far as the free-traders themselves could foresee, for a short time only?

What species of legislation is this? To make the countryman jealous of the town; to introduce the source of his desertion of the soil; to sacrifice the interests of agriculture, and thus directly to disturb the constant produce of the land, and thereby to interfere with the normal conditions of labour in neighbouring cities, the chief effect of which is seen in the reduction of wages. In a word, what is it to increase the tendency which arises from natural causes to discontentment and distress? which, indeed, would now no longer be localised to one particular branch of industry, but will spread by degrees and cumulatively over the length and breadth of the land, affecting all trades and deranging all commerce!

It is of value to revert to the arguments which Sir Robert Peel adduced to strengthen his position with reference to the Corn Laws in 1846. After referring to the recurring inconsistencies of Mr Huskisson and to the original opinion of Lord John Russell in 1822, that the free admission of foreign corn into this country would act in no other than a disastrous manner to our agriculture, he avers that it is not from observation alone, nor from the results of the experiment which had been partially conducted during the last three years, that the idea arose to react so strongly in favour of free trade, but from a large and comprehensive view of the situation—comprehensive only in the sense of its extension over a wide field at the particular time, not with respect to its subsequent operation over a period of years—that he has been constrained to alter his sentiments affecting the Corn Laws.

When the subject was rationally considered in 1845 and 1846, there could be no difference of opinion as to which side the truth lay! Are we then to infer that the subject was not treated rationally before the accession of Sir Robert Peel to power, but that it was regarded, from the selfish point of view, as a means of stepping to power?

But it might have been replied to this, seemingly the final statement of the case on the part of Sir Robert Peel,—Suppose, instead of taking a superficial examination of the two cases, of fresh meat and of corn, and arguing from general grounds which are unwarrantable, you make a minute and detailed comparison between them—suppose you draw the comparison between their ultimate effects—what grounds of likeness will you then perceive in their opposite instances, as bearing upon the general theory of free trade, when adapted to the interests of the country? And where no parallel exists between them—and this is confessed—would it not be the manly course to assume (and this Sir Robert Peel ascribed to himself in his speech on the subject, to clear himself of the charge of inconsistency) to point out the differences, to expose the fallacies, and to guard the country's trade from running along a theoretical and unconditional path?

Sir Robert changed his views; were the chances of his being on the side of the general progress of the nation thereby increased, for the grounds of the alteration were certainly insufficient to convince the merest reasoner that he was replacing a wrong by a right direction?

Why not, if he had already conducted the commercial affairs of the country under the system of protection, continue them in the face of a false opposition, which was to be met with a fierce and unyielding attitude, and with arguments which would comprise not only the present difficulties of the situation, but the whole of the future of our commercial relations? Why should the future of a nation be sacrificed for the present?

It is not difficult to unravel the grounds upon which Sir Robert Peel based the reversal of our hitherto ordinary commercial system. Having at first temporised and attempted to conciliate all parties, and hoping, with the greatest probability, to escape the final adjustment of the Corn Laws, having solved for the time being the problem of the national finances, and having laid down an income-tax from which there was no prospect of removal, except in the extraordinary and continued consumption of luxuries, and now surrounded by the increasing tide of a popular agitation, which had reached a state of fury, and with a famine close at hand, Sir Robert, in order to extricate himself from the difficulties which might possibly overwhelm him, measured all these elements in their relative magnitude and value, seized the opportunity of the predicted famine to satisfy the clamour of those who were crying out for free trade, and endeavoured, by these means, to appease the alarmed Conservative party by appearing as if he had been constrained by the adverse phenomena of nature to divert his course!

The legislation of Sir Robert Peel was thus expedient; and the most dangerous ground of principle and custom was the site where the tentative experiment was to be made. The most popular politician in the country was compelled, owing to the exigencies of surrounding circumstances, to hazard the future destinies of the nation upon the die of expediency!

The course of events subsequent to the rupture of Sir Robert Peel with the Conservative party shows the determination with which he pursued his policy. To the Whig party, now openly professing the doctrines of free trade in corn, he gave the opportunity of putting the theory into practice. But Lord John Russell, who had sounded the knell of protection in his Edinburgh letter of November 1845, was unable to form an administration. The consequence was, that Sir Robert Peel, after a formal resignation, reassumed the government of the country.

At this time there appear to have been two possibilities that might have been embraced, owing to the peculiar circumstances of the period—thus, the Parliament might have been dissolved, or there might have been a temporary coalition formed between the Peelites and the Whig party, with a view to the settlement of the question.

There was good ground for a dissolution, for doubt upon the subject of the Corn Laws extended throughout the country, and it is certainly consonant to the spirit of our free constitution that the constituencies should have the direct means of expressing their sentiments upon the measure in dispute. But it seems to be the fashion of reformers to obtrude their own ideas of reform before a people, and rather to impress them with its necessity than to gather the true development of the popular wish. Sir Robert Peel did not follow this course; and had it been on a subject that was not so intimately associated with the domestic concerns of the people, the justice of his action or that of any other politician would not be within range of being condemned. But where the general interests of the country are at stake, it is but justice that each individual interest of the nation should have the opportunity afforded to it to express its opinion on matters which are directly associated with its welfare. But such an opportunity was not granted. The feeling of the country was taken to be what it was represented as being, and it is not difficult to imagine how bias may exaggerate. If the feeling of the country was wholly on the side of free trade, it was because free-trade rhetors abounded, not because the people reasoned. There was thus an evident source of making an erroneous observation, which it was the part of a prudent politician to remove. There was the simple remedy of appealing to the polls, but Sir Robert relied upon the

G

efficacy of hypothetical argument and a false account, and hence by this conduct failed to exclude a very probable source of error.

But to the coalition there were strong objections. For not only would there be considerable difficulty in harmonising the petty jealousies and dislikes among the chiefs of parties; but the idea of a " coalition " raised up at once incongruity and disgust. The disastrous coalition, on a similar occasion, of the parties of Lord North and Charles James Fox, would be called to mind, with its pernicious results. But the strongest objection of all was, that a coalition defeats the end of government by party system, and that departure from the ordinary conduct of affairs is liable to be followed by dangerous consequences, it may be, to a subsequent generation.

However distasteful such a coalition must have been, the fact remains that the policy which Sir Robert Peel pursued amounted, though not nominally, yet virtually to the same thing. For in the critical and extraordinary position of a chief without a party, and entirely dependent for support upon those whom he had previously counted amongst his adversaries, Sir Robert Peel elected to continue the Government, with the express purpose of consummating his commercial reforms.

And under these strange and almost incredible conditions, the Prime Minister of England succeeded, with the adventitious assistance of the Prince Consort of the realms, in repealing those very Corn Laws for which he had so long and so tenaciously pleaded.

Thus Sir Robert Peel almost completed that series of reforms which he had, but in appearance only, so auspiciously commenced.

The consequences of his action were well known to him, and yet the possibility cannot but be entertained that Sir Robert, by thus accomplishing in so strange a fashion, and contrary to the foundations of popular government, the supposed desire of the people, expected, as his reward, to be borne again to power, but on this occasion, properly on the shoulders of the people.

If such an opinion were embraced, and if Sir Robert imagined that he might be able to construct a new party on a new basis, there can be no doubt that he arrogantly overrated his individual influence and popularity in the country, and the thought that these are insecure should have led him to weigh well the measure he was about to adopt.

He fell; and with his second apostasy, all hope was for ever excluded of again acceding to power.

Then the fallen statesman took up the attitude of the man who had been vanquished in a just cause. But he won the cause, though this had wrought his ruin. And now hear him proudly and defiantly exclaiming that power to him was nothing except as a means of promoting the good of the State, and in especial, the welfare of the labouring classes. To these he looked for the meed of praise denied to him in another direction. And to posterity he left the merit of his disinterested and generous measure!

But was Sir Robert Peel unconscious of having acted adversely to the interests of agriculture? The answer is found in the abatement of rents which the fallen Premier immediately made to the tenants on his large estates.

The new elections were in favour of the Whigs by a

small majority; but the course of commercial reform was continued under the ægis of Sir Robert Peel; and with the bitterest taunts from the protectionists, Sir Robert enabled the Whig Minister to proceed to the final completion of the reform of our commercial tariff.

10. *Comparison between Pitt and Peel.*—The action of Sir Robert Peel with reference to the sense of Parliament and the country, respecting the Corn Laws, may perhaps be best compared with the action of the Hon. William Pitt in 1784. There had been considerable agitation throughout the country regarding the East India Bill of Mr Fox; and on this measure the Administration of Lord North and Mr Fox, commonly called the Coalition Ministry, was thrown out by the adverse vote of the House of Lords, after its second reading. Mr Fox claimed the support of the Parliament and the sympathies of the people. The latter was open to much doubt; of the former there could be no question. But the Parliament in this case was a corrupt assembly, enslaved by the extraordinary eloquence and ambition of an unscrupulous leader. Mr Pitt was well aware of the opposition with which the Parliament viewed him; and though the Ministry of the young Premier suffered defeats in succession, he chose rather to weather the storm inside the House than place the nation at a disadvantage by a new election. For the dissolution of the Parliament was at hand; and Mr Pitt had received sufficient evidence of the support of the people, by the numerous petitions which had been placed on the table of the Commons in his favour. By such conduct would he tend to weaken the position in the country of the

party of his adversary; for thus time would be afforded to convince those who were capable of an impartial judgment of the unconstitutional nature of Mr Fox's legislation.

Thus Mr Pitt withstood the onslaught of the Opposition, while the sympathies of the people were gradually being elicited in his favour. He stood upon the ground of justice and right, and by these weapons was his victory to be won.

Sir Robert Peel, on the contrary, though opposed by the majority of the party which he had deserted, might possibly, with the assistance of his *quondam* opponents, succeed in effecting his measure in the teeth of a hostile opposition in the Commons.

In the case of Mr Pitt, the contrary sense of Parliament was obvious; in that of Sir Robert Peel it was sufficiently large and respectable enough not to be despised.

Mr Pitt had nearly the whole of the country with him, whereas Sir Robert Peel mistook the agitation of a part of the community to represent the desire of the nation.

Moreover, the position of Mr Pitt had been equal and consistent throughout: Sir Robert Peel's had been marked by inconsistency; for he had opposed, before, the emancipation of the Roman Catholics, a measure in itself wise, and based upon a large and comprehensive statesmanship. At the present he was reversing what had been a cherished policy for the last twenty years; was, therefore, such an inconstant behaviour likely to impress those favourably who regard a steady and uniform progress to be the chief feature in the career of a politician? This turncoat incident, however truly it may have been based upon the discovery of a supposed error which it had taken nearly thirty years to detect, must have reacted adversely to the prospects of Sir Robert Peel, for many would look upon him as having for the largest part of his official career acted contrary to sense and contrary to right.

Both Mr Pitt and Sir Robert Peel conscientiously held the interests of their country in their hands. But Mr Pitt maintained existing rights, and opposed only the seditious and those who raised up unconstitutional measures in the State. Mr Fox's Bill was for the reformation of the government in India.

Sir Robert Peel, on the contrary, in his efforts to advance the prosperity of the country, disturbed the possession of existing rights prescribed by Act of Parliament. He set his face directly against the whole of the agricultural interest of the kingdom.

Both were surrounded by circumstances which had an eminently dangerous tendency. Mr Pitt was assailed by the boisterous and vapid rhetoric of a politician who strove to play the part of a demagogue. Sir Robert Peel was confronted by an agitation which sought to identify the interests of manufacture with the interests of the nation.

Mr Pitt's action was directed against a measure which, if it became law, would place more power than was justifiable in the hands of an individual who was the subject of his king.

Sir Robert Peel's action, on the other hand, regarded without misgiving the introduction of a principle which was to enrich disproportionately the merchants of the country, and thus to rapidly and unduly advance their importance in the State. But the consequences of the actions of the statesman and politician were widely different. Mr Pitt by his attitude tended to weld the forces of the State into one homogeneous whole, Sir Robert Peel directly effected their disruption.

However slight may be the comparison between the respective positions of these leaders of their parties, they both offer a perfect agreement in the arbitrary character of their procedure. In the moral consequence of Mr Pitt's action there is nothing to condemn. The Parliament which he defied was a corrupt Parliament; and he is treated leniently by Mr Burke when the latter compares Mr Pitt's action of 1784 with Mr Fox's of 1793. The conditions which Mr Pitt found were not those of the ordinary course of events; the representatives in Parliament had deserted the cause of their constituents; and thus an extraordinary course had to be adapted to the new state of affairs. To blame Mr Pitt as having acted unconstitutionally is to blame him in name only. Nor is the corrupt assembly of Mr Pitt's time ever likely to come into existence again. But Sir Robert Peel has left an example which it would be unenviable to follow. He arbitrarily introduced a measure on a subject which it was universally supposed would be left untouched by the Parliament of 1841-46. His party was taken unawares by such an action, and the country had to witness the deplorable spectacle of a chief deserting the body of his party.

But it was for the good of the country! Why then did he not leave this question to be settled by that party which had embraced the theory of free trade, when it was strong enough to effect the alteration?

Did not Mr Pitt leave the vexed question of the reform to be applied to the East India Government to a new Parliament, elected under the most advantageous circumstances for eliciting the wishes of the people?

Why did Sir Robert Peel so strongly desire to repeal the Corn Laws? Because he was impelled by the motive of becoming adored by posterity!

But the sources of error which Mr Pitt successfully excluded were left open by Sir Robert Peel. Even Sir Robert might have imagined the free-trade agitation to have been exaggerated, as it certainly was. Were any measures taken to ascertain whether there was exaggeration and misrepresentation; and how much? Is the impulse of the mob always directed into the channel of right? And in the present instance, when popular enthusiasm was dependent upon the teaching of agitators, what means were used to ascertain whether such teaching was based upon sound principles, and not upon interested motives either of the merchant or the visionary?

By grasping the opportunity which was before him of appealing to the country, Sir Robert Peel would thus have precluded the possibility of an adverse criticism; of having legislated in haste, and without due regard to the full merits of the measure he was adopting.

Has not the country the right to express its sentiments upon a policy which is bound up with the well-being and prosperity of its inhabitants? But no such right was admitted by Sir Robert. He alone was the judge. And upon his judgment the fate of the nation depended! And what were the conditions under which the judgment of Sir Robert Peel was formed? A famine in Ireland, which was looming in the distance; and the fact that Lord John Russell had thrown up the idea of a fixed duty on corn. The time had come when Sir Robert Peel was being outbidden by the Whigs; the contingency of a famine in Ireland offered a pretext of applying extraordinary measures to critical times.

So long as the Whigs were on the side of protective duties on the admission of foreign corn, so long did Sir Robert continue his conscientious scruples in favour of agriculture; but these being removed, and the race for popularity commencing, Sir Robert, with his well-known avidity, desired all the honour and the glory for his own. To retain a fleeting popularity, he was compelled to sacrifice the welfare of a relatively important though small industry of the country!

11. *The nature of Sir Robert Peel's action.*—To understand fully the motives which formed the foundation of Sir Robert Peel's conduct in 1845-46, we must take a retrospective glance of a former epoch in his political career. For the antecedents of a man's conduct are of paramount importance in the display of a present action.

When Mr Canning, with sentiments disposed to the favourable settlement of the Roman Catholic question, succeeded to power in 1827, Mr Peel refused to join his Ministry, on the ground that the Cabinet ought to be united on the burning dispute of the day. It has subsequently come to light that Mr Peel had expressed an opinion in 1825 that Catholic emancipation ought to be conceded. His position, therefore, with regard to Mr Canning arrives at the juncture of a self-contradictory action with the continuance in power under a leader of whom he was envious. That there had been a feeling of rivalry between Mr Canning and Mr Peel was well known at the time; but Mr Canning, by the aid of his more brilliant faculties, had outstripped Mr Peel in the race for the Premiership. What grounds, therefore, could there possibly be, in the case of an open and disingenuous mind, for any further animosity between them?

Mr Peel, however, though beaten, and remaining ill-disposed towards his more favoured rival, still sought some plausible excuse which would relieve him from the unpleasantness, not of acting with Mr Canning, for they had already been colleagues in the Liverpool Ministry, but under him in a subordinate position.

So that Mr Peel chose the ground of the Catholic question as that which was to separate their future careers.

But that there was something underlying this apparently genuine source of difference between Mr Canning and Mr Peel is evident in the feeling at the time, that the latter had not acted generously to his former colleague; and that Mr Peel and his friends greatly added to those anxieties which terminated in Mr Canning's premature decease.

The incident is adduced to prove, how, in affairs even of the highest importance, Mr Peel was impelled by the obstinacy of his nature to seek his own individual aggrandisement, even at the sacrifice of the interests of the State. In this Mr Peel acted as his selfish disposition dictated, animated by hatred which he bore to a rival, who he persuaded himself to believe was his inferior in talent and ability.

It is possible that Mr Peel's career at the Home Office, having won for him extravagant praise, may have reacted with undue impression upon an able and persevering man. But there is a distinction, and one of vast importance, between the power of administering and the capacity to originate. And it is a curious observation that, during the whole of his official career, it was Sir Robert Peel's misfortune never to originate, but his merit to adapt measures previously constructed by others to the supposed requirements of the country. It was thus with regard to the regulation of the currency in 1819, when Mr Peel took up the propositions of Mr Francis Horner, which before he had despised, and with respect to those ameliorations in our commercial code already commenced by Sir James Mackintosh. And now, in 1842, when Sir Robert Peel began the work of reform in the commercial tariff, the lines upon which he was to act had already been laid down for him. What the country was to gain on one side by the introduction, and partial operation at first, of the principle of free trade, Sir Robert was to gain on the other by applause for his financial ability, and by the contrast which his scheme offered to the miserable results of his Whig opponents.

But between 1842 and 1846, and previously to 1842, the free-traders had promulgated the same doctrines and deduced the same results as those which appealed to the intellect of Sir Robert Peel in 1845 and 1846!

It must have been something marvellous, amounting almost to miraculous, which thus suddenly converted the Prime Minister's notions of a commercial principle to an abstract hypothetical doctrine!

But there was an agitation abroad, and it is of importance to remark this, inasmuch as the opportunity was afforded of acting presumably with the consent, and directly for the interests of the people at large.

There was prevalent throughout the northern counties of the kingdom an opinion that free trade was advantageous to the prosperity of the manufacturing element of the community. This opinion had gradually been diffused, from the fountain-source in the manufacturers themselves, even to the very dregs of the populace. Those now out of employment would, with the introduction of the new principle, succeed in obtaining work. Now the Whigs had up to the present been on the manufacturing side, and had advocated in Parliament considerable relaxations in the Corn Laws, till Lord John Russell in 1841 pronounced his verdict in favour of a fixed duty.

While, therefore, the opposite party entertained such an opinion, Sir Robert could continue to smile upon one side of the House and to threaten the other.

But the unlucky moment arrived when the leader of the Opposition, after mature consideration of the affairs of the nation, reversed his previous decision, and unreservedly proclaimed the absolute necessity of free admission of corn into this country. The position of Sir Robert Peel then became a critical one. The opposite party was in favour of the total repeal of the Corn Laws; Sir Robert still held a restriction on the admission of corn. And here there seems to open up the explanation of Sir Robert's course, and of what had passed in his mind and been uttered by him previously. Up to 1845, the speeches which he made on the subject of the Corn Laws were all in favour of continuing the restrictive duty. Existing rights, he iterated, ought always to be respected. But in the instance of the introduction of a new principle, this should take place by degrees, in order that the conditions of surrounding circumstances may become gradually adjusted to its action.

Is it possible to suppose that during all these years Sir Robert Peel was in reality entertaining in private the value and beneficial influence of a principle which, by reason of party ties, he was, or thought he was, prevented from admitting in public?

But let us compare Sir Robert Peel's speeches against the emancipation of the Roman Catholics, up to 1829, with his opinion privately expressed in 1825; and his speeches on the necessity of retaining the Corn Laws with the admissions which he makes throughout, towards the eve of the solution of the problem, on the probable results of the operation of a new principle.

Are we to believe that Sir Robert Peel was virtually a free-trader at heart while he was fighting the battles of the protectionists in corn?

And was he but awaiting an opportunity when he could, with the least danger to his own prospects, surrounded as they were by dangers on all sides, proclaim the new principle with regard to corn, and thus end a prolonged and deplorable game in domestic policy, in which he had been and still continued the chief player?

As Sir Robert Peel drew no distinction between the importation of various articles, as he seems to have regarded the principle as sound in its general bearings, and stayed not to inquire what were the particular exceptions which forbade its indiscriminate application, when Lord John Russell had come to advocate the cause of manufacture in his progress to the helm of the State, he was left alone to consider the outcome of what was regarded, and he took it to be, an illogical situation.

Already had the free-trade economists propounded the illogical position of those politicians who admitted fresh meat and live cattle duty free, and yet denied the free admission of the corn on which they were fed. And now there would be the whole weight of the Opposition party to expose still further the unsoundness of his policy.

Out of this miserable plight there was no other door open to Sir Robert Peel but that which led to the abolition of the Corn Laws. But even the view through this was pleasant enough in the prospect, for what he lost in the confidence of the former members of his party he would gain in the favour of the majority of the people. His popularity would still further increase, and he saw a vision of country villagers and town labourers resounding with gratitude the name of Peel.

This would console him for the loss of power, if he chanced to be unsuccessful at the ensuing polls!

But even then the shadow of Canning must have clouded his brow. Sir Robert may have soliloquised: "This measure, I believe, is for the country's good; but suppose my opponent resists it because it interferes with his party pretensions and his own individual ambition, what then? Can I complain? I refused to give my support to Canning under similar conditions!"

But there could be no doubt of Lord John Russell's support in effecting the measure. For the division in the Conservative ranks had opened up to him early aspirations of the advent of office.

12. *The origin of the conflict between manufacture and agriculture.*—We have already seen in a former section how unfavourably the final policy of Sir Robert Peel contrasted with that of Mr Pitt; for while the latter statesman strained all his energies to consolidate the forces of the country, the former politician, instead of harmonising, rent still further the breach which had appeared in the future prosperity of rival interests.

Although asserting that he was converted to the principle of free trade by the light of reason simply, the whole of the official conduct of the Prime Minister between 1841 and 1846 proves beyond doubt that his policy with reference to its introduction was based upon expediency. Such an unstable attitude was unlikely to be associated with a happy condition of the several opposite parties in the State, and it had its evil consequences; for on a subsequent occasion the cause of the depression of trade was purely out of animosity to Sir Robert Peel, but erroneously ascribed to the Bank Restriction Act of 1844; and such was the abnormal excitement induced by this wrong notion in some commercial circles, that in 1847 the Act was suspended by an Order in Council. By this means, tension was immediately relieved, and the Act remained unbroken; but still discord was rampant, and showed its existence in ascribing to false and impossible causes the distress under which the country was then suffering.

The depression of 1837-41 led to the question of its causation.

Sir Robert Peel's generalisation that a low state of interest and inordinate speculation are the invariable antecedents to a depressed state of the markets, was supplied in order to prove that depression in general was not due to the adverse influence of the operation of the Corn Laws. But this generalisation was exclusive of these causes of depression which are without the sphere of man's power.

It appears just to ascribe these paroxysmal conditions in the normal progress of our trade and commerce to the operation of natural causes, some of which can directly be traced to the designs of the human intellect, while others are without the sphere of human action. Thus, deficiency in harvests, when this is due to the inclemency of the seasons, is without the power of man; while those tendencies to insane speculation can very well be controlled by the appropriate remedy, and its disastrous effects thereby limited in extent.

Up to the time of Sir Robert Peel, it had been the opinion of most practical politicians that the existing system, under which the trade and commerce of the country were conducted, was the best under the circumstances.

Then it was in vain to discuss the merits of a fresh system of things. Under the idea of protection was conveyed the feeling of national self-interest, and by its influence the monopolies of the country were jealously guarded. Our commercial relations with foreign States were founded upon the basis of reciprocity. In these days the goodwill of statesmen was consigned to the region of probabilities, and mutual obligations formed the means of international commercial intercourse all the world over.

But in the course of time there appeared a tendency on the part of certain politicians and statesmen to relax a system that seemed to bear with too great a burden upon those nations which supplied us with the larger part of the corn we consumed, on the ground of the vast importance a foreign supply of corn was to this country.

Of such a disposition was Canning, who introduced a sliding-scale, in order to remove what he conceived to be too stringent an operation of the existing Corn Laws. But this scale was rejected by an enormous majority, nominally on account of the opinion entertained by the leading men that it was not sufficiently protective enough, but really because they considered it undesirable to tamper with the bulwarks of an important industry of the country. And so was Huskisson characterised by a similar though inconstant tendency. But it must not be inferred from the limited policies of these eminent statesmen that they were ardent advocates of unconditional free trade. They were promulgators of the doctrine of free trade just in the same way as any comprehensive politician was then, and is now, a free-trader, when all nations agree to be free-traders. But their policy sufficiently proves that they would have unhesitatingly rejected any arrangement which would have eventually a beneficial effect upon

H

the interests of surrounding nations at the expense of their own. For what relaxations were made during their periods of office were based on the foundation of mutual loss and gain. And the reason why the Corn Laws were the subject of a proper and temperate degree of relaxation was that the alteration would be attended with advantage to the prosperity of the country, because it removed a tendency which, at the commencement of the operation of the Corn Laws, did not act to any serious extent, but which now, after these laws had been in action for some years, appeared in greater force, and had come, in their opinion, to oppose the real intention on which they were constructed.

In this we again perceive the policy of self-interest. It is curious to notice how former legislators, in their relations with our colonies, acted on the principles of nearer acquaintance and intimacy. Then, colonial corn was not exported to this country to anything like the extent it is usual to see nowadays.

The vast resources of some of our colonies are being gradually utilised, and it is possible that the framers of this wise reservation in favour of our colonies perhaps foresaw the time when this country would altogether be supplied with the produce of her colonial acquisitions.

But if such opinions were seriously entertained by those gifted with the faculty of looking ahead, they were disastrously unheeded by the majority of thinkers at the time.

What an argument, therefore, can be turned against the hasty legislation of 1845 and 1846! But the times were extraordinary, and impending famine demanded that extraordinary measures should be taken!

The exigencies of the case could, with the greatest ease and confidence, be met by allowing the ports to be open to the admission of foreign corn for a definite time by an Order in Council; the precedent of 1826 would apply to the instance in point, and permit the free admission of foreign corn on the discretion of the Government for the requisite period. Even in 1846, when the Corn Laws were repealed by Act of Parliament, but were not to be suspended till 1849, the ports were opened for six months to meet the special requirements of the times!

It is strange to notice how Sir Robert Peel came to the conclusion that before their abolition, if he suspended for the time being the operation of the Corn Laws, he would not be justified in reimposing their burden upon the country! Why not? He had the precedent of 1826 in his favour; but perhaps he believed that, in the agitated state of the country, the people would not lightly accept the return to the former conditions of the importation of corn after the burden of the Corn Laws had once been removed.

And yet, while they were in the transitionary stage of repeal, the Corn Laws, as they remained in their modified form from the adjustment of 1842, were suspended by an Order in Council. What, then, was it that drove Sir Robert Peel to this inevitable conclusion? The agitated state of the times. It was necessary, in his opinion, that the so-called wants of the people—in other words, the free-trade doctrine of the manufacturers—should be appeased.

From the attitude of Mr Canning and Mr Huskisson and their school, there cannot be drawn, without introducing an arbitrariness into the opinion which is foreign to a just contemplation of the facts of the case, the slightest inference that they were on the side of free trade, in the sense that political economists of 1842 were free-traders, or that they advocated its unconditional operation. But some few, and especially the Hon. Charles Pelham Villiers, extolled the virtues of the principle of free trade in the abstract. The Hon. Mr Villiers was particularly pertinacious in his advocacy of the doctrine. There was not a blessing, however free trade might operate, whether conditional or unlimited, that could not be traced up to the fountain of this benign principle! His annual oration in Parliament became, in the eyes of the protectionists, an annual farce. But soon the majority against his singular views was gradually reduced, and ultimately they reigned supreme. And no doubt can be held of the fact that the position of the Hon. Mr Villiers constituted an important link in the antecedent chain of free trade, which proved of the most inestimable service to the cause.

Whether or not the Hon. Mr Villiers supposed that free trade, acting so beneficially upon the commerce of our own country, would be followed by other nations, is open to considerable doubt; but this is certain, Mr Villiers advocated the principle of free trade from the noblest motives. He, unlike Mr Cobden, was purely disinterested in the immediate operation of the principle; he took only a comprehensive survey of its course, though that was imperfect and obscured, and heralded in its introduction the germ of a constant commercial prosperity of the nation.

But it may well be inquired, Did Mr Villiers examine into the nature of the after-effects of the progress of a principle which, when once in a condition of full development and in the possible event when its action might be limited to one country, would be surrounded by dangers in all sides? For we were to gain by the operation of the principle of free trade. Then who were to lose? The answer is afforded by the speeches of Sir Robert Peel! Far greater harm would be inflicted upon the commerce of other nations by this arbitrary procedure than harm resulting to ourselves. With respect to ourselves, he asserted that "every shilling abstracted from consumers by monopolies and protection diminishes the abilities of those consumers to contribute to the exigencies of the State;" and with reference to the foreigner, "take off imposts, and then you will be able to contend to greater advantage with your foreign rivals." In the gross, therefore, it was Sir Robert Peel's opinion that we should be the greatest winners.

But was such a policy as this likely to attract the admiration and esteem of surrounding nations, the more particularly when they had to bear the initial burden entailed by the limited application of the free-trade principle, and when certain branches of their industry were for the time being crushed, if not destroyed?

The Hon. Mr Villiers might have put the question to himself, whether the boasted universal peace which he predicted would follow in the train of free trade, even partially operating, was likely to reach a consummation when it developed, wherever its influence appeared, such deadly feelings in the breasts of foreign peoples?

Should he not have shown the way to allay and appease international hatred and hostility on the sound principles which are inculcated in the Gospel, by spreading the Christian doctrine of " loving thy neighbour as thyself," rather than opening up new sources of discord and enmity? For is the usual animosity which is evinced in the business transactions of a single nation likely to disappear when nations are concerned in commercial relationship?

Still the weight of Mr Villiers's authority was sufficient to give an air of respectability to the diffusion of a doctrine of which otherwise it would have sadly been wanting. (For a time he stood alone, and pleaded the justice of the cause of free trade with all the ardent feelings of a patriot, whose sentiments alone were associated with the welfare of his country.) The Anti-Corn-Law League stood aloof from him. Its members advocated free trade from their own selfish point of view. But afterwards, when they sought the assistance of the earnest outspoken champion of free trade, that assistance was frankly offered; and then ensued thereupon the united efforts of disinterestedness on the one side and of self-interest on the other; for Mr Villiers viewed the principle of free trade extending far and wide, and erroneously conceived that the future progress of the principle would be as prosperous as its first period of activity, while the manufacturers regarded only the depths of their own pockets. It is true that with their aggrandisement for the time the wages of their labourers would be raised for a corresponding period, and would, on the whole, be more certain for a somewhat longer one; but the extent to which such a beneficial result would reach was limited, firstly, in point of numbers, as regards the part of the community to be affected by it, and secondly, in respect to that tract of time during which these immediate benefits would be flowing.

But the manufacturers themselves had set their hearts on the introduction of the principle of free trade. The conduct of the Manchester Assembly—the centre whence emanated all those forces which acted in favour of the free-trade system—sufficiently proves the narrow motives which guided their conduct. This is shown in the way in which they combated the idea of transferring the main source of action from Manchester to London, for the purely selfish reason that they feared their cause might lose in popularity and strength; and it belongs solely to the merit of Mr Cobden that he succeeded, after many obstacles were overcome and much patience exhibited, in conferring upon the free-trade agitation the aspect of a metropolitan character.

What was the action of the Manchester Chamber of Commerce with reference to the attitude of Mr George Wood, who was their chairman, and therefore was presumably foremost in the advocacy of the free-trade doctrine? Mr Wood was selected to second the Address in the session of 1841-42; and although in Manchester he was of the opinion that free trade was the sole means of relieving the distress of the country and of deepening the pockets of the Manchester manufacturers, yet when he was removed from the sphere of narrow and selfish convictions, and was at once surrounded with an atmosphere of liberality, which was clouded with the future disasters of so precarious a system, he as well succeeded in demonstrating, to the admiration of the Peel Ministry and to the satisfaction of Parliament, that the country was in a prosperous condition in spite of the supposed pernicious operation of the Corn Laws, as he showed to the enthusiasts of Manchester that the distress of the country was directly due to the evil action of those laws! The obvious corollary of which is, that the agitation was thereby proved to be more selfish than ever in its character; that distress was aggravated, but in speeches only; and that the nation was in as flourishing condition as the circumstances of the times—be the commercial policy free trade or protection—would allow.

But, in consequence of this independent expression of opinion, the tone of Manchester, then "Liberal" in its politics, was greatly aggrieved towards Mr George Wood. The Chamber of Commerce was irate; and Mr George Wood was deposed from the position of president.

What is the probability that many others of the same assembly would have pursued a similar course when removed from the contact of such a deadly virus, the worst possible of all when the general body of the assembly was subject to its insidious influence—the selfish interest of a limb of the body politic, which the free-traders had mistaken for the trunk, leading to an unwholesome congestion, and terminating in a fatal overgrowth, for it thereby nurtured the seed of disease?

But the importance of manufacture was inordinately exaggerated; and as the case permitted it, the progress and development of manufacture was extolled at the expense of agriculture.

Thus agriculture came to be depreciated. A limb,

and an important one too, of the body politic came thus to be neglected; and when its circulation was on the verge of being strangulated, was it unlikely that it should die?

This opposition between the main branches of the industries of the kingdom being originated in this way—by the selfish attitude of the manufacturers towards those measures which kept up the price of corn, because they interfered with the temporary wellbeing of their labourers—it was not difficult to maintain the flame of passion which blazed amongst the respective champions of the antagonistic interests. There was extreme facility in impressing the ordinary merchant with the unconditional truth of the free-trade doctrine of buying in the cheapest market and selling in the dearest. Nor was there any greater trouble in deflecting the feelings of the common labouring man into that channel where he would find his highest account. The previous opposition which he had exhibited towards his master would now be turned into all the more devoted an adhesion than if he had simply been drawn, in the first instance, to the side of the merchants. Thus, when the labourer was convinced that he had a common cause with his master, and that the repeal of the Corn Laws would be altogether for his own advancement and prosperity, it was obvious that the progress of the free-trade agitation in corn, which before had been limited in extent and therefore retarded, would now, with this fresh accession of strength, be greatly increased.

The agricultural labourers were shown the blessings that would attend them by the application of the new principle to the admission of foreign corn, and the revolution which it would effect in our trade; and even the farmers were persuaded to believe that their profits would increase when their rents were diminished.

So diffused had become these false teachings of the Anti-Corn-Law League, and so violent a certain section of the mob in favour of the free-trade system applied to corn, that individual instances of violence and uproar were not uncommon. The halls where speeches in favour of free trade were delivered, by the insidious means of exposing the faults and supposed injustice of the policy of protection—and what system is free from faults?—were filled to overflowing, by a populace generally inflamed by the sophistical tricks of an ignorant eloquence.

Free trade—indeed!—would deliver them from those burdens under which they imagined, by being taught to believe, that they were groaning! Free trade was the means—the only means—of for ever abolishing war from the face of the earth, and of diffusing peace and goodwill throughout all mankind! But most of all, the nation would be prosperous under the unrestricted operation of the free-trade principle, and not only prosperous for a time, but its prosperity was always to continue! On these foundations were the harangues constructed. It was easy enough for the merchant to anticipate that the abolition of the Corn Laws would render the condition of his labourers far more satisfactory relatively than it had ever been before, and convert the possibility of his accumulating a large fortune into a certainty. The difficulty, however, of foreseeing the ultimate results of so vast a disturbance was not encountered, and hence the masters were contented with a view which was restricted to the near future.

But feeling must be aroused: as it is impossible that a movement shall spread throughout a considerable mass by reason alone. A more volatile instrument is needed, and one which can be brought into action readily. Passion must be called forth and kept aflame. And thus the necessary means were devised by which the agricultural class partly, and the landed owners generally, were held up to the excited people as being adverse to the progress of the nation nominally, really of manufacture alone. There were tyrants in the land, who ground down the wages of labour to their lowest point!

But what was this progress, of which the free-traders made such a brilliant display? In the eyes of the agricultural protectionists it was an unwholesome progress; and it was to this kind of false progress—which afforded the shadow only, a mere temporary increased circulation of the markets, and not the true substantial element of advancement, which they associated rather with the decline than with the reform of our commerce, as being the unstable and exuberant product of too active a growth—that they directed their steady and fixed opposition; for they perceived in the agitation of the manufacturers the germ of an undue growth of a single, however much it may have been the most important, branch of our industries, an overgrowth which could only be effected by a corresponding diminution in the vitality of another industry.

But the free-traders, at the instigation of the manufacturers, identifying themselves with the commercial prosperity of the nation, and openly proclaiming that England was no longer an agricultural country, pointed to the landowners, who were mainly on the side of protection, as being the mainstay of the high price of bread; for they argued that the high price of corn is maintained to increase the rents of the farmer, and so to attract more money to the pockets of the lords of the soil. The landowners therefore, and of course the aristocracy, were enriched, that the people and labourers might starve! And thus the mob were aroused into a sense of the hypothetical injustice which they were suffering at the hands of the lazy and rich.

By thus appealing to the lowest passions of an angry populace, it was but necessary only that the free-trade rhetors should make use of arguments which were based upon an obvious fallacy, and statements which had their foundations alone in the depths of their oftentimes luxuriant imaginations. They little perceived the tendency of the change by which they were endeavouring to bring about a redistribution of wealth. The vast fortunes of the landowners might, for the nonce, be arrested in their flowing course; many who were previously enriched might, by these measures, become impoverished; but those who pleaded the cause of the new principle as a means of checking the inordinate accumulation of wealth, argued with a strange deficiency of the knowledge of surrounding conditions, for they failed to discover that, in their attempt to effect their object, instead of preventing the gigantic accumulation of wealth, they but displaced the sources of that accumulation.

Suppose the rent of the arable land of the country to

be reduced according to the prognostications of the free-traders—an event which was not of unusual occurrence, and generally it may be stated that the rent of the farmers remained where it was—the value of the town land would proportionately increase with the extension of the commerce of the nation. Large offices would be required, and larger still, according to the gradual development of commercial houses, and prices would increase with the most desirable situation. Here was one source by which the landowners would recoup the loss, if that was to occur, ensuing upon the effect of free trade upon the agricultural prospects of the country. But in the meanwhile there would be a greater demand for labourers' dwellings in the manufacturing towns, and these would undergo a corresponding increase in development to become adjusted to the requirements of a temporarily over-active trade. The law of competition would appear, and tend to drive the rent of the artisan's cottage to its highest point. Another influence, too, which would react upon this and increase it, was evident in the higher wages, which, for the time, attended the immediate consequence of the introduction of free trade. The labourer would have more to pay for a home increasing in comforts. And thus, if the country landowners were to be the losers by the pernicious effect of the free-trade principle upon agriculture, the town landowners would more than recover such loss to aristocratic wealth by the additional gain accruing to them from the extension of those towns in which the prosperity of manufacture usually flourished. If, therefore, both town land and country were in the possession of a single owner, it is easy to see that what would be lost in one direction would be gained in another. The free-trade principle, therefore, in many instances, is thus proved to fall short of the original intention of some of its promoters. And was the idea present to these of the possibility of the construction of large commercial fortunes by means of the free-trade principle?

It is doubtful whether, from a general point of view, the landowners lost anything of their rent by the application of the new commercial principle; and it is certain that an increase to their wealth accrued more rapidly by the immediate stimulus which free trade gave to all our trades and industries than by any other means.

But what was the baneful effect to be foreseen, and, if possible, avoided, in the dangerous state into which our domestic affairs were engulfed by the free-trade principle? The rent of the labourers' dwellings was soon raised to the highest point. While this remained constant, the incomings of the labourer were liable to fluctuate; and when they began steadily to decline, what was open to him but to exchange his better dwelling for one of inferior comforts? The relationship between the two elements of the amount of rent to be paid, and the ability to pay it, which was kept properly adjusted by the system of protection, was now seen to be violently disturbed. Before free trade, the relationship was a true one, and true because based upon a just basis—it was founded on the equable advancement of our trade upon sure and steady lines. But now, while the country is in a state of distress—and the country has been under the severest distress during the operation of the free-trade principle—and the labourer no longer able to pay the former proportionate share of his wages for the rent of his dwelling, when rent ought to be decreased, it is maintained at a relatively high level, just as the rents of farms after the introduction of the free-trade principle were kept at their previous level; because it is the opinion of the sanguine of the commercial world that a revival of trade is at hand, and that labour will be again plentiful, and wages reach their former amount.

But what brought about this sudden increase in the labourers' dwellings? The principle of free trade. And who are responsible for the misery which the descent from a higher to a lower degree of social conditions entail? The free-trade enthusiasts.

But is the forecast—and a very poor one it appears to be—that a future prosperity awaits labour an adequate argument why, in the meanwhile, the labouring man should be unjustly the sufferer of an unequal state of things, of a disordered relationship, brought about immediately by the continued operation of the free-trade principle? The labourer's son of the present generation groans beneath the burden which the labourer's father of the past age, in a moment of blind enthusiasm—and when is popular enthusiasm not blind?—bequeathed to them. The steady course of our trade was violently interrupted, and the effects of that violence were transmitted to that very relationship of income and expenditure, on the proper adjustment of which the happiness of the labouring classes is founded!

Are those, then, who advocated protection the cause of this disastrous consequence? and are the owners of the soil to be condemned because rents are, owing to the circumstances of distress, unduly high? But who are responsible for the present disproportion between the amount of rent and the ability to pay it? Obviously those who predict a near and rapid revival of the present trade-depression, which has existed now for so long a period that it may well be considered whether or not a tendency to decline is its proper attribute. What is the work which the free-traders have done? Their first object was to cause a rupture in the harmony of natural relations and progressive development; and after this was completed, and relying upon the continued efficacy of the principle which effected the rupture to induce a second reign of prosperity, they extend all their powers to maintain it, to the disadvantage of the labourer and to the evil of the State.

But there are signs of a near revival! What are they, then? Sir Robert Peel, in the time of distress, pointed to distinct causes, the removal of which, he foretold, would be followed by a return of prosperity, and they were. The causation he described completely, and indicated how the revival of trade was to be effected. But in the present day, where are the indications of such a revival, except in the imaginations of enthusiastic free-traders. Not only are there no signs of recurrent prosperity, but the evidence of an imperceptible decline comes daily to be stronger.

Are the landowners, then, in the face of such expressions of opinion on the part of free trade, to be condemned because they act for their own self-interest? Does not the free-trader himself act for his own interest, and none other?

Ay! but the landowners, in their wealthy position, should relax rents when they become stringent, will the philanthropist cry out; they should be governed by generous motives, and exercise a benevolent disposition towards their suffering countrymen!

Did the free-traders practise these measures when they agitated for the cause of free trade? Are goodwill and charity the springs which regulate the transactions of business, either between nation and nation or individual and individual?

But the general tendency must be admitted on the part of the landowners to mitigate the hard lot of their suffering tenants in those instances where such acts of charity are unlikely to be followed by the growth of indolence. For it can hardly be called a good or a safe system to replace one evil of a certain magnitude by another of a far greater.

Look at the question in whatever way we may, it is impossible to avoid the truth of the fact that self-interest is the force which guides us in all our commercial relations, as the general rule. There may be some exceptions in those peculiar cases where the emergency of the case demands that we shall make a present sacrifice; but then, do we not make such a sacrifice in order that we may, at some future time, and when the conditions are similar, but against us, be the recipients of a second apparent act of disinterestedness?

The result of the free-trade agitation carried on by the Anti-Corn-Law League was patent. Its charms had worked. The people had been aroused into an enthusiasm, the effects of which it was sometimes impossible to check. The labouring classes were the aggrieved classes; the agriculturists and landowners, the tyrants of the nation, who ground the wages of labour down to starving-point, and who directly opposed a mighty obstacle in the progress to more abounding riches, and therefore greater happiness!

Was it possible to expose to the inflamed mob the dangers which beset a too rapid progress,—dangers which, if they did not appear in their own days—and it was probable they would in the case of the young— would at any rate certainly attend the lives of their children?

But the difference between a healthy and an unwholesome progress was not to be discriminated. The mere mention of progress in the vapid utterances of a free-trader was received with exuberant applause and demonstration, as if all progress was good. Nor was it the endeavour of the people, or of those who advocated their consistent and just advancement, to lay bare the hollow nature of the arguments which served the purpose of saluting the appearance of free trade! The people had their eyes fixed and their attention riveted upon the injustice which the operation of the Corn Laws perpetrated upon them. They were taught to believe that they suffered, and suffered unjustly. It was a clever trick!—to divert the enthusiasm of the mob into the channel of the manufacturers' pockets, and to make a nation believe that the prosperity of their country was identified with the welfare of a portion of its inhabitants!

But the end was attained. By means of the most powerful of forces—passion—the interests of agriculture and manufacture came directly to be opposed!

13. *Criticism of the free-trade fallacy, that increase in the price of corn was invariably associated with, and was the cause of, rise in rent.*—An increase in the price of corn directly tended to consume a larger proportion of the wages of the labourer. But the economists, who saw the welfare of the working classes in the lower price of bread, failed to foresee that other means would be called into existence to absorb the earnings of the labourer; and that in the alteration they were endeavouring to effect, of affording the labourer greater advantages for the enjoyment of comforts on the one side, and for saving on the other, they were but introducing a redistribution of his expenditure, without gaining ultimately their desired end.

Thus the political economists of free trade supposed that labour would receive the chief benefit from their reform; and undoubtedly this was the object which many sincerely hoped would be attained by the new system. But the opportunity of gratifying self-interest they neglected. Was it difficult to detect that, under the new arrangement, the masters would use the means of attracting to themselves too large a proportion of the wages of labour? For though wages would rise with the increased circulation of the markets, they would not be permitted to reach their proportionate level, by reason of the great reduction in the price of bread. Nor does the fact, apparently, seem to have been considered, that in the fresh distribution of the labourer's expenditure the landowners, as well as the masters, would not be without their proper share.

But let us pursue the same method of arbitrary association which the free-traders used in the last age. On some few particular occasions, an increase in rent coexisted with a rise in the price of corn. No attempt was made to explain this unfortunate coexistence, nor was the general result of the advance of our industries under the policy of protection accurately deduced, though it was proved by experience, the mistress of all sound conclusions, that the country was never so prosperous as when rents were high. A comparison, indeed, might be instituted between what has already happened in the prosperous state of agriculture and what is happening now in the instance of our large commercial institutions. Is not the rent of their offices gradually increased and increasing? Why? Because so long as their markets are active, their ability to afford a higher rent becomes greater. But there is no need to inquire into the foundations of a relationship based upon the natural progress of things—a relationship which was cruelly ignored by the advocates of free trade.

Let us proceed to take the case where a low price of bread is associated with low wages. Have these two phenomena been invariably associated? And are they likely to continue so, if they have been, during the later operation of the free-trade principle? What is to prevent any one from drawing so close a connection between low wages and a low price of bread as shall result in the relationship of effect and cause? or as collateral effects of the same cause? What will the free-trader reply? That the inference is unsound, because not drawn from a sufficiently large number of instances. But supposing this association of low wages with a low price of corn has existed for some comparatively long period, and supposing, from the outlook of trade affairs, the association is probable to continue, what explanation has the free-trader to offer? He will answer that the depression is due to other influences than that of the operation of the free-trade principle. Perhaps he will assume the unenviable position of Sir Robert Peel on a former occasion; and while believing in his heart that free trade is the source of all the distress of the country, and the decline in our trade, will be under a moral compulsion of supporting a conclusion which he knows to be false, that free trade has no material share in the causation of the present ills of the nation.

Could there be any doubt that the comforts of the working men would be largely increased, after the immediate and unrestricted action of the free-trade principle? But luxuries sometimes become necessaries, and in the conversion undergo an increase in price, owing to the ability of the consumer to pay for them. The time would arrive, however, when the surroundings of the labourer had become adjusted to the disturbance in their previous equilibrium—when the cost of various articles having increased, the condition of the working men would not be one tittle any the better than it was under the old condition of things.

The conditions which before obtained and tended to the development of thrift and the accumulation of savings are present now, but in no wise improved. Rather the reverse has occurred. For if the disposition to save be absent, no matter how favourable the surrounding circumstances, there will still remain the tendency to be dissatisfied—a tendency which will not be removed even by the continued increase of wages. For this spirit of extravagance, nurtured by the inordinate rise in wages, depends upon the inability, which by education ought to be repressed, to live within the limits of the powers of one's production. This ability to adjust expenditure to income it is that leads to content and the diffusion of happiness throughout so many families. They are content with what they are able to procure; their supply exceeds their demand; and they have the consolation of having a sufficiency to fall back upon in the hour of illness and the time of distress.

It is clear, therefore, that any permanent beneficial alteration in the labourer's condition was impossible to be effected by a reduction in the price of bread. For the time being the working classes enjoyed the benefit of the disturbance in their slow and equable advancement; but to what evils was the enjoyment of such a temporary prosperity prone to lead?

Their relative surroundings, having undergone a species of convulsion, return to their former state. Their surroundings return to the same condition comparatively, but not their disposition nor their character. For the immediate effect of the convulsion has been to foster an increase of extravagance, and an attachment to luxuries, which, in the uneducated, when once the taste has been experienced, it is very difficult to repress.

The free-traders, at the period of the promulgation of their doctrine, whether knowingly or not, refrained not only from pointing out the possible disasters that might attend the course of their principle, but they neglected as well the dangers which involved the spasmodic change in the domestic affairs of the labouring man. On the contrary, instead of indicating the evils which beset their own system, while they magnified those which belonged to the system of protection—and every system is necessarily bound up with evils—they demonstrated that the price of corn was liable to rise, and at the same time, to suit the statement of their case, they asserted that rent was liable to become increased. But they left out the place of speculation as a force which is capable of effecting the former, and altogether ignored the true causation of the latter. The two factors they associated in their imagination; and after mature consideration, the association became invariable! When they thought they became restricted to one possibility, they enunciated the problem, What is it that tends to increase rent? And they sought the solution of this question, perplexing to them, in the conclusion drawn from a relationship based entirely upon a hypothetical foundation between factors which were constantly associated but in their imagination! Corn was forced to a high price, with what effect? To increase the rent of the landlords!

Thus by a simple fallacy—by means of an arbitrary association, which expresses a relation not existing in the natural course of things—the free-trade economists succeeded in constructing a problem which struck at the position of the landlords in the State; and by means such as these they eventually created a diversion of public feeling in their own favour.

It is obvious that so forced an explanation of a natural phenomenon was framed to meet the requirements of a special object.

But the true statement of the case, however, is widely

different. It is, that rent, like every other element of a similar nature depending upon a complex relationship, the components of which are all liable to fluctuation, is prone to increase when circumstances are favourable to its rise, and to fall when they are the contrary. Rents used to increase, not because corn was kept at a high price—though it is probable that the farmer tended to keep the price of corn at a high level when the produce of his farm was less abundant, but such occasions were exceptional, and were the outcome of self-interest—but because the total produce of the farm went on increasing. And here the subject of the unproductiveness of the soil may conveniently be introduced. Land, it is well known, tends to become less and less productive when left to its own resources. Rich lands tend to become poor, and poor lands tend to go out of cultivation, when their produce is no longer remunerative to the labour which is bestowed upon them.

The unproductivity of the soil, therefore, would tend to lower the rent of arable land; but there are means which have been devised by the ingenuity of man to counteract this evil tendency. With the assistance of artificial manures, the produce of the land is kept at a nominal level, and in some cases is even increased above that level. With such an aid, then, to increase the resources of nature, the rents of arable lands would remain either what they were or would increase. And the latter would be inevitable, if the total produce of the farm was, under favourable circumstances of good seasons and skill, able to be increased. But compare such a state of things with the instance of land going out of cultivation, not because it is poor—though it is relatively poor as regards the profits to be derived from its careful cultivation—but because surrounding conditions are unfavourable to its profitable cultivation. Compare the instances when wheat stood at between 73s. and 100s. per quarter, with wheat at 30s. per quarter, or a little above it. Can it be considered possible that, under the latter adverse circumstances, the production of corn in this country can be remunerative? And if not remunerative, what results? Good land, able to yield its increase, is forced, by an adverse operation of a principle, out of cultivation, to the disadvantage of the State, and the ruin of the farmer's prospects. The chance coincidence of an increased value of farm-property and a rise in the price of corn was erroneously described as cause and effect!

On the increase of value of arable land, by increasing the productivity of the soil by means of improved cultivation, the question arises: Is the result of such improvement altogether to go into the pockets of the farmer who adopts, but does not originate, this mode of increasing his resources? Obviously not; from such a beneficial result, following upon the labour of a genius foreign to both, the farmer and landowner respectively attach their proportionate shares. For by such a distribution, the present tenant is protected from the competition of his neighbours—by these means is he enabled to retain the farm upon which, perhaps, he has been bred.

It is therefore from the law of competition, arising from the appearance of those improvements, whether natural or artificial, which chance to enhance the value of the farm, that rent is increased in amount. And this law of competition appears not only in the case of farms to increase their rent, but also in all those instances which are characterised by a similar relationship. It is this law which tends to raise the price of city offices, as well as to increase the value of town houses. What, therefore, was practised years ago—because the practice had a foundation in natural progress—in the example of farm-property, but was condemned, for an especial object, is observed to be the ordinary rule in similar occasions nowadays. Why, then, is not the same arbitrary procedure practised in the present day, with respect to the gradually increasing value of city property? The instances are quite parallel; the same law pervades both cases. If this law of competition was rudely interrupted in 1845, in the case of country land, why should not the Legislature exhibit the same tendency in this year 1886 with respect to town land? What is it that prevents this perfectly logical procedure on the part of the deliberative assembly of the kingdom? Is it the nature of the consequences which were supposed to be governable, and were undoubtedly for a certain period, which impelled the movement in 1845, and which prevents the application of the same remedy to-day? Is it purely a question of political or party expediency? Such an answer is left to the descendants of the great Whig party, who, perhaps, less wise in experience than men who are concerned in the practical conduct of affairs, are nevertheless older in the art of logical reasoning!

But the unworthy action of the free-traders in magnifying the importance of a chance coincidence, and forcibly turning it to their assistance, while they utterly disregarded the slow and steady course of natural growth, is sufficiently exposed. They proclaimed that the landowners used force to raise the price of corn; but they, with much peculiarity indeed, failed to see the arbitrary force which they themselves employed in the construction of an argument to serve their purpose! —an argument which had for its object the creation of a relationship which has no constant existence in the natural order of things. How could the free-traders ever hope to reach a secure conclusion, when their treatment of the difficult problem they handled was so imperfect and so partial? They ascribed but one cause which goes to increase rent; they ignored the complex character of its causation. They despised the influence of speculation, which is as prone to affect the corn as well as any of the trade markets of our country!

It is curious to observe that the very force which they excluded actually came into appearance not long after the Corn Laws were repealed; because the rise in the price of corn went to increase the rent of the landlords. It was in 1846 and 1847 that, the harvests being generally deficient, corn became relatively scarce, and its price reached a fabulous point. And it may be inquired, In what way does the free-trade system tend to diminish the possibility of corn reaching as high a price as in 1846, when, as may happen, there may be a deficiency in any one or more of the sources of our supply? Will free trade, in such an unfortunate state of affairs, aid in the reduction of price? As soon will free-trade destroy the ordinary relation which exists between supply and demand!

But the event goes to show that if the prognostics of the free-trade economists have not been sufficiently disproved, they have received, at any rate, a serious shock.

For the condition of the farmers, who were persuaded into the belief that with a diminution in rent they would enjoy an increase in profits—what is it now?

Is it true that at the present day small rents go with high profits? Is it a fact that nowadays small rents are associated with diminished profit; and that farms, without paying any rent at all, can scarcely be worked with profit?

But the same fatality attends all the doctrines of the free-traders. Can this be otherwise, when they are based upon erroneous foundations? when mutual surroundings are wilfully unconsidered? when the law of competition is despised, and when the influence of speculation is ignored?

Suppose that, like the free-trade economists, we should take the association of phenomena with which we are now familiar, and argue thus: Low rents and small profits on the one hand, and a low price of bread and small wages on the other, are invariably associated; therefore, low rents are the cause of small profits, and a low price of bread is the cause of small wages! What objection can the free-trade economists entertain respecting this mode of reasoning?

14. *Results of the sophistry of the free-trade rhetoric.*—The free-trade doctrine, which was nursed in the cradle of selfishness while developing into its manhood, was exposed to the evils of a disease to which it was prone;

but these were carefully concealed from the public eye by its physicians, who descanted only on the splendid career that was open to its mature growth. Yes—possibly open! But surely, if free trade is to attain the plenitude of its glory and prosperity, surrounding circumstances must be favourable to its continued development. The atmosphere in which it continues to exist must remain free from all those sources that may intervene to impede its healthy function. And such is expressed in the event that all foreign nations should agree to become free-traders. Such was the original intention of the founder of the doctrine; the idea never entered his head that a single nation alone should undertake the responsibility of becoming a free-trader! by which measure so great a source of disturbance would be introduced into the existing mutual harmony of international commercial relations as must essentially result in a new distribution of energies, the outcome of all which could not possibly be advantageous to the nation which so arbitrarily interrupted the smooth and equable course of her commerce. It was in its early development that the splendid achievements, portrayed by the vivid imaginations of its ardent and enthusiastic protectors, were to happen. But of its mature state nothing was said, because nothing was properly anticipated.

And it is marvellous to relate that even the leaders of the opposite parties in the State were the subjects of perhaps the cleverest piece of logical juggling that has ever been perpetrated on a nation.

Sir Robert Peel himself assented to the conclusion that the rise in the price of corn went directly to increase rent; and naturally remarked upon the pernicious tendency of this presumed state of things. Even that astute politician, who entered into the complex causation of national distress, and who, after analysing it into its several elements, separated those of a temporary from those of a more permanent duration—though year after year he continued to openly assert that the operation of the Corn Laws did not in any material degree contribute to the national depression, till in 1846 he finally abolished the Corn Laws as a remedy to cure the existing distress;—even Sir Robert Peel was led into the extremity of supporting the most extravagant and fallacious doctrine that has ever been enunciated in the whole history of political economy! But we have already observed the expediency of Sir Robert Peel's action, and the fact that the repeal of the Corn Laws formed part only of a complex system to relieve the general evils of the country.

But the free-trade doctrine, nurtured by self-interest, was carried by a haste which was characteristic of the conduct of those who presided over its cradle. The free-traders were not wanting in those arts which appeal to the feelings of others, by the sense of injustice conveyed, while they succeed in effecting their own selfish purpose. The populace was appeased; they were taught to believe that under the new condition of things they would never again want bread, because bread would be so cheap! The farmers were entrapped into the belief that the natural and existing order of affairs would be effectively altered for their benefit by the new principle! What was established by custom, and founded on the springs of human action—what had years and reason on its side, was to be abolished for —what? For the introduction of a new system, entirely devoid of experience, based upon imperfect knowledge of its subsequent course, promoted by partiality, and flaunted before an ignorant mob as the only remedy which could remove the source of their protracted sufferings. As if the principle of free trade could change the origin from which human actions flow!

These were the methods the free-traders employed to gain over the ignorant. And they were unscrupulous in the supply of arrogant and false promises. But for the educated another course was pursued. They were not wanting in the insidious arts of a spurious logic to convince the legislators of the country that free trade was both to be a national benefit and the one great stroke of domestic policy which was to mark the nation's history of this century. Well might Sir Robert Peel jump at the bait thus thrown out to him. But might he not have paused ere he swallowed the noxious morsel? The landlords obtain their proportionate share of the general produce of the land of which they are the owners; and did not Sir Robert Peel's father amass an enormous fortune by means of another's genius and with the assistance of labour? What was the relation of Sir Robert Peel's father to his workmen? and compare this with the conduct of the landlord to his tenants.

There was no restriction of hours in those days; against such legislative interference the first Sir Robert directed the whole weight of his authority. Nor can the conduct of that illustrious gentleman be called humane, relative to the notions which we now entertain. Did the labourer, in his days, gain a proportionate share of the produce of his labour? Test the surroundings of the workman then with those of the present time. A vast change has been sweeping their entire character. But did Sir Robert Peel the first effect any important result for good in the domestic affairs of his labourers? Look at the immense fortune he amassed—the first instance in which a commoner was rated at the upper value; what was the source of it?—the labour of his workmen. Compare the position of the landlord and his property with that of the master and his labour. Property and labour are the sources by which the landlord and the manufacturer respectively gain their wealth. Is not the same rule that applies to one to apply to the other? Is there any reason why the landowner should rest contented with a constant rental, when he sees around men less scrupulous in their efforts to grind the wages of labour to their lowest point? Are the landlords constituted in a fashion different from other men? The second Sir Robert Peel, when he cast a wrathful glance towards the landowners, who did not regard him with any degree of favour, forgot for a while that in the policy he was pursuing towards them, he was disturbing that very principle by which his own father was, by a fortunate chain of events, enabled to become the master of an almost fabulous wealth.

But the free-traders were peculiarly happy in their choice! The son of the manufacturer played inadvertently into the hands of manufacture!

Have the results so foolishly predicted by the free-trade rhetors been verified?

Have wars diminished? No, will reply the free-trader. And the reason? Because free trade has not become universal. Why has not free trade become universal? Because in the opinion of foreign nations it is not calculated to attain the object which has been predicted of it. Hence is the original selfishness of the free-trade impulse laid bare, even to its base!

But if free trade has not abolished war, it has tended to diminish trade depression. Is this a fact? Take forty years before 1842 and forty years after 1846, and contrast the number of years of distress in each period. Will such a result ensue as to justify the virtue of the principle?

Lastly, has free trade continued the prosperity of the country, as it was boasted it would? There was, certainly, the immediate stimulus to the markets; there was a temporary period of excitement, a phase of feverish activity, which occupied all hands, and raised wages. But then depression appeared, and this has so gradually and almost imperceptibly increased, that now profits have reached their lowest level—or perhaps there may be none at all. In such a state of affairs, can the condition of labour be called prosperous? And yet free trade still reigns, and the labouring man was to be for ever enriched by it!

15. *The introduction of free trade into the commercial use of this country.*—After the sliding-scale had settled in 1842 the agitated feeling of the country respecting the admission of foreign corn, Sir Robert Peel proceeded to the introduction of the free-trade principle into our commercial system. This was taken in conjunction with a Bill to renew the income-tax for a

K

period of three years. For both these measures formed part of a scheme designed by the Prime Minister, as well to relieve the nation from a constantly recurring deficiency in its revenue as to remove the burden of distress under which the trade of the country was then suffering. Which of these events was present with the greater force to the mind of Sir Robert Peel?

The taxation of several imported articles, mainly concerned in manufacturing industries, was remitted Live cattle, which before had been prohibited, were now permitted an admission duty free; the impost was removed from salted meat, and the duty on fresh meat reduced. The remission of taxes was continued during the next and following sessions, and thus the gradual application of a new principle was effected, according to the previous declaration of the Prime Minister, in order that customary and existing rights might become slowly, and with the least disturbance, adjusted to the new system. After the year 1845, the amount remitted in taxation reached £1,961,000. Then came the period during which the question of the Corn Laws occupied the whole attention of the people.

On account of the change in his attitude to the operation of laws which Sir Robert, in the year previous, had definitely asserted admitted of no amendment, in the judgment of himself and colleagues, and which, he reiterated, were not responsible for the distress of the country — the Prime Minister, having effected a final rupture with his party, found it necessary to resign. This was in December 1845. A few weeks antecedent to Sir Robert Peel's resignation, Lord John Russell had written a letter, dated from

Edinburgh (and known as the "Edinburgh letter"), to his constituents in the metropolis, in which he gave his final views on the absorbing question of the day. Lord John Russell was prevented from forming an Administration owing to the opposition which he met with in the House of Lords, and depending on the unwillingness of Lord Grey to assist the new Ministry. Sir Robert Peel consequently reassumed the reins of power, with the well-known intention of proceeding immediately to the repeal of those laws which, in 1822, Lord John Russell had upheld as necessary to maintain the prosperity of our agriculture, and which the Prime Minister had regarded but a moment before with an indulgent eye.

The mission—extraordinary both in its origin and method of accomplishment—of Sir Robert Peel succeeded, and the Corn Laws were abolished, after an opposition on the part of the main body of the Conservative party which has become historical. But in order to harmonise with the sentiments of Sir Robert Peel respecting the mode of application of a new principle, abolition was not to take effect till three years had elapsed since the date of their repeal; and in the meanwhile, foreign imported corn, with colonial, was subjected to a reduced but fixed duty.

On the same night that the Bill to suspend the operation of the Corn Laws became an Act of Parliament, the Government of Sir Robert Peel was defeated on the Irish Arms (Coercion) Bill. The House of Lords rejected the measure framed by the Prime Minister for the pacification of Ireland, as being too severe even for the requirements of the disordered state of that country. The Arms Bill appeared as a strange corollary to the messages of peace which Sir Robert Peel had triumphantly transmitted to Ireland at the end of the previous year, 1845. The apparent state of quietude into which Ireland for a time had fallen, was translated by the Ministry into the happy meaning that Ireland was at last recovering from her chronic malady. Even measures had been taken for a visit of the Queen to that turbulent country: but the regal visit was at the last moment and quite unexpectedly abandoned, for sedition and outrage had once more appeared. The previous quiet had been but the lull before the storm—a period in which fresh energies might be acquired and developed. Sir Robert was rudely dispossessed of his favourable opinion of the country; and his message of peace took, as it has been well described by a late and illustrious nobleman, the form of a Coercion Bill.

But in the speech announcing his resignation, Sir Robert was not without the means of being able to point to the beneficial results that had already attended the partial operation of the new principle. Distress had disappeared, trade was becoming more active, and the whole country wore a more contented aspect.

He had also concluded a foreign dispute successfully, so that he had the advantage of being able to leave to his successor the external relations of the country in a quiet and satisfactory condition, and its domestic affairs slowly improving.

The change of Ministry, however, did not interfere with the reformation of our commercial code. The thin edge of reform had been almost silently introduced, and the body of the wedge was being driven rapidly home. The taxation remitted during the sessions 1845-46 and 1846-47 amounted to £5,662,000; so that, from the moment of its first introduction, the free-trade principle lost to the revenues of the country the enormous sum of £7,623,000. The sugar duties formed the field on which the Whig Ministry had to fight the battle of its existence. The sturdy phalanx of protectionists withstood the reckless onslaught of the new reform. Nor was it till after every inch of ground had been disputed, that the *quondam* champion of protection, shielding the vigorous efforts of his former opponents, caused the final rout of the Conservative party.

Thus, with the assistance of Sir Robert Peel and his small but faithful band of followers, the Whigs succeeded in consummating the work of reform.

16. *The conditions surrounding the gradual application of the free-trade principle.*—Nothing could have been more favourable than the condition of the commercial world in 1842 for the application of the new principle to the system of our commerce. The country had been suffering for some five or six years from one of these recurrent depressions which are natural to the progress of trade. A war had lately terminated, and thus one element in the causation of distress was removed. As the operation of the principle was only partial, and increased in intensity during the following years till 1848, the immediate and beneficial effects of free trade slowly but surely increased; and in 1845 trade had once more assumed a prosperous state.

But no sooner had it reached this satisfactory condition, than it was again, in spite of the continued and increased action of the free-trade principle, subjected to a temporary decline. For a famine was impending, uncertainty prevailed, and the progress of our renascent trade was consequently retarded. But when, towards the autumn of 1846, a deficiency appeared in the harvests all over the continent of Europe, the commercial activity of the nation was reduced to its lowest ebb.

This unfavourable state of the markets, coming on so suddenly after the previous depression, naturally led men to consider the nature of the operation of free trade, and to doubt of its beneficial efficacy. But the causation of this depression was in no wise connected with the influence of free trade. It is possible, indeed, that the operation of the new system tended to mitigate the hardships of distress—an opinion which was entertained by Sir Robert Peel, and advanced by him as an argument against the attacks of those who attempted to deny its benign action. It was dependent upon a deficiency of the harvests throughout Europe. This determined the time at which depression began; and it was intensified and prolonged by a failure in the cotton crop, and by a monetary crisis which, in 1847, resulting from the railway mania, locked up a large part of the wealth of the country. The capital which, in ordinary circumstances, would have gone to the improvement of trade, was deflected by an inordinate speculation in railways from its proper channels; and thus the markets suffered from a dearth of money, while the wages of labour were similarly affected.

With such a deplorable state of the trade-markets, brought about by causes some of which were within control, while others, as the general scarcity of corn and the failure of the cotton crop, were without the power of man, the action of the free-trade principle, or any other principle, would be without any or but little result.

But when those causes which thus disturbed so seriously the disposition of commerce generally had disappeared; when the harvests reached their former abundance, and money began to circulate more freely after the tension which existed in monetary circles towards the end of 1847 had been relieved; when the action of free trade was allowed to proceed without the prejudicial influence of adverse forces,—then its immediate beneficial operation became very evident.

All the markets reached a state of activity which was never before known to them. The condition of commercial excitement was intense. Such a state of activity was unfamiliar even to the most experienced in commercial affairs. Supply could scarce be equalled to demand. The trade circulation throughout the country became so quickened, that the simile capable alone of describing it, is the condition of fever.

So rapidly was this feverish activity induced, when the free-trade principle acted unrestrictedly and without restraint, that in the year 1848 the exports alone reached the immense value of £133,000,000. This extraordinary result becomes all the more remarkable when it is compared with the exports of the preceding year, which amounted to £57,000,000; and the exports ten years earlier, 1837, which were of the value of £43,000,000. Thus it will be seen that the amount of exported goods in 1848 very nearly trebled their value of the previous year, and more than quadrupled those in 1837.

Was such an increase in trade activity preportionate to the increase of the population during this period? It was far beyond it: for a moment the relation between an increased trade and an increasing population was unhinged; and there were evils necessary to such a disturbance of a natural relationship which seem to have been overlooked by those who brought the interruption about.

But the beneficial action of the principle was freely established; and while the surrounding circumstances continued favourable to its action, it is obvious that so long as these responded to its stimulating influence, so long would the prosperity of our commerce, under its guidance be maintained.

Men do not, as a rule, stay to reason during a season of prosperity. As much do they inquire into the causes of that prosperity as they do into the foundations of principles in which, perhaps, they may have been bred.

What treacherous prosperity was that which gave more than enough employment to every hand, and increased wages to almost a fabulous amount? Was it likely to be associated with the continued blessings of free trade, predicted by the free-traders?

Such a phenomenon of an extraordinary state of stimulation being maintained for any very lengthened period of time is without its fellow in nature!

And what does experience teach? that over-action is followed by reaction, which is the same in amount, but opposite in tendency.

But a state of fictitious prosperity is favourable to

the deduction of false causation. Free trade being associated now with real prosperity, as it was predicted by the free-trade rhetors, the association would become still more closely riveted in the intellect of the ignorant; and a common notion would be spread abroad, to be universally believed, that free trade is the immediate cause of prosperity. Such a false conclusion, however, is easily seen to be the product of those who do not analyse, and who care not to trace effects to their proper cause.

But to the prescient eye it was clear that the time would come when the effects of the principle, accumulating, would react unfavourably to the constant action of the principle. For at the first, the free-trade principle acted throughout a sphere which was new to its action, and therefore unencumbered by its effects. But after a time, these effects, and among them "increased circulation," the mainspring whence the free-trade principle confers the blessings of its virtue upon our trade, are the direct causes of those external complications, the proper objects of legislative foresight, which intervene gradually, but none the less certainly, to disturb the original and beneficial effects of free trade.

When is the period at which the free-trade principle begins to use its former efficacious influence upon our trade?

At that time, when the increased circulation of our markets begins to diminish, owing to the demand of neutral markets being supplied by foreign competition at a relatively smaller cost.

The circulation of our markets will then fall to a

point at which certain branches of industry are just maintained in existence.

There is less demand now; therefore our supplies are less. The field of our commercial operations has become contracted.

But not only will the amount of goods before supplied by our trade-markets be thus unfortunately decreased by the unequal competition of the foreigner, but the profits before reaped by our merchants will become correspondingly reduced, and then both master and man alike come to suffer, but gradually and wellnigh imperceptibly at first, from the accumulating effects of the free-trade principle.

CHAPTER IV.

THE PRIMARY AND BENEFICIAL ACTION OF THE FREE-TRADE PRINCIPLE: TO WHAT IT WAS DUE.

17. *Graphic description of early operation of free-trade principle.*—(See next page.)

18. *The immediate effects of the free-trade principle.*— It cannot be denied that, when all those sources which tended to counteract its primary action were removed, the application of the free-trade principle to our commercial relations was attended with an extraordinary and rapid prosperity.

It appeared as if the prediction of the free-trade rhetors had come true, and that the nation had at last, according to their forecast, started on a path of prosperity, in which no obstacles were to impede its progress.

But we shall soon observe how their forecast was verified only in part. There was, indeed, an initial period of prosperity; but this was to affect but a comparatively small tract of the whole course of our industries. Obstacles had already appeared; the free-trade principle had been put to a severe strain and

156 FREE TRADE.

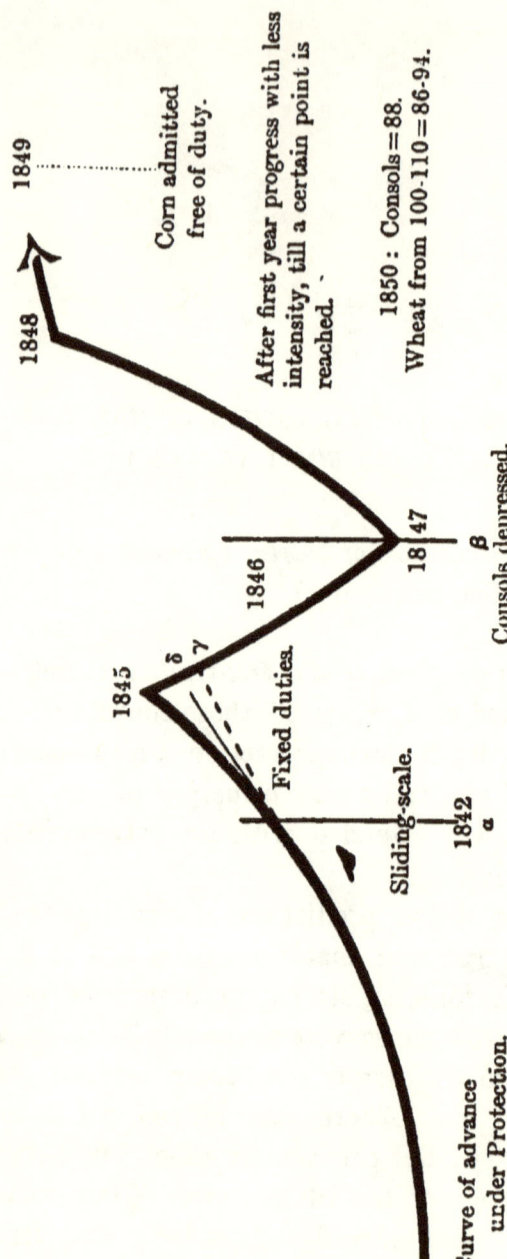

Curve of advance under Protection. Sliding-scale. 1842 α. Fixed duties. 1845 δ γ 1846. 18 47 β Consols depressed. 1848. 1849. Corn admitted free of duty. After first year progress with less intensity, till a certain point is reached. 1850 : Consols = 88. Wheat from 100·110 = 86·94.

Between α and β the new principle acts partially and with external restraints. Beyond β the principle acts unrestrictedly and without external restraints. The period of α, β, is divided into two parts: the anterior—in which the free-trade principle is surrounded by favourable circumstances; the posterior—in which adverse forces intervened to counteract its primary and benign influence.

γ denotes the natural inherent progress of our trade, usually unconsidered. δ that due to free trade. Resultant as in plan.

had been found wanting. What if other obstacles were slowly to come into existence as the direct effects of the constant action of the new principle? The free-trade principle had failed once to answer the expectations of its sanguine promoters; the same influences which brought about the first failure were just as probable to effect a second; and there were others which, looming in the remoter distance of the sphere of its operation, were appreciable only by those who were far-seeing. Was it likely to overcome those obstacles which had already caused its failure, the more especially when the virtue of the new principle was diminished by its constant action?

The gain to the nation—by a principle which was vaunted as the instrument of the welfare of mankind — was diffused even to the lowest levels of the labouring classes. Wages were raised as much as 20, and in some instances 25, per cent! The prosperity which was then spasmodic was universal throughout the body of the people. But the very circumstance of its appearance, and especially its rapid occurrence, formed dangerous symptoms, from a mature consideration of which the thoughtful politician would refrain from prognosticating for it a long continuance.

It is difficult, no matter how powerful may be the art of persuasion, to convince a populace that can call to mind the blessings of the temporary content which free trade brought in its train, that what is at once the initial and favourable action of the principle, shall ever cease to be otherwise, even when the circumstances which surround its sphere of operation gradually become adverse to the former benign influence of its action. And the reasons are not far to seek. An erroneous association is established; it is believed to be true. And more than this, people are brought up in the belief of this false connection of cause and effect. Early impressions, it is well known, are held fast—and the faster, the less the rational faculty is trained. Thus a temporary content becomes the forerunner of a permanent content, and observation is blinded to the gradual induction of adversity. And while imperceptible changes are being wrought, the populace are prudently advised by Platonic legislators "to sit still and wait for better times." What, then, will be the grand cause of agitation on the part of the people—an agitation which will be real, as it will be founded on the wants of the people, and not upon the desires of a section of the community, manufacturing or otherwise? It will be—distress. Distress—or a supposed distress—operated by insidious means to overthrow the system of protection, the principle which presided over the equable advance of our trade—a principle which was impartial, and which did not cast an indulgent eye upon any of the industries of the realm. It will be a real distress, which will move the body of the people at large, and will form the lever of compulsion to force unwilling legislators to recognise its true causation!

What was once the source of an initial prosperity can scarcely be conceived by an unthinking people ever to be the cause of a subsequent distress. For the successive links by which so opposite a condition is effected are unexplored. It is with a nation as with an individual, impulse is obeyed; and reason, the guide and prompter of all that is sound and good, is either neglected, or, if used, is basely used as the auxiliary to passion.

The time must surely come when the body of the people, having become too grossly enlarged by a liberal movement,—supposed to be a liberal movement at the time, but which had neither the character of a real nor the quality of a sound advancement, which was rather remarkable for an individual selfishness,—its wants are unsatisfied. A liberal overgrowth has resulted, but the strong circulation necessary to effect its healthy and contented state is absent. And what is the consequence? Instead of the people being happy, they are burdened with distress, and a distress for which they are not directly responsible. And the seeds of a true agitation grow in the depression which a false agitation has so successfully created—but after a period of time!

The alteration which time and the ever-fluctuating condition of elements around effect in the constant action of a principle are very slightly, and, for the most part, where partiality is insinuated, very erroneously considered in its subsequent progress. What comprehensive survey can be taken by a mob which at one time is banded against the merchant, as being the origin whence the poverty of their condition flows; and by the working classes, who shortly afterwards, as the direct result of the teaching of their masters, combine with those masters to oppose the common tyrant which oppresses both. The free-trade rhetors of 1845 would answer this query by referring to the sensitiveness of the feelings of the multitude!

And a similar course might be entered here, did not the magnitude of the question require a more worthy regard for its solution. The feelings of the populace will be sedulously set aside, and illustration, a rational product, assume the place of pathos, the source perhaps of more than half the evils of the world!

Such an action of a principle can only be displayed to the growing reason of the mob by means of a simile; and this, in the present instance, is not far to seek.

It is universally a matter of experience that in the body organism, the quantity of a medicine to maintain a constant amount of stimulation has gradually to be increased. The drug itself, circulating in the veins of the body, has the immediate effect of a pleasing stimulation; but this result cannot be maintained without such an alteration of the tissue elements, which, if kept constantly in this abnormal condition, first leads to their debility and finally ends in their decay.

To effect a similar amount of stimulation by means of an increased circulation, the drug has to be slowly increased; and the physician, in those cases of disease where stimulation is needed and has to be maintained, wisely proceeds by small degrees, so that he has always the power of increasing it largely when the occasion demands.

But the political quack, who recognised a state of disease of our commerce which never existed, and who was prejudiced into a belief that under free trade only could our commerce compete successfully with that of other nations, in a few doses, extending over a portion of time which is as nothing compared with the whole course of our trade, which he applies to the system by which our industries were for the future to be conducted, recklessly exhausted his means of effecting that intermediate condition by which his object was to be maintained. Was this treatment devised to save the life of our failing trades and industries, or was it for the good of mankind at large? Was it partial or disinterested?

In such a deplorable instance, therefore, when our trade-circulation began to decline—and no one can deny that influences have been called forth to bring about this end — what remedy was at hand to cause the renewal of its stimulation?

The action of the legislator who introduced the stimulative principle of free trade into our system of commercial relations, resembles the conduct of a man whose constitution is being slowly undermined by the constant and noxious effects of a stimulant. Increased circulation is at last followed by exhaustion; and that exhaustion, when the means which induce it are always present, surely leads to decay.

The reference of this illustration to the constant action of the free-trade principle is evident. The action of the principle wanes, because the conditions of growth soon become adjusted to its new mode of action. But if the action of the principle remains constant, there must be something to supply the demands of the stimulating influence. Trade-circulation decreases, and hence the evil falls upon the trade-markets themselves, which become slowly exhausted, and pass slowly into a state of decay.

The prosperity which was associated with the early operation of the free-trade principle, and which, from the nature of our experience, could possibly last for a definite period only, was hailed with thanksgiving by

L

the free trade rhetors, as certain to extend over an indefinite tract of time!

But cause and effect were designedly constructed to serve their immediate purpose. And when prosperity appeared, their reason became clouded, in their outbursts of enthusiasm, to the ultimate disasters of unequal free trade! What was the cause of this prosperity? The free-trade rhetor replied exultingly, Free trade! the people believed, without attempting to make the inquiry, that it was free trade.

He points to the blessings and content which he sees around him; and with all the more lively feeling of an intense satisfaction, because what he had predicted has come to pass. But the rhetor, in the exuberance of his emotion, was drawn into the fatal error of supposing that all the possible effects of a principle are direct. The prosperity of the commercial parts of the community was undoubtedly due, but ultimately and in an indirect fashion, to the operation of the free-trade principle. But there is a chain of phenomena which extends between the commencement of the action of a principle and its subsequent effects. And the links of this chain of events were either unobserved or unexplained.

Free trade is a principle, and as such it is helpless; for every cause acts through the effect it is capable of inducing. Free trade, therefore, must act by means of the disturbance which it creates in the system of relations to which it is applied. Such a primary disturbance is called its immediate effect. What is, or was, this immediate disturbance, in the instance of free trade? Increased circulation.

In what way, then, does the free-trade principle lead

to a state of prosperity? By inducing increased circulation of the markets. And the chain of phenomena is thus—free-trade principle, operating under favourable circumstances, so as to cause an increased circulation of the markets, which leads to the prosperity of trade.

Thus, if the free-trade rhetors had made it known that it was not the principle itself but its immediate effect, increased circulation, which was the source of trade activity, and therefore of trade prosperity, they would have done much to clear the way before them, for anticipating those dangers which might, and under certain conditions certainly would, beset the subsequent progress of the principle. For their attention would have been directed to the study of the question, whether an increased circulation, so brought about, was likely to be attended with a healthy state of the development of our markets,—in a word, to determine the essential difference between a natural and an abnormal increase of activity.

But it was not, in the views of the free-trade rhetors, increased circulation, but free trade itself, to which the flourishing condition of our commerce was due. They groped about for a cause, and grasped the nearest which was present to them. Nor did their bias help them to discover their mistake.

Free trade, therefore, came to be erroneously associated with the prosperous state of the country as its obvious cause; when the true statement of the fact was that prosperity results from increased circulation, of which the free-trade principle is but one of the numerous causes, and then effects it only when the surrounding circumstances are favourable.

For the principle of free trade is helpless to bring about an increased circulation, without a favourable condition of surrounding circumstances. Helpless! when these circumstances become unfavourable to the attainment of this desirable effect, the operation of the free-trade principle becomes absolutely pernicious!

Then the glory which has been shed upon the movement of free trade will be considerably dimmed, when it is understood that free trade is not the only cause of increased circulation, and that it is incapable of effecting increased circulation in all those conditions which may possibly influence its action.

A principle has been sacrificed; the true immediate cause of prosperity has been ignored. Free trade still operates; but the practical advantages of a healthy increase in circulation have, on the part of Whig politicians, been unfortunately ignored!

19. *Graphic explanation of the favourable action of the free-trade principle.*

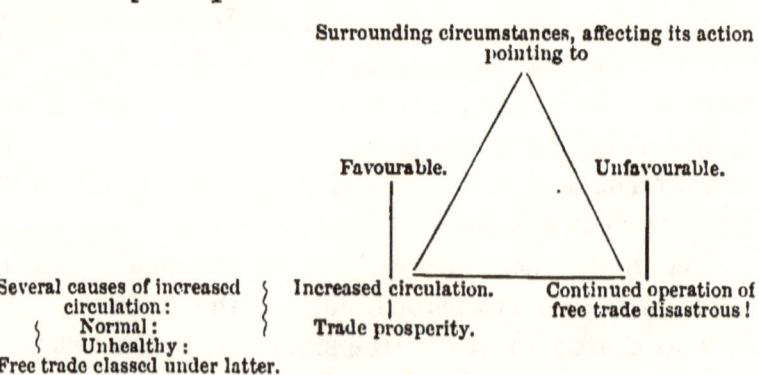

20. *The attitude of the protectionists.*—The criticism of the free-trade policy on the part of the protectionists

was sadly deficient; still the germ of the true bearing of the principle was indicated.

The protectionists, as a body, were in the position of men who were fighting for those rights which they had enjoyed for a considerable period of time, and they had come to regard as justly their own. It was obvious, therefore, that they should be inspired by feelings of animosity towards those whose object it was to rob them of their time-honoured privileges. They, too, were impelled by self-interest. Why should not Agriculture have her self-interests as well as Manufacture? But the protectionists, in order that their interests might be sacrificed with the least amount of ill-feeling, were curiously enough charged with standing in the way of the general progress of the nation,—that is, of manufacture. The relative importance of these two branches of industry were contrasted, and opposition induced, when their forces should have been concurrent. Men of intellectual ability and philanthropic disposition were called upon to sacrifice the smaller in favour of the larger element of industrial activity! Why? Because such a conclusion was the inevitable outcome of a logical deduction. Men's lives and their happiness were placed in one scale, and a logical fallacy in the other; and the balance descended in favour of the sacrifice of a small but important industry of the country, for the logical conclusions of the free-traders were swelled with the hopes of individual self-aggrandisement!

But if the main body of the protectionists were thus for their own interests, their leaders, who saw a glimpse of the ultimate disasters which would be associated with the constant operation of the free-trade principle, led the charge in the interests of the nation. These men may be likened to those who, having an insight into the comprehensive and continuous progress of a principle, imagine the various junctures when complications may arise and disasters appear. But they failed to expose in its simplicity the error upon which the new system, that was to regulate our commerce, was introduced by a former Tory Premier, aided by the united endeavours of the Whig party.

But "the selfishness of the manufacturers was exposed;" a selfishness that will be expiated by a subsequent generation. "The utter ruin of the country was predicted," but the series of connecting links were wanting.

When the free-trader was reproached by the protectionist, inasmuch as his principle contained within itself the seed of future disaster, the former replied, "Regard the present and prosperous state of the country." When the protectionist predicted that the funds would be diminished, the free-trader brought forward the actual fact of there being increased bullion in the Bank of England. And when the protectionist foretold that the poor-rates would be increased, the free-trader answered that, at the moment he was speaking, they were lowered universally throughout the country.

The free-trader replied to the future queries of the protectionist with facts derived from the present, as if he was thoroughly convinced that the present state of commercial prosperity and the happiness of the people would continue in their favourable condition.

But the protectionist, baffled by the inordinate display of increasing wealth and prosperity of the nation, and still viewing this abnormal state of trade with a jealous and unbelieving spirit,—jealous, because it thereby absorbed the attention of the country in favour of liberal reform—unbelieving, because he foresaw that this state of convulsion was not to the interest of the community in general, as being a sudden and violent interruption in the course of a gradual growth, and as tending to be followed by the opposite condition of adversity and depression,—continued his efforts to weaken the position of his arbitrary adversaries, but without avail.

For he did not trace the unerring steps by which the neutral markets would be won from us; and these were within his grasp. Our markets were in a flourishing state. But would they always continue to be so? That was the question.

And what were the collateral causes likely to effect an adverse alteration in their prosperous condition?

Energies ahead, unforeseen by either of the conflicting parties in the State!

The ability of the foreigner to become the equal of the Englishman, contrary to the dogmatic teaching of Mr Cobden, and the indication of perseverance to give it effect!

The extension of fields of industries in foreign countries, and the occasional development of new resources of nature!

The time was fast approaching when the foreign labourer would become as efficient and willing as his English compeer.

And when that arrived, foreign goods would be produced at a cost less than that of corresponding English ones, by virtue of the lower wages of Continental labour.

Then would the period be at hand when our markets would be filled with the manufactured articles of the foreigner,—articles which are within the sphere of English production, but denied production because of their comparatively high cost; and their recovery taking place from the blow which Sir Robert Peel dealt to the industries of the foreigner, its ultimate effect would thus be diverted to our own industries of a succeeding generation!

21. *The character of Lord George Bentinck.*—We have already remarked how the action of Sir Robert Peel respecting the Corn Laws led, for the second time in his career, to the disruption of the Conservative party. Those who had so generously trusted, but who had been so ruthlessly betrayed, could scarce find sufficiently powerful language with which to hurl their defiance and scorn at the apostate leader.

Of the importance of the services of Sir Robert Peel to the Conservatives there is no room left to doubt; but such, even if they reached so far as the reconstruction of the whole party, could hardly justify too extensive an independence; how much less, then, an open rupture?

But if our party system of government, essentially founded upon representation, and expressive of the notions whether progress is to be slow and stable or rapid and insecure, is to continue efficacious, it follows that arbitrariness of power in a leader, as it can be only associated with injury to those interests represented by the body of the party, is to be condemned; and that it is the first duty of the leader of a party to govern, not for his own individual glory, but for the whole interests of the nation, with the consent of each. For the disturbance which arbitrary procedure effects is limited not to the position or reputation of the leader, nor to the interests of his party, but it extends far and wide throughout all that section of the community which is directly represented by the party. The opinion of such a section of the community is worthy of respect; the members act according to the views of their own self-interests, and these, united, are placed confidently in the hands of that leader for protection. What ill is done, then, by a breach of political faith? How is confidence, the basis of security, respected? and how is a fresh sort of dissatisfaction introduced into the State?

But the precedent of Sir Robert Peel, surrounded with so much fatality, cannot be the parent of many similar examples. The morality of a conduct which is liable to so large an amount of adverse criticism is so precarious, that it is probable no statesman, even of the most self-willed type, however much he may aspire, but wrongly, to complete independency of action, would hazard both power and reputation by its practice.

With the desertion of Sir Robert Peel the protectionists felt, as they naturally would feel, very bitterly the isolation of their cause. They were now a party without a leader. Faith had been broken; and they experienced all the severest disappointment of having allowed themselves to be deceived, while they vented their spleen upon the means which had been used to cause that self-deception. But even in such an apparently fatal extremity all hope was not excluded; no, not even when their former leader had marshalled his column against them.

The times were critical, and the cause of protection was becoming desperate. In such an emergency, and when a redistribution of opinion had swept through the mind of Parliament, there was sore need of a leader to guide the abandoned party of protection through the shoals of the free-trade struggle, to avoid the mud-banks of free-trade fallacies, and to subject the facts of the free-trader to a searching examination and analysis.

And such a leader arose! In Lord George Bentinck the protectionists found an English nobleman who was true to his cause, who had the requisite qualities of pertinacity and endurance, and who adapted himself with facility to the pressing demands of the conditions of his party.

His delivery in the House is reported not to have been attractive; but what he lost in brilliancy he more than recovered in the accurate and multitudinous array of his facts, and the cogency of his arguments.

No member of Parliament was more assiduous in his duties; no leader more devoted to the interests of his followers, and these, as being concerned with the policy of protection, he identified with the interests of the whole nation.

Earnest in his manner, and fully aware of his own natural deficiencies, such was the modesty of this nobleman, called at a critical moment to a chief place in the work of legislation, that when the protectionists applied to him to be their leader, he excused himself on the grounds of the inadequacy of his ability for the appointment.

On a subsequent occasion, however, he accepted the leadership provisionally, till another should appear who possessed the necessary qualities of an able leader. Nor was it to be long before that event took place. But before it happened, the marvellous and unexampled career of Lord George Bentinck had come to an untimely end. He was found dead one afternoon in a field near his father's manor.

It is impossible to suppose that the hardships which this accomplished nobleman was inspired, like a hero, to endure for the sake of what he believed to be for the national prosperity, were without a prejudicial influence upon his constitution.

The small amount of sleep which he set apart to repair the wear and tear of a more than usually active intellect, called apparently out of a state of indolence, was less than enough to counteract the evil tendency of exhaustion which is consequent on a serious application of the mind to any subject, continued for a lengthened period of time.

But the grandeur of the object which he had in view seems to have sustained his powers. The wants of the body organism were drowned in the dangers which he foresaw would beset the wholesome progress of the commerce of his country.

And it will be to the lasting honour of this memorable politician that he died while in the service of that cause which he loved so well, and for which he worked so hard!

His self-abnegation—that quality which is the beautiful feature of noble minds—was remarkably displayed in his immediate desertion of those fascinating pursuits which had been the sole occupation of his life. But his duties required that they should be sacrificed; and now all his time and energies were concentrated upon a single object, and that, the *future* as well as *present* welfare of his country. And not the least extraordinary incident in his life is the instance which it affords to those who are students of mental development, of great talents lying buried beneath an impenetrable defect of indolence for so long a time, till they were called into existence by the requisite stimulus which the attack on the Corn Laws and sugar duties originated.

But when fully aroused, he showed the true English character in adhering to the task which he had taken in hand. But though the arguments which Lord George Bentinck used in opposition to free trade proceeded to the conclusion that the general tendency of free trade was pernicious to the trade of the country, he failed to answer the purpose for which he laboured so studiously. This was to expose the nature and mode of most of those external circumstances which would inevitably lead to the disastrous operation of the free-trade principle. But though the germ was indicated, the development of his vast design was incomplete. And the explanation may perhaps be found in the difficulty which some experience in moulding thought, when comprehensive, into language. And therefore it was with no great difficulty that the free-traders apparently refuted his arguments by appealing to the present facts of free-trade prosperity. How much more successfully would Lord George Bentinck have conducted his case had he exposed the circumstances that were favourable and those that were unfavourable to the influence of free trade?—had he shown that free trade might possibly, and would certainly, under given conditions, become adverse to the commercial interests of the nation, owing to the fluctuating tendency of surrounding relations? and had he developed, in anticipation, the successive steps through which the circumstances which relate to the action of the principle pass from the state of being favourable to its operation into the condition when they become pernicious?

The value of Lord George Bentinck's labour in the cause of protection was due to insight; but for this insight—which is essentially dependent on the faculty of arranging the various possible results of an event, and of selecting that one which will most probably happen—to be appreciated, the individual who is blest with its possession must be known and must be esteemed.

And it cannot be remarked without a feeling of disappointment, that the ability of Lord George Bentinck did not command the respect of the Whig party; it may be on account of the difficulty which he experienced in gaining the sympathies of his audience.

While Lord George Bentinck was engaged upon questions of fact and arguments bearing upon the subject of free trade in corn and sugar, his able lieutenant, Mr Benjamin Disraeli, led a merciless attack on Sir Robert Peel, by exposing the inconsistencies of his conduct. But at the same time, he defended the grounds on which the so-called protectionist fallacies were based, and stated the reasons which induced him to retain them.

The free-traders laughed to scorn the idea that from henceforth a low price of bread would ever be associated with low wages. It is true that, when the free-trade principle was in operation, as a disturbance of previously existing relations had thereby taken place, the statement of this doctrine ought to have undergone a modification. It would not be true so long as surrounding circumstances were being adjusted to its action. And it was during this time—and it was a prosperous time—that the free-trader was asked to believe that the association of a low price of bread with low wages was inevitable. But how long would this period of adjustment be?

Thus when it was stated that a low price of bread was necessarily associated (what should have been stated is, a low price of bread has a tendency, if it is not checked for a time, as by the early operation of the free-trade principle, to be associated) with low wages, it must be confessed that the advantage of the argument as thus stated, and without emendation, was on the side of the free-trader, who relied upon the evidence of facts before him, which proved that at that actual moment a low price of bread was associated with greatly increased wages.

But if the protectionist failed in the accurate statement of his case—if the ultimate progress of the free-trade principle was discerned by him, while the intermediate steps by which such a termination was to be effected were concealed from those who demanded the nature of the means to this end—the free-trader erred in rashly hazarding all upon a present prosperity, and in supposing, without any proper foundation, that a rapidly induced prosperity would continue when once begun.

So, too, with reference to the poor-rates: the arguments of the protectionists conveyed that the poor-rates would be largely increased within a short time. But was it likely, in such a forced state of prosperity of the country, that those who had advocated and succeeded in carrying the application of free trade to our system of commerce, could possibly conceive that, within their own time, the poor-rates would increase as rapidly as the protectionists, perhaps with design, predicted?

The appeal should have been made with greater intensity to a succeeding generation; the imagination of the free-traders should have been aroused, and the consideration of the influences which might check their temporary prosperity undertaken!

After the premature decease of Lord George Bentinck, the chief bulwark of their strength, it might have been thought that the position of the party of protection, previously weakened, would now be paralysed.

But his immediate successor proved himself a man capable of constructing a great party, and inspiring it with single and disinterested purposes. Mr Benjamin Disraeli kept alive the spirit of the old party, while he was repairing the foundations of the new one; and in a motion which, in 1850, he tendered to the House for a committee to inquire into the state of the nation, he reiterated—and it is characteristic of the courage of his opinions that these adverse sentiments were delivered in a period of the most unexampled prosperity—all the arguments which had been advanced before by the party of protection against the continued operation of the free-trade principle.

But it was a herculean task to attempt to convince men, tasting the blessings of a long-deferred prosperity, and especially those who were directly concerned in its causation, of the fatal nature of the enjoyments they were experiencing—not fatal to their own generation, and herein was contained the insidious nature of this prosperity, but to the one after. And much of the value of the speech was lost in the bitter sarcasm he launched at the head of Sir Robert Peel. It exposes more the contradictory nature of the late Prime Minister's conduct rather than the grounds on which the foundation of the free-trade principle might have been destroyed. One of the two chief features, however, of the whole of the free-trade controversy, consists in the fact that the protectionist did not separate clearly enough the near from the remote effects of the operation of the free-trade principle, while the other rests upon the attitude of the free-traders who refrained from regarding its action in a comprehensive fashion from the prospective point of view. No anticipations of danger were made, and consequently no provisions for it.

Between antagonists thus pursuing so obviously different courses, it is not to be expected that there was much in common.

As Sir Robert Peel met with an unfortunate death in this year, it is just to observe that the speech above alluded to, by Mr Benjamin Disraeli, was made before the accident which led to a fatal termination.

CHAPTER V.

CRITICISM OF THE INDIRECT AND DIRECT OPERATIONS OF FREE TRADE.

22. *The origin of the free-trade principle.* — The principle of free trade had its source in the fertile imagination of Adam Smith. The initial success which attended its operation has added more than a due share to the lustre of the author of the 'Wealth of Nations'; but let the precarious state of conditional truths be kept in mind. Adam Smith himself fell into an error respecting the definition of the element of rent—an error which was pointed out to him by his countryman, the philosopher and historian, David Hume.

The free-trade principle, as propounded by its author, was an abstract principle. There had been no previous experience of it; and its efficacy was altogether dependent upon the development of certain conditions which were assumed to accompany its progress.

These previous conditions were definite in the imagination of the founder of the doctrine of free trade. And are they to be overlooked in the subsequent and arbitrary application of the principle to the development of fresh conditions?

What were the original conditions? That England should take the lead in giving universal effect to the principle of free trade; and that the advantage to her trade by such action would be such as to force surrounding nations to follow her example.

It is possible that when first enunciated, the course of subsequent events, if free trade had been introduced, might have been that which was depicted by the great economist. But it is also clear that, with the addition of new factors and the modification of old ones, the probabilities affecting the subsequent application of free trade would be greatly varied.

In the opinion of Adam Smith, the gain to Great Britain accruing from free trade was fully established. The doctrine was essentially founded on the basis that the change in international commercial policy would be associated with an increased prosperity to all nations, but to England more especially than all the rest, because she would recover, by the lead, a certain supremacy which she would afterwards be able to maintain.

But let the relative considerations of such an action on the part of England, and actions on the part of surrounding nations, be carefully analysed, and what is the result? That by this manœuvre England has raised the level of her commercial basis, while the bases of surrounding nations remain relatively to England lower after the introduction of the free-trade system universally, even though they may have undergone, so far as they are themselves concerned, an absolute elevation.

If therefore, before the application of the free-trade principle, there was anything approaching to equality between the commerce of England and surrounding nations, it is obvious that after its introduction that equality—a semblance of equality—would be converted into a disadvantageous inequality.

Is it possible, then, that under circumstances which must inevitably terminate in this increased inequality, the legislators of those nations should, in the promotion of the happiness of mankind, according to the theory of the free-traders, which in this case means the advancement of the commercial prosperity of the people of Great Britain and Ireland, voluntarily abandon the interests of their respective countries?

Are we to suppose that men are to be found in high stations who will contradict the fundamental law on which all commercial transactions are based?

So flagrant a selfish action could not fail to be seen in its true bearing by those who watch over with a jealous eye the prosperity of their country. Such prefer the more certain course prescribed by a long experience, and estimate the vast difference between a slow and constant advance and a bound, which for the time being might bring them the enjoyment of extended action, but the end of which, perhaps unrecognised, is threatened with the uncertainty of a fall.

To follow the progress of the principle as it was delineated by Adam Smith, leads, as truly as a hypothetical case can, to the prosperity of this country.

But then it is a hypothetical case, in which the immediate and the remote future will have to be taken into consideration. And was it certain that when applied to all possible conditions, of which those of 1842 formed one, the event would take that course which Adam

Smith portrayed? For Adam Smith's opinion was limited to the existing state of commercial relations which obtained in his day.

And if not, and if this country found itself in the solitary position of being the free-trader of the universe, was it not the duty of Adam Smith, the parent of the doctrine, and who therefore, we may suppose, was filled with the natural affection of the father for the normal development of his child,—was it not his duty to foresee how these alterations in surrounding conditions might intervene to spoil the growth of free trade? for he, if any man knew, was well acquainted with the fluctuations to which the commercial elements of nations are prone. And thus picturing all the possibilities of these future conditions which might at a subsequent period attend its progress, if put into practice, ought he not to have separated those which would assuredly be associated with disaster to its operation? Ought he not to have pointed out where danger may assail, and the extreme instance in which the principle involves in ruin that nation which, under peculiarly unfavourable circumstances, may have adopted it?

But what says Adam Smith of the ultimate condition of that country which alone embarks upon the system of free trade? The conditions under which the free-trade principle was promulgated and effectually put into practice, had undergone an immense change as compared with what they were in the times of the author of the doctrine. This country then depended largely upon its own agriculture for the supply of corn; manufacture had not yet absorbed nearly the whole of the attention of the nation; steam had not yet appeared to add its disturbing influence upon the commercial relations of nations.

It is a fair question to propound whether, under the vastly altered circumstances, the weight of Adam Smith's authority would have been found on the side of those who introduced his favoured principle into our commercial code? For it is clear that the action of a principle is bound to alter with an alteration in those circumstances which surround its sphere of operation; and therefore the imaginary influence of the free-trade principle in the days of Adam Smith could not, by any means, be similar to its real action in 1842-47.

But there is difficulty about the virtues of principles. What is predicated of the efficacy of a given principle in one century is liable to be maintained as true by a generation of a succeeding one; and the tendency is aggravated when those who are to gain by the application of the principle advance their cause by the influence of those whose sentiments respecting its action refer to a state of affairs totally different from that in which the principle is promulgated.

But a fatal error hangs round this tendency to such a belief and the arbitrary procedure of those who force authority to their side.

For such, who give an indisputable assent to principles so enunciated, do not readily understand that principles which may be efficacious at one particular period of time may at another be adverse, owing to the fluctuation of old and the appearance of new elements to complicate their operation. And thus by an inadvertence, which is removable, to the exact functions of a principle, much hurt may ensue!

Another ground presents a site for the attack on Adam Smith's doctrine, the more particularly in the case where this country alone is a free-trader, but also, though in a less degree, if free trade reigned universal throughout the world. This ground is the tendency of the principle to act perniciously upon the native industries of the country. For the principle directly tends to the consequence mostly of supplying the demands of neutral markets, to the neglect of less extensive branches of industry, and to the inordinate exhaustion of our resources. Nor is this the only way in which the smaller industries of the country suffer by the system of free trade. The foreigner is able, by means of the cheapness of Continental labour—and it is questionable whether those who were responsible for the introduction of free trade properly anticipated the evil results which would ensue upon too rapid an advance in wages in their own country, when contrasted with the comparatively low wages of European countries, and the effect of this difference upon the price of various productions of labour—nowadays to send over to this country more than our demands require as far as these smaller markets are concerned, with the natural consequence that such industries are gradually being pushed out of the great labour-market of the kingdom. And thus it comes about that the workmen of our country are denied the opportunity, and this the Legislature should see is efficiently afforded, of contributing the produce of their labour to the welfare of the community. Small prices rule this system of commercial transactions to such an extent, that the English labourer, shut out by the foreigner's competition from the market which has been familiar to him, is compelled to seek some other mode of employment or starve!

And when other means of occupation are restricted, and depression, constant and paroxysmal, reigns throughout the labour-markets, how are his chances of starving considerably enhanced!

With such an adverse criticism of the prospect of free trade under given conditions, and supposing that it was known to Adam Smith that in 1842 the agricultural interests of the country were undergoing a steady decline since the commencement of the century; supposing, too, that no means had as yet been devised to counteract the gradually increasing unproductivity of the soil, but that he had by the aid of his powerful imagination depicted the gigantic development of our colonies, and their ability to supply the mother country with the requisite amount of corn, can it be believed that Adam Smith, with such a view of the future possibilities of the action of a fresh system, would have given his consent to the introduction of a new principle, even should it have been his favourite principle of free trade, when the dangers which beset its progress were, after the initial disturbances of its action had passed off, like to become so numerous and so great? Is it to be expected that the illustrious economist would have legislated so disastrously for his country?

23. *The morality of the free-trade system.*—Judging the question purely upon a scientific basis, the grounds

on which the legislator introduced the free-trade principle into our system of commerce, were not founded on the propositions of its original inventor. It was applied as a supposed remedy for the evils of the times —evils which had been unjustly and arbitrarily laid at the door of protection. Adam Smith enunciated his principle as being peculiarly applicable to an already prosperous state of our commerce. But of this nearly all could be certain, that its first effects would be associated,—whether our commerce were in a state of prosperity, as in the times of Adam Smith, who discovered the principle—or in a condition of depression, as in the second Administration of Sir Robert Peel, who applied it,—with a temporary elevation of the fortunes of our trade. And in the latter instance, how easy was it to dissipate, for the time being, present difficulties; and how fatal to the future progress of the nation would be the association, then erected, of free trade with prosperity! But this future progress—well, time would witness the ultimate development of the principle.

We have already seen how it happened, that Sir Robert Peel adopted the free-trade principle to our commercial relations on the ground of expediency.

What a contrast this new legislation to all that preceded it! Before, practice was based upon experience of the needs of individual interests of the community; the sum of these formed the total interests of the nation. But the policy of Sir Robert Peel undid all that previous legislation had done for the welfare of our commercial interests; the State now interfered to settle what the individual interests of the nation required. And the information upon which the authorities of the State proceeded was derived exclusively from an interested source—the demands of only one of the numerous interests of the country, the present interest of manufacture.

It is strange that England, the country which had set the example of protection in her international commercial relations, and which nations in their own self-defence so prudently followed, should be the first to interrupt the slow and equable, and, better than all else, the certain advancement of her trade!

To interrupt the continuance of relations which had existed for so long a time, and which had proved themselves capable of bearing the strains of the severest depression, on the authority of Sir Robert Peel, for the sake of an abstract principle, the early action of which was predicted as the sure cause of so much prosperity, but prosperity of an unwholesome nature, but whose remoter effects were hidden in the clouds of the future, the course and magnitude of which were not even so much as described, was an experience, the future hazardous character of which was risked for the sake of tiding over present difficulties and dangers; the difficulties being the disordered state of the revenues, which had been progressively increasing in the hands of the Whig Chancellor—and the dangers arising from the growth of the popular agitation with reference to the false notions then propounded regarding free trade. But the real basis of that agitation might have been exposed, and the agitation dissipated in a moment!

But Sir Robert Peel, as Prime Minister, stood between his duties to the party as their leader, and his duties to his country as its guide. He found the influence of manufacture overwhelming; and instead of analysing the causes of the agitation, he determined to make use of the popular enthusiasm to effect a double purpose. And thus the political machinations of the manufacturers succeeded at last!

To satisfy the thirst for gold of the manufacturers, and indirectly to gain the applause of the mob, this interruption in our trade was undertaken, at the certain risk of destroying the agricultural prospects of the country, and with the certainty of receiving the continued opposition of all foreign nations.

Our trade relations with other nations formed part of a whole, the harmony of whose action was rudely broken.

Why? To fill the pockets of the manufacturers. Is this in accordance with political morality, to act unjustly and arbitrarily towards the commercial prospects of other countries; to destroy their industries, in the words of Sir Robert Peel; to increase discontentment among foreign neighbours, and thereby increase rather than diminish the enmity of race?

Is it a moral action on the part of the Legislature to destroy a weaker industry in order that a larger one may be solely benefited by its destruction? Would Englishmen have agreed to this course at the time, had they been cognisant of the future distress that was to follow prosperity so unnaturally acquired?

Is peace to extend throughout the world by the operation of such a principle, the immediate effect of which was to create a feeling of animosity among the rival industries of that country in which it was first introduced?

24. *Why have surrounding nations remained protective?*—The boasted efficacy of the free-trade principle had blinded the greater part of the nation to the possibility, under certain circumstances, of the pernicious results of its future action. It is not difficult to assign to each of the several parties to its contraction—the legislators, the manufacturers, and a large part of the body of the people—their respective shares in effecting its introduction into the commercial code of the country.

But, generally speaking, its application was associated with one of two alternatives—either the people, or the majority of them, who were forced to believe in it, allowed themselves to be self-deceived; or the glories of the free-trade principle were so extravagantly and baselessly portrayed, for the ulterior purpose of concealing the partial selfish motive which formed the source of its advocacy. And the expression, partial selfish motive, is made use of to indicate the attitude of a section of the community which, instead of advancing with equal steps all the interests of the nation, pleaded with so much success the cause of only a part of them,—the larger part, it is true.

But the fact remains that, notwithstanding the almost supernatural virtues ascribed to the operation of the free-trade principle, surrounding nations have remained protective; and the grounds on which they have retained the system of protection may well be considered, especially when the initial and successful course of the principle of free trade must have tended to shake the confidence of those who failed to foresee its final results.

The conduct of surrounding nations, at the time of the introduction of the free-trade principle, was founded on the basis of national self-interest. It regarded rather the equable progress of their industries, with the gradual advancement of the people under it, than a sudden and violent interruption, the consequences of which, if they did not attend their own, would certainly reach the next generation.

It fully proves that the wise legislators who prescribed it foresaw the time, not far distant, when the free-trade country, having spent the produce of the energy of surrounding nations, would begin to prey upon its own vitals. For now there was the opportunity presented to the foreigner of applying protected labour to free-trade machinery; and not only of attracting the mechanical inventions of the free-trade country, but also trained artisans, who are induced to convey the knowledge of their arts to the workmen of foreign countries.

But it was only natural that the countries under the protective system should suffer during the early period of the operation of the free-trade principle on the commercial system of England, and should continue to suffer, till they had learnt at the hands of the free-trade nation to supply all their wants. The gain thereby to England, though temporary and surrounded with every kind of danger, would be the corresponding loss to other nations. And an immense increase in capital in consequence accrued to the nation whose commercial system was thus disturbed from out of its former and steady course. And the increase of capital has not been without its advantages, for it has served to enable our merchants to pursue their trade at a disadvantage. Profits have been gradually diminishing, and their capital has been slowly consumed; and thus, what the father gained in his successful commerce with foreign countries, the son slowly returns, but in an indirect manner; for he paid high wages so long as the hope remained of the accumulation of profits, and some of these high wages go to the purchase of foreign manufactured goods.

But this damaging influence upon the industries of the foreigners by the early operation of free trade was not unknown to the promoters of the principle. Sir Robert Peel himself declared that many of the industries of foreign countries would be destroyed, and pointed to this result in an exulting manner as being the immediate outcome of free trade; just as if this was one of the means by which free trade was to spread peace and goodwill over the face of the earth!

By free trade, therefore, we should become the great market of the world; by the free importation of raw materials we should be the better able, as a manufacturing community, to cope with the rival trade and commerce of other countries.

By increasing competition of the markets, out of labour, we should raise the wages of the labourer, and therefore add to the prosperity of the masses of the country.

But what errors led Sir Robert Peel to incline to this prospective action of free trade, for must he not have held this to be the permanent result, however insufficiently grounded, of the principle?

The error, propounded by Mr Richard Cobden, that

the energy of the English labourer, and the superior kind of his work, would always bear the same relation which they *then* had to the indolence of the foreigner and the inferior quality of his labour. But is not this to suppose that relations shall continue fixed, which we know must be ever fluctuating, from the mobile nature of the elements related?

We are to suppose that the distance between the Englishman and the foreigner, in their relative capacity to work, is to be always maintained; and this, too, whether improvement takes place or not; for if the foreigner improves, so does the Englishman. But although there is no absolute limit to improvement, there is a relative limit, and in the race to this goal there is no means on the part of the Legislature of this country of checking the pace of different nations. These means were removed when we permitted our machinery to leave the country, against the ulterior purpose of the manufacturers! There being no check then, we are to suppose that the same features which had characterised our own industries, and the workmen employed in them, are to be denied to others, who are in every respect gifted with all these forces, the usage of which has led to the advancement of the English artisan. But does not the supposition compel us to the belief that similar forces in the foreigner, other conditions being equal, cannot admit of the same degree of development as they can in ourselves? Is not such a notion altogether absurd, and based upon an absolute want of knowledge of the comparative progress of the elements of society? Because we advanced slowly, the means to that advancement being gradually evolved, is this an argument that the people of other nations shall also undergo a slow progress, when the means for their development are ready at hand and have but to be utilised?

The free-traders would have had a good argument had they been able to show that, in the relative advancement of the commercial interests of their own and other countries, these means were developed with unequal strength, and that their own means would be always more efficient and more powerful than those of their neighbours. But how can such a result be gained when our machinery, the produce of the genius of the nation, is exported duty free, and our artisans leave this country to advance the industries of foreign climes?

And yet this is the doctrine which Mr Cobden held, and maintained in the Parliament of the United Kingdom! This, however, was not the only error; there was another one which was brought into the foreground. It was that this country would continue to be the central market for all the goods of the world. Neutral markets would remain for ever open to our commerce, and therefore the prosperous career of that was established on a firm basis—as firm as the free-traders could make it. Why? Because we could now compete to greater advantage with our foreign rivals, for we had crushed them, and thus were left without any rivals! The work of free trade was done when it was shown that our markets had reached a height of prosperity which they never would lose.

But besides the falling into error in these particular directions, where the power of the imagination was needed to vary the possible combination of the consequences, immediate and remote, of phenomena, and to provide for dangerous results, it was taken for granted that no new and unforeseen difficulties would arise to complicate and probably to endanger the progress of our trade. In short, the conditions surrounding the operation of the free-trade principle were supposed to remain in a state similar to what they presented during the first period of its action to subsequent generations! Such a treacherous conclusion, however, based as it is upon the assumption that relations will continue to remain as they are, in spite of the disturbance already introduced into their midst and the Liberal notion of continual reform, obviously lent itself to credulity. Although the conditions on which these relations were based were admitted by the free-traders to be capable of fluctuation, still these relations were supposed to remain for ever the same!

But what would be the true course of the disturbed relationship is as follows: the surrounding conditions would remain, for a time only, favourable to the operation of the free-trade principle. It required foresight to enable the legislator to anticipate how much and in what direction these fluctuating conditions might change —what new elements might appear, whether to stimulate or to counteract the action of the principle—and what consequences such possible alterations might have upon the future progress of free trade.

Such a foresight was seen in the resentment with which the free-trade manufacturers regarded the too enlarged policy of Sir Robert Peel, when he allowed the mechanical implements of the country to be exported free of duty. And it was practised by those who presided over the commercial welfare of surrounding nations, when, uninfluenced by the primary beneficial action of free trade as saviour of this country, they judged that its prosperty was of but a temporary duration; and that the present sufferings under which they groaned at the hands of the powerful but arbitrary Minister of England, would be slowly but certainly turned into content and happiness, as their trades and industries gradually recovered from their former state of depression and partial arrest. For they perceived the seeds of inherent growth in their industries, and determined the direction in which that growth should take place.

Let it be admitted that the present state of their commerce was injured by this attitude of England; if they followed in the train of free trade, would their relative position be one jot improved? Not in the least. Besides, by such an action, the prospects of the future gain to be derived from the maintenance of the protective system would be dissipated. Better to undergo the temporary crush of this arbitrary procedure, and be certain of the future and not far-distant spoils of a spendthrift and extravagant policy! If free trade be capable of conferring the immense advantages ascribed to it, upon the trade and commerce of nations, why did not the nations in 1842-47 follow the lead which England gave? Because the so-called glories surrounding the free-trade principle were dissected with the cold hands of reason; because the consequences of its action were analysed; and because the possible combinations which might affect its future course were arranged in order, and their policy for good or evil ascertained. And to what did such a treatment of so important a problem tend? That it was far better to be content with the gradual progress of trade and industries. Besides, was there not the consolation, that their present loss will surely be counteracted by future gain? A stimulus was thus afforded, and new energies were called forth; fresh powers were awakened to remove the injustice that had been so cruelly, and apparently so wantonly, thrown upon them.

Do men ever work with so much patience and so much force, as when they are urged to wipe off some evil which they have never deserved?

Thus what the British politician failed to discern—for his action proceeded to a greater extent than his advisers had determined and hoped—the wise legislators of surrounding nations observed in silence. They perceived the tendency towards improvement in the industries of their countries; and foresaw the time when their national energies would have undergone such considerable extension as to place them upon the footing of equality with the first commercial nation in the universe; and when the labour of the foreigner would equal, if not excel, that of the free-trader, because not spoilt by the excesses into which a temporary but inordinate prosperity has thrown him. They predicted the time when the neutral markets would gradually become the sole emporium of their merchandise, in the same way as before the free-trader absorbed all the profits of the commercial world; for they would be able to supply the customary articles under the protective system at a cost much less than that of the free-trader. And not only would they have the satisfaction of underselling the free-trader in neutral markets, and of replying to the original message of free trade, but there would be the possibility of invading even the markets of the free-trade country itself; a procedure which would be assisted by the extension of bounties in the instance of those industries, grown and growing, which could not, by virtue of their inferior state of development, compete unaided against their stronger rivals!

All thought of the former crushing of their trade and industries would be, for the nonce, forgotten, in the intense satisfaction that all this they would be enabled to do with the direct assistance of the free-trader. Free-trade goods they tax, and this taxation is set aside to assist and improve the growing industries of their country.

What gain then has England made in the long-run by the action of the free-trade principle?

Our markets abroad are disappearing, because competition has appeared in such strength as to shut our merchants out of their former monopoly; our trade is shrinking, profits diminish to such an extent that in some markets it is impossible to make any profits, and wages proportionately decrease.

And still the forces are constantly acting which have brought about these grave and alarming signs!

If they continue, with their potency for evil, as they are likely to do, unless some phenomenon appears to act in our favour, can it be otherwise than that this decline in the trades and industries of our country will lead to a fatal decay?

25. *Philosophical considerations of free trade.*—The difference in the origins of the protective and free-trade systems is this,—while the former gradually grew out of the requirements of the commercial relations of the nation, and therefore had for its basis the process of induction, free trade was altogether the product of the imagination, and is classified amongst the deductive principles.

Before the introduction of free trade into our commercial code, our legislators based their actions upon the experience of the past. What experience was there of the efficacy of the free-trade principle, and what certainty of the ultimate results of its operation, except what was secured from the selfish calculating process of the enthusiastic free-traders?

And upon what foundation was that calculation based? That the circumstances which surrounded its action would continue much in a similar condition to what they then stood. But was such an assumption based upon a true determination of the subsequent alterations which these surrounding circumstances must in the natural course of affairs undergo?

When Sir Robert Peel posed as the theoretic legislator in 1842-46, he administered a remedy, the immediate consequences of which were foretold almost to the very letter. But what measures were taken to elucidate the subsequent action of the principle? Such were hidden in obscurity!

The protectionists, on the other hand, pursued the method of practical politicians. They based their measures upon what had gone before—upon experience therefore; and they were content to follow the paths of experience, on which they could rely with greater certainty, than step into the partially explored territory of theory. But they had the mortification of discovering, too late, that the Minister who had delivered great speeches in favour of protection, and who had on innumerable occasions entirely exonerated the Corn Laws from the unjust charge of being the cause of distress, had in the meanwhile been maturing plans for the reversal of a policy in which he had taught his followers to maintain the highest trust.

But it is to be presumed that Sir Robert had satisfied his scruples for logical accuracy, when after having pursued the experimental method for three years, and having escaped the observation that the period over which the action of the principle had extended was favourable to its operation, he arrived at the final conclusion that the free-trade principle, being right in the abstract, and also successful so far as he had up to that time allowed it scope of action, ought therefore to be admitted, free and unrestricted, into all the commercial relations of the country.

As if the observations prolonged over the ridiculously short period of three years were sufficient to interrupt the course of a system which had been found equal to the discharge of the embarrassments that had been thrown upon it, and, in the words of Sir Robert Peel, had already successfully overcome greater strains than the present distress placed upon it!

But the final conclusion was not based upon this single observation alone, there were some other considerations as well. But amongst them is not to be found the favourable state of surrounding conditions. The new principle was growing, as it were, upon a virgin soil. But no means were devised to renew the exhaustion which the principle would in time effect.

Sir Robert Peel allowed the free-trade principle to be right in the abstract; and though his admission was apparently an honest one, yet in the same speech that he makes the admission, he noticed the contra-indications to its application. But what is the meaning of a principle being right in the abstract? It means simply this, that, with given conditions, a principle is found to work with the greatest possible benefit to the system into which it is introduced. It is exactly upon these given conditions that the whole of the merits of an abstract principle is placed.

But do these given conditions remain constant? What sound statesman would legislate recklessly upon a measure, when the direction in which the given conditions might fluctuate were not wholly within his grasp? No consideration of abstractedness would have impelled the intemperate Fox to legislate on the basis of abstract principles. And the evidence to be derived from the attitude of William Pitt during the first illness of the King in 1788, suffices to indicate his opinion upon the nature of the *abstract* in politics. For what he inculcated was, to collect from past history what had happened on occasions which had more or less resemblance to the one with which he had to deal, and with the assistance of such material, to legislate on the lines which had already been laid down by his predecessors.

Thus Sir Robert Peel could find no precedent, either

in the career of the greatest statesman of the party he had deserted can boast, or in the opinion of the champion of the party of reform, to which for a time he became attached, and by which, since, he has been claimed, despite his want of moral courage to resist the Tory opposition to Roman Catholic emancipation.

Is it possible that Sir Robert, acknowledging the times to be critical, and therefore applying an extraordinary remedy, and finding no precedent for the arbitrary application of an abstract principle to our commercial system, established one on the questionable grounds that other Ministers would have acted in the same way if they had admitted the state of the nation required it?

It is obvious that, whether or not a principle is right in the abstract, this mere rectitude is not sufficient to justify its introduction into practice.

When we state that a principle is right in the abstract, we refer to all those possible conditions which we revolve in our minds when we consider the principle as being in operation at a certain point of time.

But the power of reading the future is a peculiar one! Will not those conditions alter? have they not the sources of fluctuation within them? And who without the possession of profound knowledge and the liveliest imagination can portray the appearance of new conditions, with the decline, and it may be the disappearance, of some of the older ones? And when the surroundings thus change, is it to be supposed that the original effect of the principle is to continue uniform? Such is obviously contradictory. It is absurd to conclude that the total results of the action of a principle shall remain constant, when the conditions which surround it are subject to variation.

Regarding, therefore, the free-trade principle from the abstract point of view, Sir Robert Peel could only be convinced of its favourable action just so long as the circumstances which related to its operation remained in a state similar to that in which they were when the principle first commenced its progress.

To suppose that this state would remain constant, was to suppose that the course of things, which are ever fluctuating, shall remain fixed and uniform; and to evince an ignorance of the progress, if not of this, at any rate of the commerce of other countries.

Was Sir Robert Peel aware of the inconstant character of the function of the free-trade principle?

And did he take any means to prevent the principle from assuming an appearance of a pernicious nature?

It is an error which, it has already been remarked, is with difficulty eradicated, to suppose that free trade, being a cause constantly in operation, must always be associated with that degree of prosperity which marked its initial action, or any prosperity at all! And we have adverted to the circumstance that a principle is of itself powerless either for good or evil. It begins only to have effect when it is applied to certain conditions.

That effect which characterised the appearance of the free-trade principle, and to which is undoubtedly due the stimulus which all our markets received at the time, was "increased circulation." And "increased circulation" was the immediate cause of the prosperity of our trade. Now the relation between free trade and increased circulation is that of cause and effect. But how is free trade in reality related to the condition of prosperity? Obviously through increased circulation.

Thus free trade is not the proximal cause of prosperity, but the source of its origin, increased circulation; and this only during the existence of conditions favourable to its appearance.

But though the same cause must always have the same effect, this effect is concealed by the contingent appearance of collateral causes. The total immediate effect of a cause, then, depends altogether upon the nature of the external conditions upon which the cause first begins to operate.

We have seen how these conditions may be favourable to the induction of increased circulation, the source of prosperity, by means of the free-trade principle.

But these conditions do not always remain favourable. Why? Because collateral effects in the commercial world appear, as the immediate results of the operation of the free-trade principle, to counteract the tendency of the countries where the consequences of its early operation were adverse to the progress of their industries, with this final result, that forces are at length established in those countries which are opposed to the pernicious influence of the principle upon them—pernicious for a while to them, but favourable to us. As, therefore, the influence of the principle in these countries ceased to be less and less pernicious, so must its real nature become more and more disadvantageous to the commercial interests of the free-trade country.

What means, it may be inquired again, were taken by Sir Robert Peel to grapple with such probabilities supposing that any one of them, or all together, came into action? How did he contemplate the adverse effect of the other protective nations upon the isolated free-trader? The free-traders themselves, to their credit, thought that they were safe and secure in the possession of one ally, and that—the monopoly of the native machinery of their country.

Such an extraordinary piece of legislation was never for the moment entertained by Pitt, Canning, Huskisson, or any other statesmen who held the present interests as well as future welfare of their country in their hands. But what was the previous attitude of Sir Robert Peel to this abstract principle of free-trade? Sir Robert, when discussing the relative merits of the abstract principle, himself declared that, in a new state of society, its application would without any doubt be desirable.

What was the place, then, of this abstract principle in all the old conditions of the community in which rights of a general nature had grown up, and in which a branch of industry, founded upon those rights, ought to be maintained, and which both himself and Lord John Russell had already declared should be maintained? For is it not the object of good government to advance the industries of the nation, in order to diminish the sources of discontent?

Now Sir Robert Peel asserted clearly, and apparently without hesitation, that such rights ought to be maintained! Was it with a view to appease the growing distrust which the party of protection were beginning to display against them?

But whatever may have been his motive, it is certain

that what Sir Robert Peel proclaimed one year as being essentially bound up with the interests of the nation at large, his action contradicted in the next!

Had the consequences, remote as well as immediate, been subjected to a larger amount of analysis, is it probable that Sir Robert would have hazarded the prospects of his country's commerce upon the slender amount of experimental observation which was available? And was sufficient attention afforded to the operation of the principle when surrounding circumstances were, as they certainly would become, adverse to its action?

Was it safe to trust to the insecure hypothesis that surrounding nations would follow in the train of free trade? And if they did not — as there were more than enough grounds to suppose that they would not —after the loss they had sustained by the powerful disturbance produced by the first period of action of the principle, in what way would this principle react upon our own trades and industries eventually, when, as there was no solid reason to expect the contrary, instead of increased circulation of the markets, there should happen in some future time to be depression of these markets, or, it might be, absolute stagnation?

When the source of demand was being gradually cut off, would there not be a tendency to a congested state of the markets—a condition implying an inordinate production? Would not such a congested state be the first sign of the ultimate pernicious action of the principle?

But such an alarming disturbance would be read differently by different minds. Thus one might suggest that it was the fault of the producer—he produces too rapidly.

But upon what does he exert his powers to stimulate production? Upon expectation. It is expectation which really fails him; an expectation based upon a previous experience of the demand of his market.

Such a congestion points to the local arrest of the former increased circulation of our trade. What follows? The congestion must be relieved. But this can be done only by diminishing the degree of production; of correlating the amount of supplies to the smaller demands. Hence, with the diminution of supplies, the large number of workmen thrown out of employment.

Now does the pernicious action of the free-trade principle appear naked for the first time. Before, this adverse action was concealed, and its effect counteracted by the adventitious increase of the circulation of the trade-markets. But this wanes, and the exhaustive influence of the principle becomes gradually perceptible.

But the same forces are still at work which caused the temporary congestion of our markets, leading to reduced activity. It is clear that what has then caused congestion in the first instance, will, if not checked, produce decline in the next. Thus the amount of trade production will generally diminish; and to decline will succeed an inevitable decay!

26. *Effects of free trade.*—When any change is contemplated in the ordinary progress of things, it is requisite that, however much their ordinary, and therefore regarded as common, progress may be scoffed at by certain reformers, whose motives for such a destructive

purpose are not always upon the surface, the exact nature and working, immediate and remote as well, of the change should be narrowly discriminated. And all the more needed is this process of discrimination, when the primary effects of any alteration are of a favourable kind. For under these circumstances, those who are to be the present gainers by the new system, are likely to be blinded to the possibility of its future and prejudicial action. But the keen discernment of the legislator here interposes to balance the various actions of the new principle. It is his to regard the ultimate as well as the near consequences of a falsely introduced principle; to analyse the constant action of that principle, as well as its fluctuating operation; to imagine the possible changes its application may effect in those circumstances which surround its action; to determine which, if any, of these circumstances are constant; and, most of all, to maintain the equable growth of the various elements of his country's industry, and to foresee evil results! He will not be entrapped into the espousal of a system, however fair it may be in appearance, because it confers prosperity on the present, but is likely to be associated with disaster in the future. Rather than introduce such changes into the midst of affairs, the termination of which he cannot gauge, will he, in the language of Bishop Berkeley, "leave things as he found them," and be wise. For is not the future of his country his especial care? Are not violent measures avoided in the instance where too powerful a stimulation follows the application of any particular remedy, because he well knows that this must be followed, if the condition of surrounding circumstances are capable of fluctuation, by a corresponding reaction in the opposite direction? Thus will exhaustion ensue; and where is the wisdom of interrupting the natural progress of affairs, when the results of such an interruption are without his control? Is it prudent for a legislator, who has the interests of millions of his fellow-creatures to serve, to risk the future for the sake of the present?

But such apposite reasoning, depending not upon the immediate, but upon the remote effects of the free-trade principle, working under restriction, seems never to have entered the heads of those who took the most prominent place in the free-trade controversy; whether in or out of Parliament. What only concerned those who were amazed at the wonderful operation of free trade, as it was described at the time, was the prospect of immediate prosperity which its action would certainly, but it was not stated *indirectly*, effect. It was sufficient to know that free trade would be followed by blessings which would be bestowed upon the greater portion of the community.

Thus the near effects of free trade, acting partially on the whole commercial world, were described as altogether tending to the growth and welfare of our manufacture. Then was the opportunity afforded of lauding the relative importance of manufacture and agriculture, and it was abundantly embraced. But only the immediate prospects of the manufacturers were considered. It was supposed that these foreshadowed the whole of the future of free-trade prosperity. It was the fatal method of arguing from insufficiently known grounds, and without the assistance of all possible data—thought of the future was drowned in the enjoyment of the present! It is worthy of observation that the immediate effects of free trade upon agriculture were admitted by the free-traders to be adverse to the interests of agriculture. Even the free-traders could not shut their eyes to the fact, that the free-trade principle, when acting partially, brought disasters in its train. The immediate operation, therefore, of the free-trade principle may be summarised as acting beneficially towards manufacture, but adversely against agriculture. And it is of importance to recognise the double influence of the principle. It is as if the true ultimate action of the principle in all directions had been portrayed, at the commencement, in one only; to offer a sign, which might or might not be accepted, of its disastrous tendencies!

But the free-traders were not at a loss to persuade the farmers that the certain reduction of their rents would recoup them for the losses which a fall in the price of corn would entail upon them. Rents would be lower; therefore profits would be higher, according to the opinion of some economists, who, however, appear to have no regard for the rigid conditions which such a generalisation demands. It is obvious that for profits to remain high when rent falls, the conditions which effect this reduction must have no prejudicial influence upon one of the factors of which the relationship is composed. It is clear that the circumstances which attend the sources of profit must remain in a state similar to what they were before rent was reduced, or, if they do continue in a similar condition, to be at any rate favourable to the production of profit.

But suppose the case in which the sources whence profit flows become gradually dried up by the application of a new principle to the ordinary system, and imagine the extreme instance where the sources of profit remain idle in the hands of the farmer, and cannot become converted into profit, when there is no remunerative market for his corn, will any amount of reduction of rent compensate the farmer in such a deplorable state of his affairs?

However, the farmers, like everybody else, were deceived by the false and interested arguments of the free-traders, and the deception once begun has continuously proceeded with the prosperity of the misled Liberal party. For the results of error can only be escaped by a further addition to error!

Was it certain that rents would fall? It was certain enough that the tendency to fall in the price of corn would continue to operate and gradually ingravesce, and the farmer acted upon the hypothesis "that rent would fall," and admitted the source of his own destruction.

As the price of corn fell, so would the actual value of arable land tend to recede. But the question was, When would the tendency begin to operate? Though the tendency existed, rents might still, and would most probably, in the generality of instances, remain about the same as they had done during the system of protection, for the immediate necessity for reduction was not at hand. The gradual and almost imperceptible lowering of the price of corn would scarcely, after the first and sudden reduction in level, be felt by the farmer. Capital would come to his assistance in a bad year, and the deficient harvests, blamed as the source of his misfortunes by the free-trader, ever ready to advance a false cause. Thus his hopes would be flattered, and the farmer reduced to the uncertain position of relying upon the sufficiency of his harvest for his income. And so would the several links in the chain of a downward progress be passed, till the corn-markets of his own country were closed to the admission of his corn. The corn-markets of a nation shut to the admission of home-grown wheat! This was the event to which the action of the free-trade principle led! Ye wise legislators in times past, who filled the mouths of the people with cheap bread in one generation, and closed the avenues to labour in the next!

Thus the fortunes of the farmer, being grounded on so insecure a basis, his ruin was slowly, but none the less surely, being wrought, and with him the material prosperity of the owners of arable land.

For the rents of farms would, in course of time, undergo an actual decrease, though the actual value of land would, by the united endeavours of the landowners, be maintained at the nominal value.

Such is obviously the outcome of that self-interest which is common to all the members of the human species.

But the reduction would not happen in a way which the free-trader anticipated, and which the statesman, concerned in the interests of his country, would regard with favour, nor would the terminal result of this untoward course of affairs meet with his approbation.

If the tendency of the free-trade principle acted in the direction of decreasing the value of the arable land of the country, and thus verified the actual prediction of free trade, but not the method by which that event was to take place, the free-traders could hardly have foreseen that such a downward course in the level of rents, when it began to happen in a manner entirely unconceived by them, would be necessarily associated with the downfall of the prospects of the agricultural labourer. Nor did the free-trader, in his gigantic endeavour to effect a redistribution in the spoils of labour, and to direct a large proportion into the channel of the producers themselves—but, nevertheless, not a just proportion, for the manufacturers amassed more than their proper share—anticipate that the alteration he was intent on inducing would inevitably result in a far greater aggrandisement of the landowners than the mere increased rent of farms would of itself effect. The manufacturers were hoarding up riches in one age that the landowners might become so much the more prosperous in the next.

For the value of town land, the rents of offices and manufacturing mills, would gradually increase. The landowner, shut off in one direction in making up his income, would find, if he were fortunate in the possession of town land, his account balanced by the increase of his town rents, which would be slowly raised, according to the increased ability of occupiers to pay a higher rent. At first there would be a strong current flowing from the springs of the landowner; but when the eddy had subsided, the exaction of produce would find its natural path into the purse of the owners of the soil. For where there was the ability to pay increasingly higher rents, as in the case of the flourishing state of manufacture, this would be utilised, and the time surely arrive when, as the inevitable outcome of these temporary depressions to which all trade is naturally subject, some of the manufacturers would early find themselves, and all subsequently, in a position similar to that poor situation of agriculture during the initial operation of the free-trade principle. There would be no profits, because of the temporary or permanent contraction of business, but their rents, nevertheless, would continue the same.

Thus the remote effects of the constant influence of the free-trade principle may be portrayed. They are beneficial as well as adverse. But the tendency of its beneficial action is now diverted from the slowed stream of Manufacture.

Before, Manufacture was prosperous, and Agriculture the sufferer, and through her, but indirectly, the landed interest. But now, Manufacture is herself the sufferer, and the suffering she undergoes at her own hands; those who presided over her welfare in 1846 sowed the seeds which now bloom, and they end in a fatal strangulation. And what gains? The landed interest. What is the final production of the monstrous free-trade birth? The fortunate manufacturer whose prosperity has been established, and whose wealth has been acquired by virtue of the primary and prosperous action of the free-trade principle.

But when Manufacture was in such a flourishing condition as at this early period, what was the tendency? To reduce the price of all manufactured articles—a tendency which apparently has scarcely any limits. And what is the essential nature of this tendency? It is replete with dangers: the danger of making everything as cheap as possible does not end at itself—it leads to others. It leads to the production of inferior articles, with the expectation from a large sale of making greater profits. The energies of the workman are concentrated upon labours in which his peculiar talents are of no avail. The tendency acts prejudicially upon the skill and handicraft of the artisan.

And if the markets become unfavourable, there is opened up the source of fraud, whereby the materials of which manufactured goods are made undergo a deterioration in quality. And the ignorant buyer is unconsciously drawn into the trap of taking a relatively cheap article, with the expectation that it possesses all the qualities of the former more expensive ones.

Such purchasers, attracted by the cheapness of the goods which they buy, do not readily understand that the amount which they yield to the profits of the manufacturers of these trumpery articles exceeds that which a dearer one is called upon to contribute. And the reason is at hand. They yield their sources of profit in frequently increasing purchases.

By such dangers was this tendency to indefinite cheapening of manufactured goods surrounded; articles deteriorate in quality as they diminish in price; skilled workmanship declines. But what is the result of the decline of manufacture upon the working classes?

And may not that be called a sign of decline, when the possibility was presented of enabling foreign goods to be supplied to neutral markets on account of the relative dearness of free-trade labour?

What mercy is to be shown to Manufacture in this decline, when she showed no compassion upon the precarious state into which her elder sister Agriculture was thrown by the influence of free trade?

Then, Agriculture was sacrificed for the aggrandisement of the younger sister; now, she dies by her own hands!

The effect on the labouring classes is easy enough to depict. Trade undergoes a compulsory shrinkage in volume, and a relative decrease, when the increasing population of the country is taken into the account, and in some branches an absolute decrease. Why? because neutral markets are supplied with cheaper goods by the foreigner. Hence the field of labour is restricted, fewer labourers are employed, and increased competition of labour sends receding wages, owing to the diminution of profits, to a lower point—namely, the starvation-point, of which the free-traders made so much account, when the injustice of the landlords was arbitrarily, and without any foundation, tendered as their false cause; but now the real cause is observed to be resident in that very method which the free-traders employed to bring about the solution of the difficulty with which they tried to grapple, and which they have so unnaturally deformed.

To this extraordinary state has the free-trade principle reduced the labouring classes of this community; there is less labour for the country, for there is less demand from outside. Former supplies are checked, the markets are turgid; but their abnormal expansion, so strained for a while, rapidly declines, when no outlet appears for the discharge of these goods. Thus the means of utilising her resources are diminished; and wages, where these are present, are continually being decreased.

What, then, is the total effect of the course of the free-trade principle in this country? It has been the custom, and it still is maintained by that party in the State which is interested in the permanence of the falsehood, to declare that free trade is associated with nothing else than the prosperity of the nation. Where is the prosperity at the present day?

But those who care, if able, to conceive the comprehensive working of a principle through successive periods of time, some favourable, others unfavourable to its action, while surrounding circumstances are constantly fluctuating, will recognise that the path of free trade has been entangled with disaster from the very first moment of the commencement of its operation, though these were obscured by its initial but indirect success.

The immediate effect of free trade in corn upon agriculture was disastrous, but the sphere of its influence throughout the nation partial.

The remote effects of free trade upon manufacture, the ultimate result of buying in the cheapest market and selling in the dearest, the most insidious doctrine that has ever been preached to the world, is still disastrous; but the sphere of its operation is general throughout the land.

27. *Scheme of the continued operation of the free-trade principle:—*

The free-trade principle acting with restriction: surrounding nations protective.

	Manufacture.	Agriculture.
α Immediate effect.	Prosperity.	Loss.
	Neutralised by collateral policy of surrounding nations, who act in their own self-interest, as we did in 1846; and leading to subsequent	
β Remote effect.	Loss.	Loss increased, because soil cannot be cultivated at a profit.
γ Total effect.	Loss to the nation.	

Free-trade goods are subjected to an import duty in foreign ports, and to counterbalance the cost of an increasing consumption of corn, there remains the produce of a constantly diminishing manufacture.

28. *Effect of the doctrine of free trade upon several parties privy to it.*—The party of reform, as was to be expected, came in for a full share of the popular ovation which followed the successful operation of the free-trade principle when it began to act freely and without any restriction in the commercial circles of this country, and after the primary sources of disturbance to its beneficial influence had been removed. The liberal spirit had effected so great a change in the whole aspect of the trades and industries of the nation—the liberal reform in our commercial code had been the

ultimate means of conferring the blessings of plenty and content upon so large a proportion of the inhabitants of the country—that it was not extraordinary to predict that the Liberal party would enjoy a lasting popularity among the labouring classes! Yes; free trade and prosperity, being arbitrarily associated in the public mind, the Liberal party would retain the confidence of the country so long as the prospects of commerce remained favourable. But just as in the period of depression, which was wantonly exaggerated to meet a special object, the free-trade party grasped the opportunity presented to them to further their own interests, in their selfish view that these were the interests of the nation, so when free trade came to be intimately associated with a constant decline, would thinking men turn the channel of their meditations, and with more or less compulsion, into the causation of the present distress, in order to determine the successive links which thus have been brought about. In 1845 and 1846, the Liberals, and among them Sir Robert Peel and his followers, discovered the cause of the then depression, which cannot be compared in its magnitude to the present decline, in the adverse operation of the laws which related to the importation of corn. And what cause have the Liberal party to account for the distress of to-day?

The Corn Laws have been abolished—the source of all depression, the origin of the starvation wages of the labourer. Still depression reigns, and with it, unhappily, decline. We have seen free trade associated with prosperity to the manufacturing interests of the country, and we are experiencing the unfortunate co-existence of free trade with distress, from the decline in all our manufacturing industries. Can free trade, then, alone be the cause of prosperity and decline? Obviously not. Free trade as a constant cause has a constant effect. But it may have other evanescent effects, due to the action of the principle upon surrounding conditions, to the disturbance in them leading to an increase of trade circulation. And when these collateral effects have had time to subside, then the real and constant tendency of the principle becomes apparent even to the prejudiced eye. But it is clear that the Liberal party are not in a position to advance the true cause of the present distress. For if once they yield to the consideration of the working of their favourite principle, they begin to doubt their chances of continuing the government of the country! And thus is explained one of the objects of the Liberal party in discrediting the means by which the cause of the distress can only be deduced—by observation and inference.

But the false remedy which the Liberals used has been and still is assiduously so wrapt round with an apparent disinterestedness on the part of the Liberal leaders, and obscured by a primary success, that there is needed only this presence of distress to dispossess the public mind of a false association. For the Liberal leaders are naturally concerned in the bolstering up of a false idol, at which they have persuaded the ignorant man to kneel.

The mercantile classes have had their desire; and what now have the manufacturers themselves to say? Free trade caused Manchester and other industrial towns to rise rapidly in the scale of prosperity. But what has become of that prosperity, which was to continue always, at the present day? What prevents Manchester from still increasing at the same rate she did during the early period of the action of free trade? Her markets are contracted; her labour is unoccupied; her wages are reduced. The place which not long since was the scene of a feverish activity is now comparatively inactive; exhaustion of her efforts has succeeded to their too severe stimulation. What prevents Manchester from even reaching such a degree of prosperity which the relation of her population to the amount of her trade demands, is the difficulty of obtaining markets for her goods. And this arises from an unequal and therefore unfair competition.

But when markets fail in one direction, ought they not to be sought in others? And what is left to this country except the opening up of new fields, of extending the region of our former commercial activity in new countries? But against this humane system of colonisation—the only remedy near at hand to rid us of a redundant population—against the means of extending our colonial possessions,—what is raised? The whole voice of the Radical section of the Liberal party. The system is denounced as a pernicious one, when in reality it contains the germ of new powers—for does it not increase the responsibility of the Imperial Government at home?

The means of relieving distress at home and of increasing the extent of Christian civilisation are denied, because the enormous benefits which they confer upon the nation are counterbalanced by the increased responsibility of the Ministers in power—as if such an increase in responsibility was so heavy to bear! and as if any comparison between this increase of responsibility and the good accruing to the nation from the development of our colonies could with any show of reason be maintained. But what is to be said of such a shrinking from the burden of responsibility, which naturally devolves upon us with the increasing growth of the empire, when those who refuse to recognise the relationship are concerned at home in the design of means for destroying those proper relations, on the recognition and maintenance of which, this kingdom reached formerly such a high degree of prosperity? Is it difficult to analyse the efforts of these extreme politicians —the failure to construct abroad, but the energy to destroy at home? It would indeed be an extraordinary phenomenon if Manchester, the cradle of free trade, as she has been falsely called, should be the first to discern the unequal place she and her compeers have in the commercial markets of the world, and to demand *that* protection for her markets and her labour which the legislatures of other nations grant to theirs.

Does it not sound strange in the ears of the short-sighted reformer, that free-trade labour starves, while labour under protection enjoys its steady and onward course of prosperity?

But this free-trade labour was once prosperous, and was the source of much injury to labour which was conducted under the natural system of protection. Now it seems as if labour under protection is the cause of the premature decay of free-trade labour. It is an endless repetition; the effects of our adverse attitude towards other protective nations in one generation, recoil upon ourselves in the next!

Labour once enjoyed a high wage under the operation of free trade, while surrounding circumstances helped this to remain benign. The increase in the wage of the labourer rose too rapidly to offer the idea of the increment being founded on a secure basis. All the elements of stability were wanting; and the working classes, with the legislative assistance of the country, entered upon a mushroom-like progress. Their acme of prosperity was reached; they had choked all the springs whence their supplies were fed; there was the large superstructure overground; the stem which supported was fragile; free trade had induced too rapid a circulation, with a consequent overgrowth; and the foreign markets which supplied it with nourishment were fast disappearing. Must such a structure fall with a crash?

But before the period of the limitation of the markets had arrived, the penalty of stimulation and a forced prosperity had to be paid. The labouring classes, while they were receiving constantly diminishing wages, yet had the same rents to pay. And the result of this untoward change was evident. His expenditure was reduced, the means of bringing up his little children contracted! What a contrast, this rise and fall, to the steady progress of labour under the protective system! And what is the ultimate effect upon the condition of the labouring classes? After having been rudely taken out from their normal position in the chain of a natural progress, and advanced to a position for which they are unprepared, they have receded further back than they were at the commencement of the action of free trade. In this lower condition has the continued operation of the free-trade principle plunged them; and is not this abnormal descent hard to bear, after the slight glimpses they have had of better things? Let the two methods of progress, under the natural means of protection, and the artificial system of free trade, be contrasted by the unprejudiced intellect, and which will be chosen? That which has stability and certainty!

How dearly those farmers, who were led into self-deception by the arts of the free-traders practising upon their credulity, paid the penalty of their ignorant folly, very soon became apparent when they discovered that the course of events as depicted by their seducers did not come to pass. The price of corn was lowered, but the level of their rents remained the same; nor was this changed during a long period when the fall in the price of corn was gradually increasing, for this was imperceptible. Nevertheless the farmers were roused into a condition of alarm for their future welfare, as well as that of the agricultural labourers, whose prosperity was dependent upon their own. But the natural relationship between master and man was broken, and the Liberal party lost all hope of the subsequent support, what little was left, of the agricultural interest. The agricultural labourer was taught by the party of reform to look to legislation as the sovereign cure for his ills. And what remedy have the Liberals advanced to entrap the support of the starving agricultural labourer? What can be honestly put forward as a means of improving his precarious position, by those who have regard for knowledge and for truth? But the ignorant agricultural labourer is impelled by the very insecurity of his situation to accept any promise, however falsely it may be founded. And thus he falls into the net which Liberal stratagem has purposely constructed for him. But for what? To advance his cause? Not by any means, but to keep the Liberals in power. For the town Liberals are supposed, by the greater advantages which they enjoy, to be on the side of progress, and therefore to belong naturally to the great Liberal party. But education will slowly evince the means of distinguishing between what is true reform, founded on a firm basis, and what is artificial progress, supported on the — swelling phrases of the Liberal leaders!

The agricultural labourer is compelled to desert the soil! he feels the hardship; the separation of a lifelong intimacy is keen. He cries against the injustice under which he suffers. And his cry is taken up, and echoed by the Radical party. Sympathy is aroused. But let us examine the grounds of this sympathy. Before we begin to feel, let us proceed to reason. For on what are we to display emotion? On what is false?

The Radical leaders endeavour to rouse enthusiasm, of course based upon injustice. But what is the true source of the agricultural labourer's distressful state? Is it the unjust action of the farmers, who deny a proper share of their profits, as the former manufacturers did, to the labourers on their farms? No; the farmers are not in a position to make any profit at all. Is it the consequence of the legislation of the old party of protection? How can it be this, when it can be fully proved that when Sir Robert Peel introduced the principle of free trade into our commercial relations, our commerce was increasing at the rate of five millions of exports during each period of five years under the protective system, more than sufficient to provide for the natural increase of the population during that time. What, then, is the cause ? It is the free-trade principle, harboured by a Conservative Premier, and safely landed by the Liberal party into our commercial code. It is free trade which has been the source of all the disasters to our agricultural interest.

And is it not strange to discern at this time of day a Radical leader still censuring the system on which the ownership of land is founded? But it is easily explicable. He has to fasten on some cause, and he cannot blame the free-trade principle. He must, like his predecessors, only in a more extravagant degree, call up to his side false causes, and support them by as false arguments. He must instil enthusiasm, create sympathy, and deceive those who are willing to follow in the path which he so skilfully, and with such obvious designs, opens out to them. For he knows that when he has gained, by any means whatever, the sympathy of the masses, he will be powerful enough to guide them; but to other fields than those of their ultimate prosperity, as the action of his immediate predecessors, the free-traders, sufficiently proves.

CHAPTER VI.

THE DESCRIPTION OF THE DIRECT EFFECTS OF FREE TRADE.

29. *Graphic delineation of the effect of the principle of free trade upon the progress of our commerce.*—On the opposite page is the course, graphically depicted, of the free-trade principle upon the progress of our commerce. It will be observed that it is divided into two parts—the upward curve corresponding to that period when the principle was acting with surrounding favourable conditions; the downward curve representing the adverse operation of the principle, after equilibrium had been established, and the pernicious tendency began to operate, uninfluenced by the beneficial operation of the most advantageous collateral effect of the principle, increased circulation.

It is important to observe that, during the ascent of these small curves, a false argument might be raised, and it was on some occasions, tending to the conclusion that our commerce was once more in a state of increased activity. So it was with reference to the paroxysmal falls of which they form a part, and to which they are

FREE TRADE.

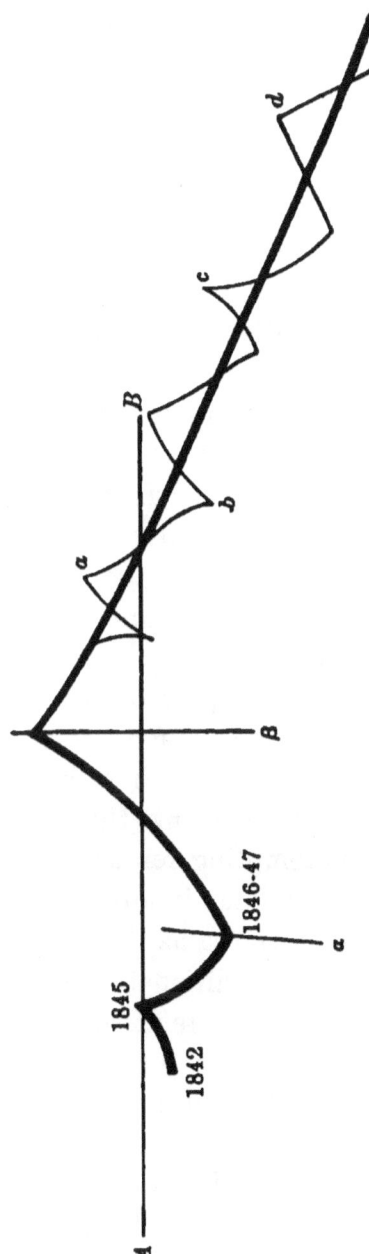

Between α and β is the period of the beneficial action of the free-trade principle, characterised by increased circulation, an inconstant effect of free trade.

Beyond β is the period in which the principle is not assisted by this effect of the principle, hence constant action of the free-trade principle is evident.

AB = the level, slowly ascending, of course, of our commerce under system of protection.

$a\ b\ c\ d$ mark paroxysmal depressions in downward course of free-trade principle.

necessarily related; but it is quite clear that of themselves they form no trustworthy guide to the true elucidation of the course of our trades. For this to be effected, regard must be had for the highest level our trade line reached during the most prosperous career of the free-trade principle, and for the normal line of advancement of our trade under the system of protection; where, too, our trade is stated to be undergoing a revival, this increase must carefully be compared with the volume of our trade in previous years, an allowance being made for the proper increment which belongs to the addition to the population of the country during the period in which the revival has or is taking place; and likewise a comparison of profits must be instituted, for although trade may undergo an increase in volume, if the value of an equal amount of manufactured goods decreases in succeeding years, it is obvious that the loss must be borne in part or wholly by the producers, and therefore that labour must in reality suffer, though the markets may remain in a buoyant state. It is by allusion to these elements that error is only to be avoided. For it is tempting for the Liberal party to point to an increased volume in any branch of our trade, and forget to add at the same time, because it would dim the hopes their unconditional statements create, that the increase is merely a relative one, and not absolute; that it is relative to a former level of depression; and that though the increase means a greater activity to the markets, yet it is not associated with higher profits, nor with the increment of any prosperity to the labourer's reduced condition.

But in all instances it is of paramount importance to

detect the constant tendency to decline; and when speaking of the action of free trade under unfavourable conditions, to separate the constant element of decline from those other causes which tend to raise the fortunes of the markets and raise the expectations of the manufacturers for a while.

30. *The congested state of the markets.*—The immediate effect of the free-trade principle when it began to act without any external impediment, as that which occurred in the years 1846 and 1847, was a congested state of the markets; and this congestion was the direct result of increased circulation. It was a congestion of a kind which came not within the experience of any— it was the reply to the increased and increasing demands from foreign sources. And so long as these demands continued, so long would the trade circulation continue active.

But the growing industries of neighbouring nations were either unheeded, or, if taken into consideration, regarded with a contemptuous eye. For the majority of Englishmen—and amongst them men of political fame—never for the moment thought that the labour of Continental nations could ever compete, on a level even of equality, much less than on terms of superiority, with the advanced and well-established labour of England. And so it was, but for a time only. What the free-traders expected to have an indefinite course, was very soon found to have limits assigned to it; and among these limits, the bounties which foreign protective nations confer upon their growing industries. Cobden's dictum, the result of his comparative researches into the relative value of English and Continental labour, was taken to be true eternally. It was a bold statement to offer that, because an Englishman's labour was three or four times the value of that of the Continental labourer, that this same difference should practically remain a constant quantity. And it must be added that the dictum required credulity alone to become convinced of its truth.

Then no thought was taken of comparing these possible conditions where Continental labour was equal in value to that of the Englishman, but of less cost, and was competing with English free-trade labour in those markets which had been for so long the monopoly of this country; and no proper consideration was given to the bounty-system of protective nations, which would afford the foreigner an earlier opportunity of competing on terms of equality with his English rival. How clear it would have been that only one result could follow so unequal a competition, and that in the labour-market the race for supremacy between free trade and protection is won easily by the latter!

Let us contrast for a while the tendency of England's arbitrary procedure in the application of free trade to her commerce, to the actual injury of foreign trade and industries, with regard to its possible influence on our national spirit and the feelings of other nations.

The consequences upon the wages of the English labourer were remarkable, and the labouring classes entered upon a path of prosperity, which, alas! was to terminate but too early. English labour then was dear, but that on the Continent remained, relatively to a slow advance, checked by a sudden arrest of their industrial activity, much the same as before. With what a longing eye, therefore, would the foreign labourer regard the more successful condition of his English brother! Why should he not be as prosperous? Why does not the foreign Government, which presides over his welfare, effect for him what the British Legislature did for the labour of this country? Why? Simply because the course which may be adapted, apparently with success, to one country is not suited to the requirements of another, on account of their national condition as regards means of subsistence and the ability to supply each its own wants, being present in varying degrees.

When the Englishman's labour came, therefore, to be the especial object of a legislative interference, was there not a ground presented on which the foreigner might stand and raise the cry of despotism against the Government of his country? There was but a seeming one only: it was a ground which a temporary feeling of relative injustice created; but, as it was based upon emotion, so it could be removed by reason. Foreign labour might be cheap, but there could be no doubt of the security of the advance of her prosperity. It would be slow, that was true, but yet it would be equable. Let this certain state of things be compared with the unstable condition of labour in England, and what was the result? That the course of British labour was surrounded with dangers, one of which would be supplied by the gradually increasing ability of the foreigner to compete with and eventually to outrun the Englishman.

And what kind of danger is nourished by that party in the State, the end-result of whose legislation is the decline of labour after it has experienced so great a degree of prosperity? Does not this downward tendency create a feeling of dissatisfaction amongst the working classes? Does not dissatisfaction at home become heightened by the knowledge of the continuance of a normal prosperity abroad? and does not this dissatisfaction lead to discontentment? and discontentment form the germ of agitation, the result of which alone is determined by popular enthusiasm? May not this popular enthusiasm be directed into a wrong channel? May it not be utilised by designing men to work out their own particular objects?

The English labourer now turns his anxious eye in the direction of those markets which have despoiled him of his occupation which, before, in his day of prosperity, had regarded him with jealousy! What if this procedure on the part of a single nation, the leading nation in the commercial world, had terminated in the rupture of the customary relations between a foreign people and its Government? What a hollow and wicked movement it would have been! But the difficulty was overcome by convincing those who, by reason of their limited powers, cannot take a comprehensive view of the progress of their affairs, of the paramount necessity of a gradual and equable advance in their onward course, if they are to hope for security in the present, and if they have a proper concern for the well-being of their children in the future! But how often is it to be expected that such a view, grounded upon the natural progress of one of the elements of society, will be entertained by a mob, whose thoughts are only for the present, and whose movements are under the influence of a predominant passion ? Is not their passion liable to be inflamed by the specious declamation of would-be demagogues ?

To effect a calm reasoning where the emotions are in a state of violent perturbation, is perhaps impossible; but it is certain that if the feelings of the multitude can be aroused through the influence of a supposed injustice, they can be commanded by a regard for its ultimate and best interests. If the control of the people was difficult in bygone ages, because of their illiterate character, it is, or ought to be, capable of being more easily effected nowadays, if this age of education has brought forth the results which those look for who preside over the improvement of the masses ! It is a question whether, under the system of protection, there was ever the opportunity presented for a congestion of the markets: the tendency, however, existed, but it was never brought so powerfully into action as to be associated with harm. But the congestion which was effected by the introduction of the free-trade principle took time to subside, and in its course towards a diminishing degree of local activity of the markets, the original impetus remained for some time without control. What was this impetus? The expectation of the merchants, based upon their belief that events would pursue a course similar to that which they had just experienced; a belief which depended upon the false predictions of the free-traders. And when this expectation of a continued prosperity— it is hardly credible that men should have been found to believe so obvious a contradiction to the laws of progress—was associated with the desire for gain, what a powerful impetus it supplied ! But when the demands from the neutral markets began to decrease, while the supplies to the home markets continued the same in amount as before, then the tension of the latter would gradually become evident. And would it not increase till those who controlled the circulation of the expanded markets perceived that there was an over-production going forward, and that such could only react with disadvantage to trade?

What an opportunity was here afforded for the Liberal party to step in and give their solution of this economical phenomenon of over-production! For was not this over-production directly the fault of the manufacturers themselves? How generous for the Liberals to censure those whom they were most anxious to befriend! But blame must be localised, and localised early, so that the diffusion of a false cause may turn to the advantage of the Liberals themselves. For it is easy to see there is another explanation of this phenomenon of over-production, which has its source in the original disturbance which the free-trade principle, ever shielded by the reform party, effected.

But what kind of over-production was this which is blamed by the Liberal economists as one of the chief sources of derangement of the markets leading to depression? It was clearly a relative over-production—relative to the amount of production, which had occurred previously, during the initial period of prosperity of the free-trade principle.

Demand was diminishing; but it requires some time to elapse before those who formerly supplied recognise the fact that there are now fewer calls upon them. The markets were capable of supplying the same amount of goods as before; but what was happening was that a less and less proportion of goods were sold. Hence the markets became overstocked; and the cry was raised, "Over-production is the origin of the malady affecting our trade."

But those who raised the cry care not to trace the source of over-production to its proper cause—which was the increased circulation which followed the stimulus given by the free-trade principle to all our trades. What was regarded as the fault of the manufacturers, and for which they were freely blamed by the free-trade economists, was in reality one of the collateral results of the free-trade principle. For assuredly there must have been some ground for the merchant to continue his powers of production. Men do not, except in the fancy of the free-traders, continue to produce for an imaginary market! What ground, then, had the merchants to continue this relative over-production of their stock? Expectation. They did not perceive the true course the affairs of their markets were pursuing: a constant tendency, become for the first time apparent, though its previous action had been obscured, was mistaken for a temporary and minor adverse influence. They were urged on by the hope of better times. The fatal conclusion was embraced, "the tide will turn"; and then, with the disappearance of impediments, their swelling markets must be relieved.

Now, would this expectation, thus falsely raised upon a tendency, supposed to be constant, of the free-trade principle, be admitted to have failed them till the tide of demand had continued far in its ebb, and when during a period of depression they were led to consider the causes of their misfortune? Then they would be compelled to admit that the neutral markets were no longer their monopoly; that they had ascribed a false cause to the origin of their falling markets; and that they had reasoned wrongly because they had decided erroneously. The present depression was the commencement of the decline of their trade. The downward course might on occasions be interrupted by the appearance of temporary causes which would tend to raise the drooping spirits of those who had already hazarded an adverse forecast respecting the ultimate condition of our industries, and to weaken their former opinions; and these would certainly be utilised by the politician as a present indication of the revival of trade. But the decline had been brought about by an unfavourable competition; and when unequal competition thus appeared to be gaining in strength, and when its influence was recognised as a factor in the causation of the depression of our markets, then the tendency to a relative over-production forthwith disappeared; and instead now of there being an expanded market, this became contracted, and with the contraction of the markets the sphere of labour tended to diminish and wages to decrease.

But is there any over-production nowadays? If there is, there must be some cause for it. But can it be present in any large amount sufficient to disturb the course of our trade in any material degree? For a general tendency to exist there must be some general cause which is able when conditions are favourable to give it effect. And we have just traced how this general tendency to a prejudicial over-production has disappeared: it is now a phenomenon of the past!

There may, however, be some local tendencies which confine their operation within a limited sphere of action. Is it just to bring forward local and minor causes to explain general and large results? How can a tendency of small intensity produce an effect of great magnitude?

To the argument that over-production leads as a chief cause to the depressed state of the markets of to-day, the reply is forthcoming that, though over-production may have some influence in a few particular branches, yet that it has no appreciable influence upon the whole downward tendency of our trade. It is obvious that when over-production is advanced as a chief cause of depression, a partial cause, and one very minor in its influence, is mistaken for a general and more powerful one!

Increasing and unequal competition in neutral markets has gradually limited the area of our supplies—it has even encroached upon the supply of our home markets. Thus when our merchants enter the monopolised markets of old, they leave them with constantly diminishing profits. But if the volume of any particular trade does not actually shrink because the tendency is checked, it is evident its conduct is not so successful because profits are not so large. And it matters not whether the volume of trade begins to contract and goes on contracting, whether profits are reduced, or whether both these factors are continuing their existence side by side, the end-result is the same. The total loss is borne wholly or proportionately by labour!

31. *Decline follows congestion.*—There is abundant evidence to show, and this on the figures which the great master of British commerce himself supplied, that the progress of our trade, even during the troublous times of 1837-41, was normally and therefore gradually increasing. And who will deny that extraordinary increase in circulation, in an already increasing trade, which pervaded every department of our industries, immediately after the free-trade principle—which, while its beneficial action was being impeded by adverse forces, was regarded with distrust—had begun to operate without any restriction, and when every source of opposition had been removed?

The comparative ideas of the course of events may thus be described. A normal progress, called normal inasmuch as its source is inherent within the sphere of our trade-activity—an internal force of growth as opposed to a temporary stimulation applied from without—was going forward in all our trades and industries, though, at the period 1837-41, the line of advance was interrupted for the moment by one of those depressions called paroxysmal and dependent upon normal causes. And this kind of progress was regarded by the party of protection as being the true progress of our industries. But the other party in the State, which has taken up the position of being the reformer of the nation, foresaw the increased activity which would result if free trade were applied as an external stimulant to our trade relations. This species of progress, associated with an unhealthy congestion of the markets —the effects of which could not be induced without a proportionate damage to the markets—was styled the real progress of the nation, and therefore its cause was introduced as the reform of the age into our commercial code. But on the demand of whom? Why the manufacturers themselves. Well, then, was not this a force inherent within the sphere of our trade-activity? Did not the protectionists apply for the protection of the State, and was their application refused by the Legislature?

Now, the demand is, instead of protection, "give us free trade." And we granted the application, coming from within our growing industries, say the Liberals, just as the protectionists did in days gone by.

But this specious reasoning is of the Liberal type; it is on the same level as the increased profits and reduced rents, and the false association which they made between free trade and prosperity. The whole aspect of the question changes when the differences in the nature of these demands, for protection and free trade respectively, are taken into consideration. For the older legislators perceived that the call for protection was universal throughout all the industries of the country; besides, what was the nature of that protection which they demanded? Did it introduce an element of disturbance into the normal growth of our trade? No; it rather prevented external forces from interfering with its proper development. Compare the grounds upon which protection was based with those by which free trade was introduced. Free trade was granted on the application of the manufacturing interest alone, for those farmers who consented to its introduction were persuaded by false promises; and it operated after the fashion of an external stimulant. Thus the difference between protection and free trade may be summarised:

protection offered the best condition of surrounding circumstances for inherent normal growth of our trade; adverse external influences were neutralised; while free trade, on the contrary, acted not upon the ordinary powers of growth of our trade, but upon its extraordinary capacity to respond to intense stimulation, with the result that in the overgrowth which was produced, those proper sources of its natural development were consumed. And thus the overgrowth was left to decline.

We have already traced the normal progress of our trade; we have seen an external stimulant applied to it, with the consequence of congestion due to overstocking of the markets; we have deduced the cause of this over-production, the offspring of a false expectation; we are experiencing now the contraction of our markets and labour declining.

The relation between "increased circulation," congestion, and decline throughout the field of development, is a well-known phenomenon; it is observed in every kind of growth, whether of the individual organism or of the concurrent action of various forces spread over the area of society; nor can trade-growth be excepted from its general tendency.

And what is this tendency? It is that, within certain limits, activity of forces may increase to the advantage of the community within which they operate; but that if they extend beyond these limits, over-activity surely leads to exhaustion and then decay. And what is the means by which nature effects this result? A fatal congestion, the product of excessive stimulation.

But before the adverse course of our trade can be studied, it is necessary to recollect the features of its natural growth. And these are: first, that it is slow, due to the gradual operation of forces which thereby gain in stability and strength; and secondly, that it is equable—that is, adjusted to the increasing demands of an increasing population. What, then, happens, when this steady line of advance, due to inherent activity, and agreeable to the practice of the majority, is interrupted by an artifice which is designed by a few to have certain effects, amongst which are enrolled their own selfish interests? This happens — that the future growth of our trade is disturbed from its former groove, because the conditions which relate to its development have undergone an entire alteration. Her future, therefore, is thus disjointed from the past; she enters upon a new course. But upon what does the continuance of her prosperous career essentially depend? On the favourable condition of surrounding circumstances. Are these conditions within our control? Obviously not, for they are the outcome of the attitude of foreign Ministers and the progress of foreign trades. Thus the progress of our trade now depends upon the stimulation which it receives from outside sources! What a strange contrast to the course of affairs under protection, when the growth of our trade was dependent on inherent forces; what a curious sequence of the true and the false!

We are thus led to the point where the Liberal spirit of the nation forsook the old lines of a steady and equable advancement as unsuited to the times, and replaced it by a state of activity, the consequences of which they could not gauge, and the cause of which they could not increase nor diminish. But if development was going on, as it was declared by Sir Robert Peel; if this gradual increase of growth was certain, as the increasing exports of the country fully proved, was not such a secure condition far better than a temporary increased activity of growth, which assumed so large a proportion, that the wants of the labouring classes were far more than comfortably supplied? And what was the character of this precocity in our trade growth? It was fundamentally insecure; and the reason—because we no longer held the means of its growth within our control.

Was it a prudent piece of legislation to hazard a certain growth for an unstable activity, however much prosperity this might have been the means of creating? But the die was cast, and prosperity reigned.

The consequences of such an artificial disturbance to a normal growth, we are led to gather from an inquiry into the altered working of the many smaller laws, which are collected into the general law of the development of trade. One of these laws is that the trade-markets must be maintained in an efficient state of activity. But the new system of free trade entirely interfered with the normal circulation of the markets, and left them in the future to be the prey of an unequal competition, which gradually shut off the sources of their supplies. Hence deficient circulation in the long-run, and this would be associated with decline.

But let it be admitted in favour of this Liberal free-trade reform in our commercial code that there are exceptions to the general association in natural productions between slowness of growth and durability of structure, are not such exceptions in the region of a much less certain degree of knowledge than the vast number of instances which conform to the law?

And under such circumstances was it wise to risk the certain advancement of our trade, under a system which has seen this island attain a degree of prosperity unexampled in the pages of trade history, for its present excessive stimulation, the terminal results of which could only be disastrous, if the disturbing influence, which was the ultimate cause of that activity, were turned, by the united endeavours of protective nations, into a lever, by which they could effect the gradual descent of our trade?

But what man, in the common affairs of life, risks his fortune on the chance of an exceptional result? Such an one, without any dependants, would be enthralled by folly! But let him be surrounded by wife and children. What man, gifted with domestic affection, if he were of sane intellect, would gamble away the prospects of his home. Would he not be called reckless, abandoned, frenzied? What is to be said of that party, then, who risked the subsequent trade progress of their country upon the chance of an artificial remedy being able to supply a sufficient amount of stimulation to maintain the increased development of our industries, upon the hollow prospect that an increased circulation, thus induced, would continue for ever; and upon the false foundation that the remedy thus applied was the cure for the existing distress of the country? Does any man speculate with such little foresight, fenced round with such slender data, in the ordinary affairs of life, who is characterised by the qualities of wisdom and prudence? Can a legislator be called wise who deserts the known paths of experience, a better mistress and teacher than free-trade economists; or a patriot, who thus evinces so little regard for the ultimate welfare of his countrymen, however much he may have been gratified by the temporary wellbeing of the labouring classes, whose evanescent prosperity he lived to see?

If there had been nothing else to guide the politician in the conduct of the commercial affairs of his time, might he not have looked around him and ascertained the working of parallel forces in other spheres, and the effect on them of the change he contemplated in our commercial relations? To deduce the generalisation might perhaps have been impossible, for this would require an extensive knowledge of many sciences. But the tendency of the sequence of stimulation and permanent decay, when the former is excessive, might have been detected in many instances; and this had proved an argument why a new principle should be shunned, whose working is associated with so much disaster.

Such an act of observation and comparison was apparently ignored; but the observation of those who succeeded the free-traders of 1842, and who were still wildly attracted by the abstract fascinations of the new principle, has hardly been conducted with that accuracy and impartiality which the study of a science demands.

Thus, when a clamour arose amongst the trades-people respecting the depression of their markets, it was merely a temporary affair, a paroxysm, a natural recurrence of depression.

Thus the free-trade principle has not interfered with

the tendency of natural forces to create depression. Temporary depressions are admitted, even during the progress of the free-trade principle! But what comes of the boast of the original supporters of the free-trade system, that it would wipe away all depression for ever from our markets? It is left for their more sanguine successors to palliate and to distort. And yet in one sense the prediction of the older free-traders may be said to have come true; depression has been swept away from the face of trade, for the means to its causation are being continually narrowed, but in its place free trade has left—decline!

But the signs of decline the free-traders totally fail to see. They admit the fluctuations in the onward course of trade; but to the factor of decline they deny an existence. Under these circumstances it may be observed, that though our trade-line undergoes a recurrent rise, this rise is inadequate to meet the requirements of the labouring classes, for its highest point is continually receding.

And in the case of the upward tendency of our trade-curve under protection, and its downward tendency under free-trade, how is the difference in direction explained by the free-trade economists?

This general tendency to decline has been in operation for many years; its presence is irresistibly demonstrated by the gradually increasing number of the labouring classes without occupation; and what grounds are there for an immediate revival? Sir Robert Peel depended upon the inherent energies of the country, while the nation was suffering a temporary distress under protection. He offered the highest hopes of a near revival; perhaps he had the stimulant of free trade ready for application! What is the attitude of the Liberal leaders of to-day? There is distress, a constantly increasing distress, and free trade does not operate with stimulation, for it has lost its former efficacy. What other stimulant can the Liberals provide?

32. *Differences between the present trade conditions and those of* 1842.—In every instance of the operation of a principle, it is requisite, if that operation is to continue successful, to examine the various stages through which these external conditions which influence its action are likely to pass; and thus to determine the sources of its mischievous bearing, leading either to means which will check their prejudicial tendency, or to the abandonment of the new principle. For it is not enough to assume that because those circumstances were favourable to its initial operation, that therefore they shall continue in a similar state. Such an arbitrary conclusion, as we have already observed, is totally opposed to experience. For the merest examination of the disturbance which was created by the application of the free-trade principle to the ordinary existing system of our course, would lead to the observation that, in the course of its action, collateral tendencies were being called into being which might or might not react disadvantageously at some period of its future operation.

What were some of these collateral tendencies? They were the forces which protective nations were gradually putting forth—to aid England in the continued development of her prosperous career? Rather to divert some of the sources of that prosperity which attached at that time to this nation, into the industrial channels of their own country! This was, and is still, the immediate object of the legislatures of foreign nations. Each naturally tends to protect the development of its own internal resources; to promote the occupation of the people; to increase the markets; and by maintaining the contentment of the masses, to deflect the popular attention from theories dangerous to the safety of the State. For this reason, if for no other, is it the object of good government to afford as tranquil a condition of the people as is possible under given circumstances; and the best means employed to attain this end is the maintenance of the normal progress of native industries, and their protection from external injury; the sources of which were so violently increased by the application of free trade. For it is a historical inference that no people rise against their governing body, except when they are in a state of distress; except when some calamity, perhaps unforeseen, has attended them to the deprivation of the ordinary means of their subsistence. Thus the future being involved in darkness, there being nothing to expect but the continuance of distress, numbers combine to defeat, as they suppose, the tyrannous designs of their governors, and where strength is, there will be victory.

The attitude of surrounding protective nations is, therefore, easily explicable. Is the free-trade principle as suited to the requirements of the development of their native industries, as it was to our own for a time? Will the free-trade principle, when applied to their commercial systems, assist them in the attainment of that object which is closest to the hearts of true patriots? In other words, is the free-trade principle capable of producing those beneficial consequences which some enthusiasts, during the free-trade agitation of the third and fourth decades of this century, predicted of it? We have the reply to those vain boasts of a former generation in the present action of protective nations. Are the conditions relating to the trade-development of those nations the same as those which affected our own at the time when free trade was introduced into our commercial code? Obviously not, on account of the vast differences between the relative internal resources of different countries. The system of free trade was peculiarly suited to a particular phase of our industrial growth; that is not an argument why it should be associated with the same result when it is applied to far different trade conditions. And this is the main reason why not a single nation has followed England in the so-called progressive, but unknown, path of free trade. Progressive in what direction? Free trade leaves the issue to be decided by the course of time: protection decides in favour of a steady but certain advance!

But the inquiry may be made, Why have protective nations, whom many ill-reasoning and unforeseeing enthusiasts of 1842 judged would be pressed to follow the glorious (but insecure) example of free trade in this country, taken the advantage of enriching themselves, as they certainly do by virtue of the imposts which they place upon imported articles, instead of spreading peace throughout the world? Because, although they may enrich themselves, the increase of each is but relative as compared with that of other nations who likewise pursue the policy of protection by a unanimous consent. In this way they discover a method of turning the arbitrary procedure of the isolated free-trader into the direction of that object, which was one of the grounds for the introduction of free trade universally, and this is effected at the expense of the free-trader. They have retained a present security, with the opportunity presented to them of increasing its effects, after they had overcome the initial hurt which free trade inflicted upon them; a certain progress, so far as this can be certain, to the chance of running into decay after a period of unusual activity—in a word, they have preferred the substance of true development to the shadow, rendered inordinately fascinating by a fluctuating prosperity, of artificial growth!

With such considerations as these, it was easy to foresee that the subsequent progress of the free-trade principle would be beset with difficulties, and dangers arising from the attempt, which has been followed with success, to dissociate the pernicious tendency of the principle from its inconstant beneficial consequences, and to lay bare, in all their nakedness, the evil results which would assuredly be associated with its partial operation in the international world of commerce!

We have already seen how the free-trade principle was checked in its early operation by the adverse influence of a combination of causes. Towards the end of 1845, after being in restricted action for three years, its results were regarded as satisfactory, though no account was taken of the normal element of our trade increase. But in 1846 and 1847, when there was a deficiency of the crops throughout the continent of Europe, people began to think that, after all, the free-trade principle was no more efficacious than any other principle. Then came the commencement of the period in which free trade acted without external restraint, in which the normal element of the trade-development of the country was consumed. Commercial circles doubted the potency of the free-trade principle for good; and to explain the distress of the country, other causes, perhaps advanced for ulterior designs, were introduced, and amongst them, the Bank Restriction Act of 1844. But if the efficacy of the principle was doubted, there can be no defence for the error. Nobody can hold that the free-trade principle was inefficacious. But what is to be called in question is the ultimate advantages to be derived from that efficacy, and the ability of the principle to continue its efficacy?

For after a time, when surrounding conditions came gradually to a state of equilibrium out of the disturbance into which they had been thrown by the appearance of a new force, and during which period of disturbance a spurious good was done to the commercial interests of the nation, it was obvious that the resultant effect of the free-trade principle could not be similar to what it was at the outset of its action. Why? Because those conditions, capable of fluctuating within themselves, which tended to modify its operation have varied. They are now no longer the same as they were before. But in what direction have they varied? Towards the interests of this country? To answer this question in the affirmative is to assume that nations are not self-interested, and that the commercial intercourse between nation and nation is not what Sir Robert Peel declared it to be, similar to that between individual and individual.

But is there any particular reason why protective nations should treat us kindly, a nation, or the legislators of that nation, who showed no mercy to foreign trades and industries on the authority of Sir Robert Peel?

It is impossible to suppose, from a comprehensive view of the question, and taking into consideration the working of several forces all acting simultaneously, and all concurring to oppose the trade-prosperity of this country, that the principle of free trade can be associated for ever with those successful results which it exhibited during the early period of its progress. Increased circulation was an inconstant effect of the original action of the free-trade principle, and formed part of the disturbance above described. Where is that increased circulation now? Is not this sufficient to demonstrate that surrounding conditions vary, and that the action of the free-trade principle will tend to become restricted to its constant result?

To create an increased circulation there must be some force. Where is that force? Free trade, it will be replied. But the principle of itself is powerless: it can only act for good through one of its effects, and that particular effect is increased circulation.

Are the present conditions relating to the operation of the free-trade principle favourable to the production of increased circulation? We have traced the reasons why they are not.

The great difference, then, between the conditions of 1842 and the present is, that in 1842 the principle was untrammelled by the ultimate consequences of its own effects, the chief of which was increased circulation. Now the free-trade principle is in constant action, with the same constant result which it had in 1842, but which is not obscured by the beneficial consequences of the contingent effect of increased circulation, for the favourable conditions, on which that effect was contingent, have disappeared.

That increased circulation, the cause of prosperity, has passed away, but it has left the markets in a far deeper depression than if they had been subject to an ordinary recurrent or paroxysmal depression. Nor is it difficult to perceive that free trade without increased circulation is a political bauble; but a bauble fraught with the surest danger to the unhappy people who groan beneath its burden.

It may be inquired, on the part of those who defend the operation of the free-trade principle, If free-trade once caused an increased circulation, can it not do so again? And the reply will be, Yes; if the conditions which relate to its action can be reduced to their former state!

But if this is impossible, cannot our trade receive some other legislative stimulus? The additional stimulus to increase the circulation of our trade may, indeed, be looked for from the Liberal party, who were the chief means of applying to it the free-trade stimulant. But it will be looked for in vain.

The truth is, that free trade has stimulated till it has lost its original power. Our trade, therefore, without external stimulation, lapses into a sluggish condition; some stronger stimulant is needed to arouse it from inactivity.

FREE TRADE. 251

Has the nature of this extra stimulant been indicated by the Liberal party—the stimulators of trade?

When Sir Robert Peel and Lord John Russell stimulated the trade-activity of their country in the fifth decade of the century, did they keep back in hand some other remedy to take its place after free trade had failed to do its work? Did they recognise this stimulant property of the free-trade principle? And did they forecast the final results of undue stimulation?

33. *Observations on the present decline.*—The great difference between the present depressed state of our markets and their previous states of depression lies in the absence of the "use" of capital nowadays. Capital is idle, or diverted into other channels, which should be utilised in the circulation of trade, because experience shows that its returns are less favourable than if applied in other directions. The importance of this observation is unquestionable; of its accuracy there can be no doubt.

If we look around and search for these elements, which, in the opinion of Sir Robert Peel, invariably lead to depression, do we find an apparently favourable condition of the trade-markets? Not the most sanguine of the free-traders in the country can admit such a state! Is the money-market regulated by a low state of interest? By no means.

The factors, therefore, which were constantly associated by Sir Robert Peel, and which led him to make the generalisation that an apparently prosperous state of the markets, combined with low interest, results invariably in inordinate or "insane" speculation, which ends in depression, are absent in the present day. They cannot be adduced as the causes, therefore, of the present depression.

And this simple observation would of itself tend to the conclusion that the present depression might be different in its character; that it would not present the same features which characterised those periods of depression induced by the method described by Sir Robert Peel.

What is the nature, then, of the present depression which accounts for its being thus different from its predecessors? We will proceed to the solution of this question by the comparison of instances.

The period of depression between 1837 and 1842 was brought about mainly by inordinate speculation. There were other minor causes which operated to increase the result, but these are too insufficient in themselves to require a separate discussion. The conditions favourable to the acquisition of capital led to an extraordinary circulation of it; but this circulation of capital, though at first it diffused to the labour-markets, finally resulted in the disordered relations of supply and demand, because the grounds in the generality of cases of speculation were fictitious ones. But there was no dearth of capital at the commencement, and it was not until more capital was required to complete the object of the speculations of the merchants that interest rose, and then the burden of the speculation fell upon the originators of it. And thus the designs of the speculators became frustrated, and the labour-markets suffered as the result. But the new element of the present depression is not that capital is wanting, or is locked up, as it was during the railway mania of 1846-47, by which the trade activities were made to suffer from a diminution in the supply of capital, while the labour-market was kept in a flourishing state. There is no dearth of capital at the present day, the new element continuing the depression and leading to decline is that capital is not forthcoming; it is locked up, but not in railways; it is put out to those more certain speculations which yield a larger return than the languishing trade activities of the country.

This capital is a real quantity; it expresses in part the gigantic addition to the wealth of the country which the early application of the free-trade principle yielded to manufacture. It is idle now, or diverted from its proper channel, to increase the industrial activity of the nation by the inequality of competition. The same amount of profit is no longer possible—and this was large—and even a remunerative profit is becoming by degrees more scarce. What then? Are not the capitalists self-interested? If capital yields not a sufficient return in one direction, it is diverted into more favourable ones. But though this gigantic increase to the wealth of the nation was gained at the expense of the foreigner, let it not be supposed that it is remaining at the same level. How can it, when the pernicious action of free trade, now a source of exhaustion, is constant?

But this source of exhaustion is slow, and therefore tends to be wellnigh imperceptible in its operation. And what a danger there is in this gradual tendency towards decline! for the true gravity of the condition of affairs is thereby apt to be neglected or misrepresented.

Let the evils of the system of protection which the

free-traders were so ready to exaggerate be compared with the evils derived from the constant operation of the free-trade principle. Will it be denied that the free-trade principle has its evil effects as well as other principles?

But in the eyes of the Liberals the free-trade principle is the only known exception to this universal rule! Attack the virtues of the free-trade principle, and they at once refer you to the prosperity of its initial action; they point to the increase in the wealth of the country; continue the false association between free trade and trade prosperity; proclaim that as free trade has already operated advantageously to the interests of the country, it must always do so—for how can free trade cause both prosperity and distress? and promulgate the fatal error of ascribing to the cause itself the consequences of one of its effects—and an effect, too, which is possible only when surrounding conditions are favourable to its action. Where can the free-traders point and say that there is increased circulation of the markets? And when they have discovered the fortunate market, let them compare *this* increase with *that* increase which characterised the same market during the first period of the operation of free trade. Will they then contend that the free-trade principle still retains, in the same degree, the property of stimulating the markets? Will not the conclusion be, Does the free-trade principle at present stimulate at all?

Sir Robert Peel's generalisation demonstrates that, during the course of the protective policy (leaving out the unproductivity in various degrees and kinds of the resources of nature), one main element tended to the causation of depression. There might be other sources, but speculation carried to an inordinate extent was the chief factor leading to distress.

And it is curious, here, to remark on the expression of opinion entertained by that great authority on domestic affairs, respecting the continuance of the system of protection. Sir Robert Peel himself proved as certainly as it could be proved that the activity of our industries was gradually increasing. Who knew so well the immediate effect of free trade upon our trade-markets, but who judged so ill its ultimate results?

It was in reference to this difference between the constant progress under protection, and an artificial rise through the influence of free trade, that he let fall that explanation which now so unfortunately can be turned against himself. He said, in one of those memorable speeches immediately antecedent to the introduction of free trade into our commercial relations—speeches which are characterised more by their endeavour to cloak his own inconsistencies than by any real attempt to discover truths—that " a constant and injurious process was going forward."

As an absolute statement, his own observations proved it to be false. It was relative therefore, and relative to the " what might be " of our commerce under the influence of free-trade.

And now let us turn to the actual facts which the study of the progress of free trade supplies us with. We perceive that the main elements leading to depression are two, as compared with the single chief element under protection. And these, speculation, as in the course of our trade when protected ; and " a constant and injurious process," which is the ultimate outcome of the continued operation of the free-trade principle, as we have already and sufficiently shown. Inordinate speculation still determines the ups and downs of the trade-curves of the nation; but the constant exhaustion of the free-trade principle leads to a permanent depression, which, as it increases, ends in decline.

It is of the first importance to recognise the existence of this latter element relative to the course of our trade, and to deduce its single cause. For accuracy of observation, in fields which are open to misrepresentation which is unlimited, apparently in the case of the prejudiced, and to confusion, which finally ends in complete obscurity, is paramount. Look around and discern the various circumstances which relate to the stunted development of our trades, gather all the indications in which such a procedure terminates, and then collate these with accurate observation of existing facts.

For before the cause of decline can be certainly deduced, the single observation on which it is based must be acknowledged as true.

How like to that course of decline in agriculture will the present advanced depression of our manufacture now appear—how strict the parallel! And the cause of the decline in both, unequal competition.

But it will be asked, If free trade thus results in unequal competition, and is the direct cause of the exhausted condition of the trade-markets, why was not the tendency observed before? And the answer has been given.

It was not observed before, because not felt; the tendency, though present, was checked—by an increased circulation, which was temporary. When this ceased to counteract the influence of an adverse tendency, this latter grew into power; and it will begin to be the more observed when its consequences have been experienced in an increased and increasing degree.

34. *The more simple explanation of the phenomena above described.*—To explain the constant tendency of the free-trade principle, partially operating to the prejudice of the free-trade nation, it is necessary to revert once more to an illustration, which served a similar purpose in a former section. But let it not be supposed that any subtle analogy is intended to be drawn by the usage of a simpler means of illustrating our present meaning.

Nor is there any opportunity for the merest reasoner to fall of his own accord into a possible trap, which it might be supposed has been constructed for him! Our purpose is to explain what is less known by means of that which is more known : and this, we presume, is the object of explanation by illustration. Reasoning from analogy, it may be stated, is beyond the scope of the following description.

We may compare our markets to the tissue-elements of the body-organism, and free trade applied as a stimulant to them. Free trade acts by increasing the circulation of the trade-markets, and by raising, therefore, the functional activity of those markets. Is there any harm resulting from too excessive a stimulation leading to an excessive display of functional activity? Yes; for maintenance and growth on the one side and function on the other proceed with an inverse proportion.

R

If function be inordinately developed, maintenance suffers the loss. And thus in the case of the trade-markets, whose growth and function proceed in a similar manner, if the solid element of gradual growth is sacrificed for a temporary and excessive stimulation, expressed in the over-activity of the tissue-elements of the body of our trade, the maintenance of those elements becomes proportionately depressed, and perhaps their growth impossible. And what results? In the first place, exhaustion; and in the second, if the power of repairing the mischief which has been done be interfered with by the constant demands of stimulation, decay.

By the aid of this illustration we have attempted to show that the action of free trade upon our commerce was not directly upon the trade-markets, but through the intermediate means of increasing the trade-circulation. This species of commercial activity, therefore, inasmuch as it is derived from without, and the result of legislative interference, must obviously vary with the constant action of the free-trade principle; it must, from the knowledge which our experience supplies us with in parallel instances of stimulation, decrease—for there is no instance of any force in natural operations not tending to seek a condition of equilibrium with surrounding forces, and in the effort decline may ensue.

From greater activity, the free-trade principle has already passed through a phase of diminishing activity, till it reached a period when its action was, for a moment, adjusted to the operation of surrounding influences.

When this period was attained, fortunate would it

have been for the trade interests of this country had these surrounding influences remained the same.

But these influences were, by their fluctuation, the very means by which equilibrium was effected, and by which the activity of the free-trade principle was reduced.

Did anything appear to check the adverse operation of this principle? Nothing; and therefore what had already diminished the potency of a principle for our good would, if they still continued to advance in the same direction, eventually destroy its beneficial action altogether—that is, that part of the operation of the free-trade principle which reacted to the prejudice of foreign nations. It was by these means that those nations, remaining protective, and originally depressed by the initial action of free trade, succeeded in removing the burden which an arbitrary procedure unjustly placed upon them.

Let the different states of the progress of an element be contrasted in the two opposite instances, in one of which the forces leading to an increased activity are applied from without, and in the other, where they are derived from within.

In the former case, it is seen that the amount of progress must certainly vary with the degree of stimulation to which the element is subjected; and it is well known that the rapid tendency of elements, whose nature is marked by a great degree of mobility, to reach a state of equilibrium, to adjust themselves to the action of a constant force, is particularly characteristic of them.

In those instances, therefore, in which such elements become habituated to the action of a constant stimulant force, some other means must be devised to continue their stimulation; and, of course, some force of greater intensity than the last one applied. But in the second case, the source of activity is inherent in the elements themselves; and the extra supply of energy which it is capable of inducing is diverted into the channel of growth. Hence we have the means both of activity and growth resident within the tissue-elements of the markets of our commercial body; but their course is gradual, as the survey of the career of our trade under protection clearly demonstrates. Whereas free trade acts as an external stimulant, which, if recklessly administered, tends to be followed by exhaustion and decay.

And here we may interpose the explanation how it was that the excessive activity of the initial operation of free trade interfered adversely with the normal progress of our markets. All their energies were consumed in increased functional activity; there was nothing left for their proper maintenance and for their ultimate growth. This view of the operation of the free-trade principle it is important to keep in mind: that it acted solely upon the trade-circulation of the markets, first causing their inordinate activity, and finally ending in decline, because trade-circulation is depressed—the depression being caused by the accumulation of those other collateral influences which the principle calls up in its train.

There is another point to be considered, as regards its explanation, with respect to the operation of free trade.

We have already observed what were the effects of this principle upon its surrounding conditions at its first introduction, and how it created in them such disturbance as led to a very remarkable determination of the trade-circulation to our markets. The subsequent operation of the force, however, which brought about this sudden alteration, was without our control, though the expediency of its application was determined by the judgment of our legislators. How, then, should we be left if the ultimate action of the principle tended against us, and we were powerless to destroy its pernicious influence?

It is not difficult to see that the Legislature of 1842-47 was in this position. It had, in itself, the power to call certain effects into existence by the application of the free-trade principle. But having done this, it stood aside helpless, to observe the course of those effects over which now it had not control! It had supplied the only stimulant that it possibly could to the supposed (but falsely supposed) sinking condition of our trade, with the result that the subsequent progress of the body of our trade was left entirely in the control of those foreign Powers who should determine the special direction some of the effects of that stimulation were to take.

Each nation, like each individual, in commercial affairs is bound to act in accordance with its own self-interest. And if the free-trade system, which regulates the commerce of these realms (and the principle of which was applied because, at the outset, it was perceived to act for our own advantage), thus reacted to the prejudice of foreign industries, is it wonderful that protective nations should offer such resistance as is in their power to these evil influences upon their commercial welfare?

And when all protective nations combine, and are of the same mind still, in spite of the praise which has been so lavishly but so uselessly conferred upon free trade, will not the united effect be all the more disastrous to our own interests—those interests which we served so well for such a short time, but which thereby we appear to have ultimately sacrificed?

And here the true character of Mr Pitt's legislation comes more strikingly into the foreground. It was his great ambition that the two nations should be placed on a level of equality, that thus the sources of jealousy between them might be destroyed. By his endeavour, free trade with some restriction was granted to Ireland in 1786; but though a great step had been made, yet the final one had to be taken, for the commercial affairs between the sister islands, though apparently improved, were not yet in a satisfactory condition. For there were still two centres whence the subsequent progress of British and Irish commerce might be directed, and these might at any time be opposed. It was essential, therefore, to the combined prosperity of both countries, that these two centres should be reduced to a single one, in order that they might preside with all the greater effect over the entire commercial prosperity of the United Kingdom.

When Mr Pitt introduced the free-trade system between Great Britain and Ireland, he saw that the legislative union of the two kingdoms was not far distant. There could therefore be no possibility of any alteration in the commercial union so happily inaugurated, when legislative union was at last completed, though in the interval between commercial and legislative union there were some remote chances of the scheme becoming destroyed.

But when Sir Robert Peel introduced free trade into our relations with surrounding nations, what security had he that the adverse conditions, which would certainly come into existence, if we alone remained free-traders (and that event at the time must have been regarded as something more than possible), would be under the sphere of his or his successors' removal?

And if such removal was not within the highest degree of being probably effected, into what an extraordinary danger did he allow the course of our commerce to enter!

35. *The analogy of the free-trade principle partially operating, as it has worked throughout the world of commerce, in a single town.*—As the course of the free-trade principle, and the method by which it works, has been illustrated by examples which are more or less well known, and as the ground of analogy has not been assumed; so, now, in order that the operation of the principle may be the better understood, it is proposed to give a description of the analogous action of the principle of free trade, working within as small dimensions as we can conveniently take, but still surrounded by the same influences as exist within the larger sphere. In this way, we shall endeavour to afford a comprehensive survey of the continued progress of the free-trade principle.

Let there be a large town which shall represent the whole commercial world, and in it trade-institutions for the mutual interchange of goods, in various stages of growth and activity. These trade-institutions are representative of national commercial interests; and we will suppose that all of them have, up to a certain stage of their development, proceeded under a common rule, and this rule is expressed in the term protection. Each institution has protected itself, so far as it could, from the dangerous tendencies of external forces.

But at a certain epoch, when that trade-institution which had reached a higher level of activity and prosperity than all the others, looked on its advancing rivals, a convulsion of opinion took place within it. Some of those concerned for the welfare of their institution are inclined to continue the same system, by which they have already attained their present state of prosperity. But others, too eager to magnify the first indications of alarm, cast about to devise some means by which dangers, which only their disordered imagination felt were looming in the distance, might be dispelled for a time, and their sources, with the greatest probability, removed for ever!

And they find the measure for the prevention of danger in this remedy. It had been the custom to place an impost on all articles, including raw materials coming from another trade-institution into their own. It was these imposts that they intended to remit. This, then, was the remedy. Instead of continuing to protect the native industries of their own institution, they saw their account in the free importation of those articles which were mainly concerned in the development of their chief industry, manufacture. But they still kept, at one period, a restriction on the admission of produce of manufacture; such a slight restriction, however, that in course of time its influence would inevitably come to be nugatory, and hence, not in accord with the intention by which it was maintained; for it was maintained to "protect" manufacture.

The immediate effect of such a change of policy was instantly grasped by the manufacturers. They saw at once that a larger share of the whole trade of the town would be deflected towards their own trade-institution; and endeavoured to secure for themselves a footing on the path towards prosperity. Thus their action became peculiarly selfish. But this they succeeded in hiding, by attracting the notice of those who really had the whole of the interests of the institution at heart. Thus they strengthened themselves at home, by exaggerating the tendencies of the future of their trade; and amongst their neighbours, they still appeared to wear the garb of disinterestedness; for those sentiments of hostility, which the rivalry between the various trade-institutions created in the town, would, by the introduction of this new principle of governing their commercial relations, soon be dissipated in the increased activity which it would succeed in giving to all.

But her neighbours did not regard this policy of their leader with kindness. For they saw that, as the conditions which affected the growth of each varied, what was applicable with advantage to one was not certain to be followed with advantage to all. They therefore kept aloof, and smiled at the apparently disinterested fashion in which the fresh scheme had been advocated; while they shuddered at the loss which so unjust and arbitrary a measure would assuredly inflict upon them. Thus what was pleaded the requirements of the civilisation of the town demanded, came, by the adverse attitude of the majority of the trade-institutions in it, to have a partial operation.

Let us now revert to the conditions in which the older institution found herself at the time, when many who were attracted solely by their own self-interest, discovered dangers which had nearly reached, and were still rapidly approaching, the whole community.

She had to rely upon outside sources for the materials of her manufacturing industries, as well as for a large proportion of the necessaries of life. She was unable to supply enough corn to feed her people. The consequence of this was, that the price of bread was relatively higher than among her rivals, who depended in this respect upon their own resources. But then, the product of her manufactories had acquired so great a reputation, and commanded so large an external market, that by the gain which accrued to her from her increasing exports, she was more than enabled to counterbalance the loss which a foreign supply of corn entailed. Then, again, the wages of her labourers were relatively much higher than those of surrounding institutions.

These two factors, therefore, were those which were taken most into consideration—the importation of corn and the exportation of our manufactured produce. And it was easily seen that if the price of corn was reduced, while the exportation of our manufactured goods was increased, there would result a high condition of prosperity to the institution. For the labourers now would receive a proportionally higher wage, and their income would come, in an additional manner, to exceed their expenditure in the fall which the price of corn would undergo, if the tax upon its admission were removed.

The bearing of the new system thus involved, in the main, these two events. To hasten the acquisition of the one, it was considered wise to inordinately raise the industrial activity of but one of the branches of her trade, that by these means she might compete to greater advantage with her younger rivals. Thus one source of immediate danger would be removed, and in the interval following the initial operation of the new principle, it would be expected that either surrounding nations would be compelled to offer us the same advantages as she had given them, or else some new means elucidated to prevent the onset of future dangers.

And to sanction the demand of the other, it was brought forward that an agitation then on foot, and founded on a supposed injustice by which the price of corn was kept at a high level, would thereby be dissipated, for conflicting opinions would cease to work ill when the trade-institution was surrounded with peace and plenty.

Thus came it about that the present only was regarded by the legislators of that trade-institution at the epoch of the introduction of free trade. It was certain that the measure would be associated at the first with an increased prosperity to the community. But the causation of this increased prosperity was unrecognised. And the consequence was, that certain avenues to a subsequent depression, and, it may be, the decline of the institution, were left open. And it was these which the legislators of the surrounding institutions detected and utilised.

Finding herself at this disadvantage with reference to the question, and fearing that in the subsequent growth of the institutions she might be shut out of these markets which were neutral to both, she proceeded to apply what she considered to be the best remedy to counteract so pressing a probability. Nor was she without advisers, and those popular ones, on the paramount value of the course she was pursuing. For they argued that the reputation of their manufacture must continue; and that with the advantage which the new policy would afford them, they need fear nothing, for the quality of the work of their labourers exceeded that of the working classes of her rival institutions.

There can be no doubt that by forcing such a system, there was the probability, but it was a very remote one, that the neighbouring institutions, whose development had come to be regarded as of some importance, might follow in the same path. But observe how greatly the new principle would operate in her own favour. For now she would be able to procure her raw materials at the least possible cost—that is, in other words, she would buy in the cheapest market, while the exportation of her manufactured goods would still command the same high price in neutral markets; and in cases of competition, by means of this new policy, she would be enabled to undersell her rival neighbours.

Indeed it may be inquired of this free-trade institution, was not her free-trade system made use of to undersell expressly her protective rivals? Did not this idea of underselling underlie the whole scheme of increasing the chances of a successful competition, when all these chances were at first in her own favour?

But for a time only would such an arbitrary procedure succeed, and the surrounding institutions be forced to bear the burden of a loss which the evanescent prosperity of their successful reform entailed!

But for a time only would they suffer the burden of distress! Some means would be discovered by which they would escape out of the difficulty into which the appearance of a new principle in their mutual commercial relations had plunged them.

What were the means, then, which presented an outlet to this temporary inequality?

The rival institutions, which remained protective, had youth and a relatively greater power of growing on their side. Their labouring classes were lower in the scale of civilisation than those of the community which was leading the van of civilisation in the town, and, consequently, their wages were lower.

It was on this point of wages that those who guided the fortunes of the growing institutions depended. The wages of the older institution were high, and would be increased by the immediate effect of the free-trade policy; and therefore when prices were lowered, the opportunity of making such large profits as before would be diminished, and one of two alternatives would present—

1. Either the older institution must decide to rest content with a diminishing profit; or—
2. Wages must inevitably be reduced, or else both these phenomena will exist simultaneously.

Now, what dangers involved the reduction of wages in the case of the older institution? And what comparison would be framed between the slow progress of the protective institution, in which wages would gradually increase, and the dissolute condition into which the commercial affairs of the free-trade institution had fallen?

These formed the foundations of the attitude which the protective institutions determined to assume. In the course of time, their means of producing manufactured goods would be enlarged, the more especially as the free-trade institution suffered its native machinery to leave its manufacturing centres. Perhaps this action was impelled by a desire on the part of free-trade legislators to appear less selfish than they might be thought to be, as well as to give some opportunity to their neighbours to do likewise.

But besides the increasing power of producing the free-trade manufactured goods, they would be in a position to pay high wages to competent workmen from the free-trade institution to teach their labouring classes some of those manufacturing arts which were unknown to them. And when these began to flourish, and when they began to gain a footing of equality with their more fortunate free-trade rivals, then would the central authority step in, and give that material assistance which the growing industries of the respective nations required. Their early struggles would be assisted by bounties. But how do these bounties arise? From the taxes which are imposed upon free-trade goods. And the final result arrives, that the product of these protective industries can be raised at a cost less than that by free-trade labour; and hence are exported to neutral markets, where it comes, by a curious change of place, to be the turn of the protectionist to undersell the free-trader!

What, then, must eventually become of that free-trade institution, which thus may truly be said to have sown the seed of her own misfortunes? Can she any longer depend upon the produce of her manufactures for the raw materials of neighbouring institutions? And what results, when the value (not the amount at first—that will follow) becomes seriously diminished (as it is bound to do when unequal competition appears in neutral markets to send down the price)? The contraction of the sphere of her operations at home. And with what alarming conditions is such a distressing state associated? Wages reduced; labour unoccupied, and profits gradually diminishing, or, it may be, profits impossible to be acquired!

But the protective institutions still remain protective, and, from the taxes which they impose upon all goods admitted into their community, derive an important source of their revenue. Besides, as these increased—and they did increase largely during the early operation of the new principle—the legislatures of those institutions would be enabled to remit certain duties levied upon articles produced within their own industrial spheres; and thus would they be able to lighten the burdens of their respective communities.

But the free-trade institution relies upon her merchandise to supply that wealth which is necessary to procure her raw materials, and to assist in the maintenance of her general wants. If this merchandise is reduced in value, if the markets are depressed, if labour is thrown out of employment by reason of the unequal competition abroad of rival institutions, how is she to continue the wellbeing of the social elements of which she is composed?

She has less wealth now, by reason of the cumulative

exhaustion effected by her commercial principle, to purchase raw materials. What capital would, if the circumstances were favourable, circulate in the trade-markets, is diverted from them, because other sources of speculation yield larger returns. Hence those institutions must obviously suffer which have been wont to export a large amount of their raw materials into the free-trade community. With a diminution of manufacturing industry, labour becomes proliferous, and therefore cheap. But the free-trade institution is a manufacturers' institution; and the free-trade system was introduced to indulge the expectations of the manufacturers of a past age! For manufacture, the other industry of the country was sacrificed! And now, see manufacture on the altar of Doom!

Without manufacture, at the present, as the free-trade community cannot grow their own corn at a profit (and it seems that the same disastrous result is attaching to the prospects of the manufacturers, who find it more and more difficult to make any profit), the free-trade institution is placed in a pitiable plight. But her misfortunes do not end in herself, for they extend to those other institutions which have to depend for their own upon the prosperity of the free-trade community. What, then, becomes the ultimate situation of the free-trade institution? She passes gradually into a state of decline! The determined opposition of her protective rivals has been of a nature to overcome the severe but temporary blow free trade, partially operating, dealt to them.

They have recovered from these. Still they are not exempt from the occurrence of natural phenomena.

Each of the protective trade-institutions is liable to the recurrence of depression ; and it is well for those institutions to be able to distinguish between a paroxysmal depression, which is more or less partial, and remediable by natural processes, and the serious existence of a decline in all her trades and industries.

Periods of depression of the trade-curve of the various protective institutions may coexist, and may be associated in their causation. But will it not be difficult to discern between the effects of a temporary depression and the beginning of a constant decline ?

It is of paramount importance to make accurate observations with respect to those antecedent conditions which end a temporary and permanent depression respectively; and in those instances in which depression in one trade-institution is associated with depression in another, to determine the sequence of their occurrence. Then, when all the facts are collected, and in particular the exact succession of the wave of depression through the whole of the town, the cause may be deduced.

But there must be no blindness to the fact that when a large commercial institution begins to fall, its decline must of necessity be implicated with the distress of many branches of industry in neighbouring institutions, especially those on whom she formerly so largely relied.

To observe this succession of the wave of depression following on the downfall of a large manufacturing community is of the utmost importance ; for it is clear that depression will be coexistent in many trade-institutions, and this mere fact of coexistence may be taken

s

as an argument to show that the free-trade principle is not the cause of depression. Thus in the free-trade community there is observed to be depression, which has the character of permanency, and therefore takes on the nature of decline; there is also a depressed state of the trade-markets in surrounding protective communities. Hence free trade cannot be the cause of depression, because depression exists in protective institutions. But against this argument may be adduced the truth, that the same effect may have very different causes, and that protection was blamed by the free-traders as being the chief source of depression in the fifth decade of this century. This reasoning, therefore, is not sufficient to show that free trade is blameless in the matter of depression; and the fact that England first began to suffer from the effects of depression during this present long and continued period, and that this depression travelled to those countries which looked to her for support, rather inclines the just reasoner to conclude that the initial cause of depression was, and is now, resident in the free-trade community, and that it is essentially involved in the alteration which was effected in the ordinary progress of her commerce.

Thus will it be seen how the policy of this free-trade institution ultimately retarded its growth; that the huge overgrowth, which it succeeded at first in constructing, decays from want of sufficient maintenance, inasmuch as the sources of its nourishment are being slowly dried up.

When we apply this analogy to the actual commercial affairs of the universe, it is easily perceived that England is the free-trade institution.

36. *Causation of the present distress.*—There have been, and are still, many explanations of the causation of distress.

One was, that agricultural depression precedes and is the source of all other depressions.

But though a deficiency in the produce of the soil may enter into the causation of paroxysmal depression, it must not be forgotten that its intensity is as the extent to which the deficiency reaches; and that, although a poor harvest may for a season be associated with a certain amount of depression, it cannot, except in the case of a famine, possibly be the cause of subsequent distress. For agricultural depression to become a prime factor in the causation of distress, it must be that the harvests continue deficient for a period of years, and that the deficiency reaches below a given level.

Such, however, is contrary to experience. For harvests may be deficient owing to the inclemency of the seasons; but agriculture and every other industry depending upon similar relations, is prone to be characterised by rises and falls in its progress, hence there appear the increased product of the good years to counteract the deficiency of the bad.

But as regards the importance of agriculture to enter as the prime factor in the causation of distress, a special feature which has marked its course must be taken into consideration.

There is to be considered the fact that, since 1800, the agriculture of this country has been undergoing a gradual decline, according to the economic law (which is still retained) of the gradually increasing unproductivity of the soil, and the recurrency of depressed harvests.

Now, although agricultural depression cannot have, generally speaking, any influence in the causation of trade-depression—though it may tend to increase the ill consequences of the latter, but only in those very sparse instances where villages are dependent entirely for their corn upon the sufficiency of the harvest—let us assume that agricultural depression is the chief factor in the causation of distress. We have, then, to believe that a force which has been continually diminishing in intensity can produce the same results as when it existed with increased powers.

But paroxysmal trade-depressions renew their course in spite of agricultural depression — the distress of 1837-41 is stated to be as severe as any of those which had preceded it. Was the cause of this, then, agricultural depression?

But let us take the period of our agricultural progress since 1842, when the free-trade principle began partially to be applied, and let us compare the gradual course of the decay of agriculture up to this period with the rapidity of its decline subsequent to it.

What conclusion are we to infer? That before 1842 corn could be produced at a remunerative profit to the farmer; and that, after a certain time, during which the farmers of this country struggled manfully to keep alive an industry, doomed to destruction by reason of an unequal competition brought about by free-trade, the soil can no longer be cultivated at a profit; and therefore, that agricultural depression becomes constant, relative to the inability to cultivate, not to the scarcity of produce.

The legislative policy of 1842 and subsequent years

has thus resulted in a permanent phase of agricultural depression. And if agricultural depression be the cause of the whole depression of the country, the policy of the head of the Tory party, supported by the body of the Whigs, is to blame!

But of this there can be no doubt: that however certainly the agricultural prospects of the country were undergoing a natural decline, this decline has been greatly exaggerated by legislative interference of a mischievous character. Thus in the downward curve of agriculture since 1842, two elements must be enumerated; the gradual tendency, due to natural processes— and the rapid tendency, derived from the pernicious action of the free-trade principle. The price of wheat has fallen from 60s. in 1850 to 30s. in 1886! Under such a slow but continued fall, what chances has the farmer had of maintaining the importance of the agricultural industry of the country?

The introduction of this rapid element of decline into the course of our agriculture was the inevitable outcome of Liberal reform — a peculiar kind of reform which had for its object the elevation of manufacture by the depression of agriculture. And what is the final result of the free-trade principle? It has succeeded in ruining first the prospects of agriculture, and then those of manufacture.

Then the Liberal spirit of Parliament, assisted by a show of disinterestedness, but stimulated underneath the cloak of selfishness, pronounced against agriculture. But the means they devised were to further the condition of the agricultural labourer. What is the fact? As the natural consequence of their reckless policy the farmers are ruined, and hundreds of thousands of labourers have deserted the soil.

And now, as the cause of their poor condition can be directly traced to the former Liberal reform in our commercial code, it seems marvellously inconsistent that the pioneers of this species of reform, called the Radical section of the great Liberal party, should be making out a case for the claim of those who have been so much injured already by their experimental policy.

But do not the Radicals forget, for the while, that the agricultural labourer has already been under the protection of the Liberal party? In 1842, there was no end to the declamation that the agricultural labourer was to be enormously benefited by the new reform. What is his position now? But the Liberals will reply, "Yes, but events have not turned out as we anticipated they would!" Then who is to blame? the Liberals, for their false prognostications! What, too, is the position of agriculture?

But the example of the free-traders of 1842 is still followed, and the agricultural labourer is still deceived! Certainly the times are changed. *Then* it was the cry for cheap bread—as visions of foreign corn, freely admitted, floated through the fancy of the bewildered mob, and home-grown wheat was neglected. *Now*, where is the use of crying out for cheap bread, when there are no wages with which to buy it? Bread is cheaper; the Liberals are proud of this *one* effect of their reform.

But they little imagine the immense disturbance they have made in the machinery by which wages are derived, and which has resulted in the paralysis of labour. Bread is cheap because corn is admitted free.

But corn cannot be admitted free without a prejudicial influence upon agriculture! The free admission of corn is but part of a general principle; and the total results of that free-trade principle are a loss gradually accruing to the country.

Bread is cheap! and so something else must be thrown out as a bait to catch the disappointed agricultural labourer. And now the Radical section cries up the enormous importance of cultivating the soil. Arable land is going into disuse. Why? because it does not yield a profit. But in the hands of the Radicals, and with the assistance of division, the land is once more going to give up her increase, and peace and plenty shall bless the cottage of the agricultural labourer. The free-trade breeze is beginning to blow cold; and the Radicals are beginning to trim their sails. Their course is already changed. It is not the low price of wheat that tends to the destruction of the farmer; foreign competition is not unequal in their eyes. How can the Liberal party ever be convicted of protecting the interests of their country!

The cause they say is to be found in the high rents, and the solution of the problem is dexterously shifted on to the subject of land.

If there is any unequal competition, cry out the Liberal reformers, you will find it at home!

But if anything is to be gained by the competition, equal or unequal, of the present day, you will find the balance making its way out of the country, replies the Tory.

And thus we are forced to a consideration of the disabilities of land. The contention of the Radical party and those who are mainly connected with the so-called reform movement, is that rents are too high. They too, like their Liberal predecessors, place all the burden of the distress at the door of the landlords. Before, the landlords kept up the price of corn so as to ensure a high rent; now, the landlords keep the rents high, in order to prevent the greatest possible cultivation of the soil.

But the arguments of those who entertain so inconsequent a notion want experience only to confute them. Just like the false notion propagated in the early days of the free-trade movement, that with low rents profits would be higher, so now the startling doctrine is diffused that high rents are the cause of the agricultural labourer's distress.

But the plain error which pervades this mode of reasoning, of ascribing to the phenomena which may be associated, but which are not invariably associated, the relation of cause and effect, is sufficiently laid bare by a cool and impartial examination of the natural succession of facts. For if high rent is the reason why no profits are possible to the farmer, and therefore no wages to the labourer, how is it that, with the present low price of corn, farms cannot be worked to advantage with a very small rent or no rent at all. But such a doctrine is sufficiently refuted by the endeavours of the landlords themselves to protect their own interests, there having been a tendency in operation for some years toward an actual reduction, if there has been no nominal reduction, of rents.

But from this actual reduction, which has been gradually increasing, what has been the result? the exact reverse of the Liberal prognostication; for instead of profits accumulating, they have been rapidly diminishing. And this leads to the real ground on which is placed the obstacle to the agricultural prosperity of the country; and that is, the increasing difficulty with which the farmers have to contend, not to make a profit, but to be able to sell their corn. This is the fountainhead whence flows all the inequality which surrounds the unprotected position of the farmer. It is not that he has a high rent to pay, it is that he is not in a sufficiently secure position so as to be able to rely upon remunerative profits, and therefore be able to pay a rent at all.

And this unfortunate position of the farmer, and with him the agricultural labourer, is the last link in the chain of disastrous events which have attended agriculture since the palmy days of protection, while yet there was a market open to them. There was the possibility of his selling his corn, even though the price at which he was accustomed to sell was gradually receding. Still, even this unhappy prospect was borne without a murmur; and while the farmer's corn was selling for a less price, the farmer's capital was gradually becoming used up. And with so strong a tide against him, the time could not be far distant when all his capital would be consumed. And then, when the corn-markets at home are shut to him, when the unequal race in which he is taking a mock part comes to a sort of termination, what is to be his end? How is it possible that, with the present surrounding conditions of our agriculture, he can still ply his trade without the hope of being rewarded with even a small profit? And this is the pass to which the free-trade principle has led the farmer, and with him the prosperity of the agricultural labourers. And while this is proceeding, while the labourers are deserting the soil, what a cry is raised against those unequal conditions which compel the farmer to dismiss his labourers? How is the fact, declaimed from the polling-booth, that the agricultural labourer, originally attached to the soil, cannot maintain himself, because rents are too high for profits to be made, and therefore is forced to seek an outlet from his distress in the town which he invades, and tends to depreciate the town labourers' wages, already reduced by depression, by increasing labour competition,—how is this fact set forth in all its injustice: "force is used to drive the tiller of the soil away from his native hamlet"! Such a condition must be false, and can have no real foundation in the true nature of things; and we are the party who set things to rights! It is true this is not a real state of affairs, but then what can be effected from the interested efforts of the artifice of man? In what way did the Liberal reform of our commercial tariff in 1842-47 set things to rights? Inadequately and for a time only. The Liberals deplore the condition of the labouring man; this is the trick to catch his vote; for they know that the landed and agricultural interest are set against their party. Those of the farmers who gave their adhesion to the disastrous policy of 1842 have had their eyes widely opened. The Liberal reformers do not point to the farmers, for they well know they will find no sympathy in that direction; and political sympathy is a mighty engine!

The farmer and agricultural labourer both have been and are now ignored. But the agricultural labourer's aid is sought to maintain the Liberals in power; and now the same scheme is made use of as in 1842, but in a modified form. The agricultural labourer must be made to feel that he suffers unjustly, and that injustice is made to lie at the door of those who are opposed to the Liberals in politics. The landlords and moneyed interests are held up to the public eye as the origin of all their distress, though now the landlords are declaimed against as acting not directly in opposition to the welfare of the nation as in 1842, but indirectly, by preventing the cultivation of the soil.

But how comes it that the Liberal party of to-day does not directly appeal to the farming interest of the country? Because the interruption of the natural relationship between master and man has been effected. This the farmer knows, and thinks his interests and position have been cruelly and unjustly neglected. The agricultural labourer was taught to believe in 1842 that his progress with free-trade was certain. But how has that forecast been verified? The Liberals, however, who first laid the train, and saw the spark which was gradually to destroy in its development both farmer and labourer, assume the air of injured men. They have done their best; they wished for the best; they sympathised with the poor condition of the agricultural labourers. What is the outcome of all this false sympathy? The condition of the labouring man is worse than ever it was before, and this during the operation of the free-trade principle, the source of every blessing and every content. He ought to look to the master for the means of his improvement. Each ought to see in his own interests the welfare of both. But no; Liberal reform, with characteristic meddlesome interference, has stepped in between them; and the result is, that the interruption of a natural relationship, once begun, has been continued by a Liberal political manœuvre. The agricultural labourer is taught not to regard the position of his master: he is to look to the Legislature for the means of redress. And thus we are led to the explanation of the extraordinary conclusion which some Radicals have reached respecting the relation of our dependent colonies to the mother country. They are to be cast off, because presumably the Radicals find enough difficulty in adjusting the disordered relations at home which their predecessors have effected for the benefit of the nation!

What should be left to be settled by natural force, the Radicals, out of a new species of sympathy, decide shall be settled by the Legislature. What ought to be determined by the central authority, the Radicals abandon as being wrought with the ruin of the nation! And thus the Radicals fall into an error, which is frequent, of the practical man, who interferes when he ought not, and abstains where it is duty. But in an age of a do-something policy this is not surprising. Agricultural depression and land disabilities are therefore seen not to be the real causes of the present distress, however much they may be distorted into an apparent source of it. It rests, therefore, by a process of exclusion, between speculation and the influence of the free-trade principle to account for the present distress. It is not speculation; for the effects of speculation are limited to one market, and the depression spreads with diminishing intervals to those most intimate with it;

and after the evil tendencies of speculation have disappeared, the trade and industries of the countries rise to their former level, or near it, in our present circumstances of free trade.

Speculation could only be cause of so large a distress as the present, where it is general and when it affects all the markets. But there must be antecedents of such a general speculation, called inordinate and insane by Sir Robert Peel; there must have been the previously healthy condition of the markets and a low rate of interest. Such a general depression from speculation is characterised by scarcity of capital; there is no such dearth of money in the present day.

The element of speculation, therefore, is incapable, from its magnitude and force, its inconstant—and an inconstant cause cannot cause a constant result—but paroxysmal nature, to explain the present constant decline in our trade; it causes the ups and downs in the downward curve. It remains, therefore, that free trade is the cause, and we shall learn this is able to effect it by its magnitude and constancy.

37. *Effect of reduction of England's demands upon foreign nations.*—When a large and growing institution ceases to demand not only the same amount, but a gradually increasing amount, of those raw materials which other countries have been accustomed to export in her favour, it follows that these countries must suffer, and suffer according to the degree of diminution in the amount of supplies. It is not enough to be told that given imports remain the same in total amount: they may vary in value, and they have done this to an

alarming extent; and if they even remain the same in amount, when they have previously shown an upward tendency, does not this indicate that retardation has taken place? For in what way has an increasing population been affecting the stationary phase of our trade with other export countries?

And these countries, too, suffer, if not an absolute loss, yet a relative one, by reason of the fact that a growing industry has been checked in its development, and therefore a possible means of employment to a portion of their increased population destroyed. But in such a case, where there is this disturbance in the amount of imports into a country which is gradually feeling the perilous effects of decline, it is clear that there must be a period of transition in which a species of equilibrium may be established. During that period depression will reign in foreign countries on account of the reduction in the supply of labour. Competition will thereby be increased, for there will be more hands than labour to supply them, and wages will consequently be diminished.

Thus, then, foreign depression may to a certain extent be explained, and so far as it is concerned with depression at home. But the sequence of depression must be observed. The course of depression in this country tends to the appearance of depression in other countries. The two depressions, therefore, stand in the relation of cause and effect.

And now mark the direction of Liberal reasoning! The mere existence of depression in a foreign and protective country is adduced for a favourable comparison with depression in our own. We are suffering; well, then, so are other countries! But nothing is said as to the true causation of either of these separate depressions, nor their immediate connection with one another!

The Liberals then deduce the inevitable conclusion from the following statement of these facts: We see depression round about us, in those nations which are protective, and we who are free-traders are likewise suffering depression. It is obvious, therefore, that neither protection nor free trade can be the cause of these depressions.

This is a rather curious corollary to the free-trade reasoning of 1842, for in *that* protection is the sole source of depression. But sentiments alter with times, and Liberal reasoning grows to a greater amount of truth! This Liberal reasoning is on a par with that of the free-traders, "cheap bread causes high wages."

The grand cause, therefore, of depression is unknown, or due to the seasons, or due to some trifling inconstant influence, just to soothe the inflamed ear of a mob, while they are being lectured about the injustice under which they are suffering.

But it would be well if the populace were for a while to view a matter dispassionately which so intimately concerns their welfare. The cause of depression is unknown, because the Liberal demagogues are unwilling to own to it. It is free trade or nothing! And how can any conscientious Liberal desert the flag of free trade, under which the nation prospered so magnificently, but under which the nation is also suffering so egregiously! For every effect which is general and of great magnitude, and constant, there must be a cause, which is constant and sufficiently large to produce it. What other cause is constant, what other source is of sufficient magnitude to account for the present depression? Let the Liberals reply!

But in the meantime the Liberal party inadvertently allow themselves to fall into an error of observation. In the comparison they institute between the depressions of this and foreign nations, they presume that the nature of the depression is similar in each! But such is not the case. The depression in those countries which feel the downfall, gradually induced, of British manufacture, is a temporary depression, and is capable of being removed by the energies of their respective peoples. But in the instance of our own, the Liberal eye is shut to the fact that the depression is composed of two elements, one of which, it is true, is temporary, but the other, it is equally true, is constant. It is this constant element of depression, this appearance of decline, which is the chief characteristic of the distress which the nation is at the present moment suffering. It is this element which is so grossly and unfortunately neglected.

Sir Robert Peel, somewhere in one of his speeches, said that a constant and injurious process was going forward, referring to the commercial policy of protection. And the same sentiment was iterated by Mr Gladstone, who described the old system as a system of robbing and plundering ourselves. Sir Robert Peel's remark was made before the principle of free trade had commenced with its primary extraordinary success, and when it was certain that stimulation would be followed by increased activity; Mr Gladstone's, when this successful nation was nearing its acme of prosperity, so far as trade manufactures were concerned. Is it curious that neither of these politicians disclosed the continuous progress of free trade? But it is certainly curious that both these eminent politicians should have referred so disparagingly to a system under which the commercial policy of all surrounding nations was conducted, and under which our own had reached so great a degree of prosperity! But evils are not removed by an alteration of system—this Sir Robert Peel acknowledged. And what were the evils of his own free-trade principle? Did he unconsciously predict its ruinous bearing upon the country in the unjustifiable attack (unjustifiable for him!) which he made on protection?

But yet the comparison between the protectionist forecast and the Liberal policy must be carefully made.

The protectionists predicted that with a low price of bread there would eventually be a low state of wages. The Whigs and free-traders foretold the beginning of the new reign of commercial prosperity!

But they did not predict that this reign of prosperity would so soon come to an ignoble end!

The present united Liberal party seem, however, still in some doubt as to the proper apportionment of the shares to each of the individual factors in the causation of distress. Let us help them a little in this instructive process.

Sir Robert Peel (and his authority is claimed by the Liberals, and not contested by the Tories) very distinctly asserts that strained relations with foreign Powers form an important barrier to some commercial transactions, and therefore lead to a temporary depression. He instances the wars which had been conducted

T

by the second Melbourne Ministry just before his second advent to power. What may be urged against the foreign policy of the Liberal Administration of 1880-85, which resulted in the isolation of England among European nations? How did these insecure relations with foreign Powers interfere with the sufficiently depressed commercial business of the country? When the country was already suffering severely from distress, was it prudent to increase the causes of depression? And how might that have been maintained? By the display of a firm attitude on our Indian frontier. But an opening was made, and advantage taken of it. By this contrast it is seen how Sir Robert Peel, in his commercial policy, sinned against a great doctrine, as a subsequent Prime Minister has done in his foreign relations—"Do unto others as you would they should do unto you."

CHAPTER VII.

THE ATTITUDE OF PARTIES IN THE STATE RESPECTING THE PROGRESS OF OUR COMMERCE, AND THE PRINCIPLES WHICH PRESIDE OVER IT.

38. *Attitude of the parties in the State.*—It is not a little important to contrast the *different* methods employed by the Tory and Liberal parties in the investigation of the causes of the present distress. The Liberals seek to refer the main cause to the *disabilities* under which property in land is placed in this country, while they ignore altogether the *burden* which is lying so heavily upon our trade. The Tory party, giving to the land question the minor importance which it possesses in the solution of the problem, centre all their endeavours on the *inequalities* which have for many years surrounded, and are still surrounding, our commercial system; and therefore recently afforded every facility in their power in arriving at the true cause of distress, through the means of *a Commission to inquire into the causes of the present depression in trade.*

Thus the method followed by the Tory party is *complete* and *impartial*, and further, bears the stamp of accuracy. It includes both trade and agriculture, and rightly gives the preference to the former, as being of far greater magnitude and importance, *and altogether associated with the prosperity of this country.*

The treatment of the Liberals, on the other hand, is *partial*, and based upon *prejudice* and *error;* the prejudice arising from a *blind* adhesion to an economic principle which has become a *tradition* among their party—the error due to the false assumption that, in the present condition of society and generally, it is *the country that makes the town grow.*

A relation between town and country is founded, which is *artificial* as it is used by them. For the relationship only exists when the town is in an early phase of its development, and *ceases* when its demands become greater than the surrounding country can supply. But it is not difficult to see why the Liberals offered an *apparent* unconcern in the lately appointed Commission; for the *soundness* of their great economic principle is called in question—a principle which has supplied them with *popularity*, and has been the direct means of conferring on them a *long continuance of power.* Hence, to suppose that their great principle is no longer potent for good, is at once resented; they refer immediately to the *temporary rise* which followed the introduction of free trade into this country, *under very favourable conditions*, and resulted for the time being in so much prosperity. And they argue that this prosperity, being associated with, and as they think the immediate cause of, the rapid rise in the trade of this country, must continue so long as their traditionary principle remains in action. But the great bulwark behind which they hide themselves is the cry of a *tax on the people's food.*

Perhaps it does not occur to the Liberal party that their argument is *insufficient;* that the principle of free trade itself is not *directly* responsible for the sudden rise in the markets which followed its early introduction into our commercial relations; but that it is so *only indirectly* by promoting an *increased circulation*, which led to a more rapid exchange, and therefore a stimulation which penetrated to all the branches of our industry. Thus it is the *effect of* the principle of free trade, and this effect *an increased circulation*, which was the *cause of the prosperity* resulting from its early action, *when surrounding conditions were favourable to its development*. The principle of free trade was the cause of an increased circulation in the markets, and this increased circulation was the immediate cause of a *sudden*, and, as it has happened, an *unwholesome* rise in our trade. It is not, therefore, to the efficacy of the principle itself, *but only of one of its effects*, which is possible when external conditions are favourable to its action, that the explanation of its success is to be referred. In other words, the principle of free trade is *potent for good* or *for evil*, according to the *nature* of the external circumstances which surround its action, and is obviously potent *for good alone* when these circumstances are *favourable* to an increased circulation, and *for evil* when these circumstances have become *modified* and *adverse* to the development of this effect. For it must be remembered that these surrounding circumstances are being slowly and gradually altered during the continued action of the principle, and that one of the causes of such alteration is the remote *consequence* on the market of a primary and inordinate increase in its circulation.

It has been customary to account for the prosperity attending the first application of the free-trade principle to the commercial transactions of this country by ascribing it to the virtues of the principle itself. But this is obviously erroneous; for a principle can only act through its effects, and these are good or evil, according as the nature of the surrounding conditions are favourable or adverse to the development of that *particular* effect through which it becomes successful. And if this effect is not developed, then must the principle lose that part of its former and beneficial efficacy which was attendant upon its initial action; and if all the success of the principle depends upon the existence of one effect only, when that effect is absent, it follows that the principle ceases to be associated with success. And when the circulation in all the trade-markets is slowed or stagnant, what does this express? That the free-trade principle—after excluding collateral influences of minor importance, which naturally cannot continue *to act as* efficiently so long as the present decline progresses—does not, under the *existing* conditions, cause an increase in circulation, *by which it was originally intended to act.* The conditions, therefore, are not favourable for its successful action, and have become *different* from those which marked its first and successful application. Thus an adjustment has taken place, and surrounding relations have become imperceptibly modified, through the action of a *new principle* upon them. And as England alone remained a free-trader, it is obvious that during its progress, after the primary beneficial action of the Liberal principle *had reached its limit,* means would be sought by surrounding nations *to diminish the feverish activity of our markets*, and *divert the traffic of trade* towards their own country. This is but the result of *self-interest*, the motive which impelled the introduction of the free-trade principle into this country, and has been the *cause* of that change in surrounding conditions, from favourable to adverse, which has led to the inefficacy of the principle by diminishing circulation, and therefore to that constant but steadily increasing drain upon the resources of this country.

When the conditions are no longer favourable to the beneficial action of the free-trade principle, it is evident that our trade cannot feel that prosperity which formerly it experienced when our system was protective, and on a level with surrounding nations. And now, in our competition with foreign countries, which is carried on so *unequally* to the *interests* of this country, when anything is gained there must be somebody to lose; and it is clear that that nation which is under the *greatest disabilities* will be the *sufferer*. But this suffering, or the *commencement of the decline in our trade*, was not likely to be appreciated, even when the circulation in our markets was beginning to be depressed, while our country was still enjoying those blessings which were associated with a stimulation in every branch of her commerce. It would take some time before even a modicum of the rapid increase in the wealth of this country was slowly and almost imperceptibly squandered away by the gradual but constantly accumulating drains upon the national resources. And England was still allowed to pursue her spendthrift policy, and her loss was unobserved or unrecognised. Yet *slight fluctuations* would appear, due to the influence of collateral and temporal causes, to *raise* the spirits of the desponding merchants, while the Liberal politician would *point* to them as the *direct results of free trade*. But these, being for a time only, and resulting from the operation of normal but inconstant causes, could not possibly impede, in the event, the *steady and downward* course our trade had begun to take, while the *constant adverse* action of a principle which had lost its beneficial efficacy *remained at work*. And it is obvious that the *decline, which some while back had been in progress*, would only become *perceptible* in its fullest degree when much of our *former gain* had been slowly *drained* away; and when our trade was placed, for the first time since the introduction of the free-trade principle, face to face with those *disabilities*, no longer opposed by prosperity, from which it has not as yet been disencumbered. And thus it is that our trade will reach a *lower* level than that on which it stood when it pursued a *true* and *equable* advance under the *safe guidance of protection*.

With its former gain thus being recklessly thrown away, and now suffering from the hardships of an unequal competition, what hopes remain for our trade while it is labouring under its present burden? What is there to expect but that there will surely be a still further increase of the present distress? And what tendencies are developed, when thus trade is so *unequally* carried on between neighbouring countries, in the direction of *design* and—*fraud?*

It cannot be denied that the present distress, compared with our former unexampled prosperity, acts *all the more unfavourably* upon the condition of the labouring classes; for they are chief partakers in the general wave of depression which has spread over all the country, and become dissatisfied at the hopeless prospects before them, and discontented. And thus they form the *soil* of agitation, and are rendered an easy prey to all those false notions and false ideas which are scattered in their midst concerning the relations between labour and capital, and to the erroneous theories concerning property in land.

When a retrospective view is taken of the course of our trade during the past generations—the sudden rise accompanying the introduction of the free-trade principle, followed by the present unexampled depression—it may be inquired, Has this rise been really to the advantage of the nation? For much of our former gain by it has been drained away. And has it been wholesome? For it has introduced a source of discontent, as being one of the early links in the chain of causation of the present distress which is evident in all levels of society, but bears most unequally upon the working man, whose prosperity it is the country's object to promote, by adjusting our trade relations with foreign countries to the principles of justice and right.

And how have these, the labourer's prosperity and wellbeing, been fostered by the continued action of a principle which has become ultimately pernicious in its results?

What is the main source of the present discontent and distress? The low wages, as compared with former comparatively high ones.

Has the continued action of the free-trade principle been rewarded with success, more especially in the equable advancement of the labouring classes?

And when there appeared first this tendency to inequality in the condition of the labouring classes, when period is compared with period, is it now, or was it then, to the interests of the country to promote it?

And how far has the principle of free trade acted in this direction?

When the welfare of the labouring classes depends, and depends alone, upon *fair* and *equal* wages, what need is there to adduce the *deserted* state of the country, as it has been assumed to be deserted, and the *decline in agriculture*, as the source of the present distress? Is it to be supposed for a moment that an *increase* in agricultural activity in this country will have *any influence* upon the labourer's wages in the towns? The smaller towns which have demands upon the surrounding country will always have these demands supplied as long as the productivity of the soil is equal to the burden upon it. The larger towns are, and have been for many years, independent of the country for the supply of many of those necessaries which, in an earlier phase of its development, were solely derived from it. What then? It is in the larger towns, where the raw material is manufactured into the various goods, that the present distress is mainly evident, because it is concentrated; and how will legislation respecting the cultivation of land in this country influence the majority of those who are in distress, and who depend for their livelihood on successful trade or the promotion of enterprise in the towns? For the proposed legislation affects only a few; and even supposing these new conditions to be followed by success, what influence, more than just an appreciable one, could agricultural prosperity in this country have upon the welfare and wellbeing of the working classes in the towns, when the great relative difference in their numbers is taken into consideration?

Thus the larger towns are denied any benefit which can be appreciated from this *species of legislation*, of attempting to increase the supplies of the country, so that the town may grow; and their present wants are abandoned by the Liberal party, which refuses to investigate, in an impartial spirit, *all* the elements that enter into the causation of the present distress, and which widens the opportunity, therefore, of reaching the *true* remedy, and, as we think, fails to reach it altogether.

But whenever the principle of free trade is attacked, the cry is immediately raised, "Tax the food of the people." The Liberals forget, in their haste to stifle discussion, that the people's food would neither be unjustly nor disadvantageously taxed by the introduction of fairness in the conduct of our trade. For the penny loaf will still remain relatively the penny loaf, in spite of the renewal of the system of protection, based upon the principles of justice and right. For by the protection of our industries the labour-market will be gradually extended, and the means to obtain a proper livelihood proportionally increased. In what way, therefore, can this principle of free trade, advantageous for a time, but disastrous in the long-run, be regarded by those who see the prosperity of their country in a true and equable advancement of its trade?

If the commercial relations of our country be studied, before the application of the free-trade principle, it will be discovered that on the whole they continued prosperous under the protective system, in spite of temporary depressions, which mark its even progress, and which arise as the natural result of contingencies to which men are prone. Nor must the *opposition*, with which the introduction of the free-trade principle was stoutly resisted by those who had *the true interests of their country at heart*, be forgotten at this commercial crisis.

The Tory party, inspired by the true spirit of patriotism, predicted as the natural result of its action the decline of our trade. This prediction was founded on an inquiry into the continued operation of the principle of free trade, but it loses its influence by reason of the fact that the steps by which the fatal result was to be brought about were involved in darkness. There would be a temporary rise, followed by a period in which surrounding conditions would be equilibrated to the influence of this economic principle; and when this equilibrium had become effected, the decline would become perceptible. And how truly this Tory prediction of old has been fulfilled! Contrast the Tory prediction with the Liberal anticipation! It was the boast of the Liberals that the free-trade principle would become universally adopted; for was it not by this means that peace and happiness were to be diffused over the earth? and they shed glory upon themselves by conferring upon England the merit of taking the lead in an action which opened up to the nation the whole trade of the world; but, at the same time, added an enormous increase to the wealth of this country.

The anticipation was based upon the fact that the introduction of the principle of free trade into our commercial relations with all other countries would be followed by an increased prosperity, which was fulfilled, and that the same change would most probably be followed by other nations, which was false. The prosperity which they anticipated, they must have known would be temporary only, provided surrounding nations remained protective; and it is obvious that the principle could never continue to act advantageously from the point of view of trade-activity, not from the development of increased skill, unless other countries become free-traders.

The Liberal anticipation that it was only a question of time for other nations to follow in the train of free trade, has thus, up to the present, been disappointed. And thus, from the nature of the Liberal reform in trade, which was grounded upon expectations which were in part right but partly false, a temporary prosperity was gained at the price of a subsequent adversity —the present distress.

For neighbouring nations have preferred a true and equable advance in their respective trades, in accordance with the solid judgment and wisdom of their guides, to a momentary rise, with all its serious ultimate results.

Means were easily discovered by which the effects of so disastrous and isolated an introduction were made to recoil upon itself; and the continued existence of the present protective system, which controls the trade relations of the neighbouring nations, proves the Liberal anticipation to have been based on a hasty and shortsighted study of the results of their action.

Thus, what a vast difference there is between the Tory prediction and the Liberal anticipation!

For the Tories had the faculty of foreseeing the disasters that would ultimately attend our trade if our neighbours still remained protective, which have come to pass; and the opportunity, afforded them with such temerity, of aggrandising themselves at the expense of the free-trader. This opportunity has been taken, with the result that the operation of our free-trade principle has been continuously restricted to diminishing fields; and at the present is in full power, under such adverse circumstances as the Liberal party has never taken the proper measures to counteract.

How different the efficacy of the principle of free-trade would be, were all other countries likewise free-traders! It was with this intention that the Liberals became responsible for the lead in a hypothetical universal free trade. For then they would have retained all that prosperity with which they started; and the trade of this country would have been raised to a higher level. But not while there was anything to gain in the near future, would other nations follow suit; they foresaw, or the wise politicians among them, the advantages of remaining protective, under the new conditions which the isolated action of England had introduced into her relations with the commerce of the world—advantages which would accrue not at once, but slowly, and would possess the further additional interest of being cumulative.

Thus result those disasters, which follow sooner or later the application of novel principles to systems, the working of which in their entirety is without the control of the advocates for reform. The old lines were deserted, but the prosperity which followed the interruption was enough to claim for the principle a general belief in its continued beneficial efficacy.

How fatally at fault the Liberal anticipation here, as it was also disastrously at fault, in a late Liberal Administration—the Indian frontier and the Egyptian campaign! Can the Liberals do else than admit that their great economic principle has ceased to be potent for good, owing to the endeavours of other nations to promote the circulation of trade in their own countries. There is a very great difference between the gross results following our free trade with the protective system of foreigners, and those which would be associated with our free trade if surrounding nations had become free-traders, the anticipation of the founder and promoters of the doctrine!

With what disastrous effect upon this country has the initiative been marked in taking a course, which was supposed, but upon insufficient grounds, would become universal, it is needless to relate to those who recognise the fact that the action of a principle must vary, when the conditions surrounding its first introduction become altered to meet the consequences of its effects. For the conditions now are no longer favourable to an increased circulation; the circulation of the trade of this country has been slowly diverted into foreign channels. The conditions which surround the operation of the free-trade principle at the present day, present this difference to those former ones, under which it became the source of so much prosperity. Then, the principle was unencumbered by the results of its own action, and increased circulation had free play. Now, the consequences of one of its effects, increased circulation, by the creation of adverse external forces to weaken it, remain, to interfere with its successful working.

The free-trade principle is thus rendered inefficacious; for increased circulation, the means by which it becomes potent for good, is impossible.

And thus "to the operation of a principle, which contains within itself the seeds of decline," the present stagnation in trade and the distress consequent thereon, is directly traced.

It is with considerable reluctance that mistakes, persevered with by the individual, are ever acknowledged. And with what force will the Liberal party resist the detection of one of the sources, and a very important one, if not the most, in the action of a pernicious policy, which is based upon their great economic principle of free trade. They will refuse to recognise its evil results with as much force as the Tories of a past generation opposed that temporary rise which was certain to follow its introduction, and continued their opposition, even while it was being attended with prosperity, as being of a precarious nature, and as equally certain to be attended with subsequent distress. The principle of free trade was applied to the commerce of this country, without the consent, and not in harmony with the trade-systems, of foreign nations!

And what will follow the recognition of the ultimate pernicious action of this principle? The Liberal party know that to recognise the effects of their disastrous policy would be to overwhelm them with ruin!

And thus can be easily explained why the element of free trade was not represented on the late Commission which inquired into the causes of the depression in trade. The Liberals responsible for distress! would be quite inconsistent with their greatest hopes and boastful proclamations!

The principle has been in action a long time; and the decline of our trade has been constant and steadily increasing since the reaction of a former prosperous period has passed off. There has been some opportunity, therefore, to observe the tendency, to trace its true source, and to provide some means by which it might be counteracted, if not removed. But even this opportunity has not been taken; observation is perverted into the direction of party interest; the depression, constant and increasing, is referred to false causes; and the Liberals still remain consistent, but—at the expense of their country!

It is a curious instance, where the Liberals have shown no desire, as in all those other instances in which they are involved in difficulty, they are moved by the irresistible tendency to censure their opponents for having made things so bad, while they do not refer to the worse condition in which they leave them, to throw the blame of the present distress on the shoulders of the Tory party, who predicted it.

This, indeed, is the great exception to the Liberal rule of ridiculing their antagonists, where they have themselves no intimate cause by which to explain the unfavourable state of affairs. But such a weakness, despicable in an individual, is easily seen to be drawn to its thinnest dimensions by a party which attempts to excel itself in popularity!

But the attitude of the Liberals, which is doubtfully patriotic, is characteristic enough; for though they cannot blame the Tory party, they attempt to deride an investigation which will go to the very centre of the matter in question, and expose in its small confines, and divested from the association of other and minor causes, a principle which has acted, and still is acting, adversely to the interests of the country. And when the disabilities under which our commerce is suffering are removed, and with them the distress which is prevailing equally throughout the country, then will our trade resume its former condition of prosperity, but by slow degrees, and return to that true and equable advancement which has been, through the unfortunate influence of a principle, so violently interrupted for a while!

FREE TRADE. 307

39. *Graphic display of the operation of the free-trade principles, with variation of surrounding conditions.*

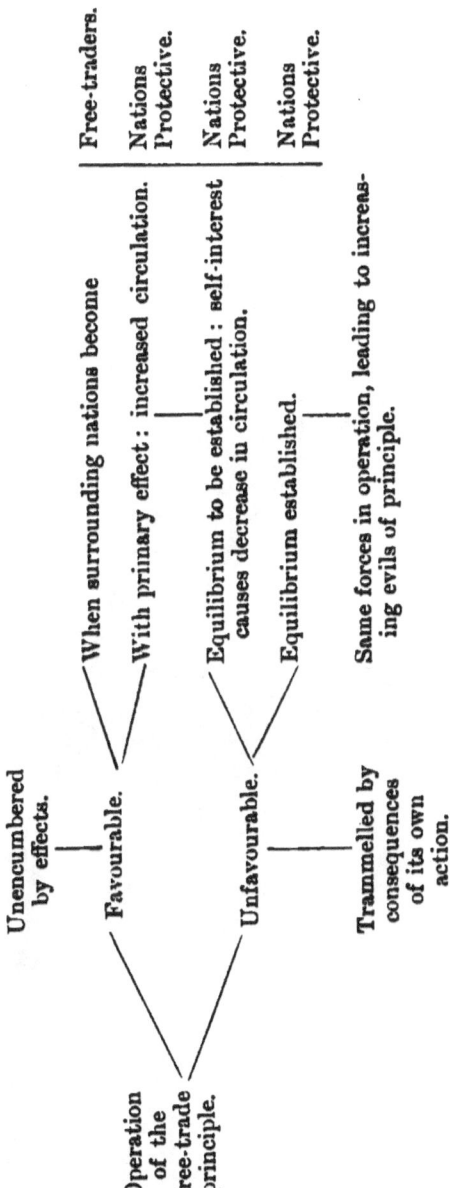

308 FREE TRADE.

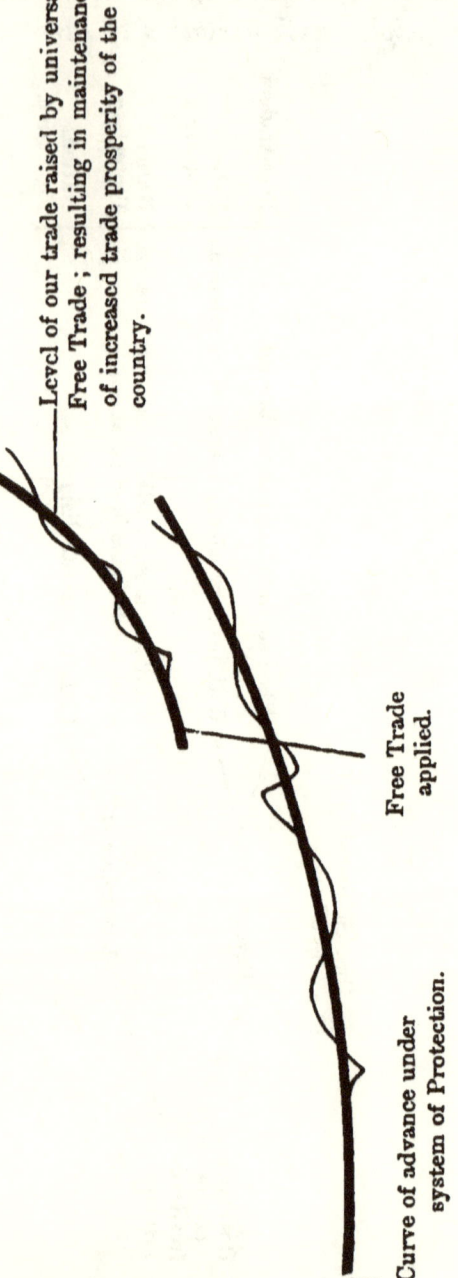

40. *The result depicted, if the Liberal anticipation had been fulfilled.*

FREE TRADE. 309

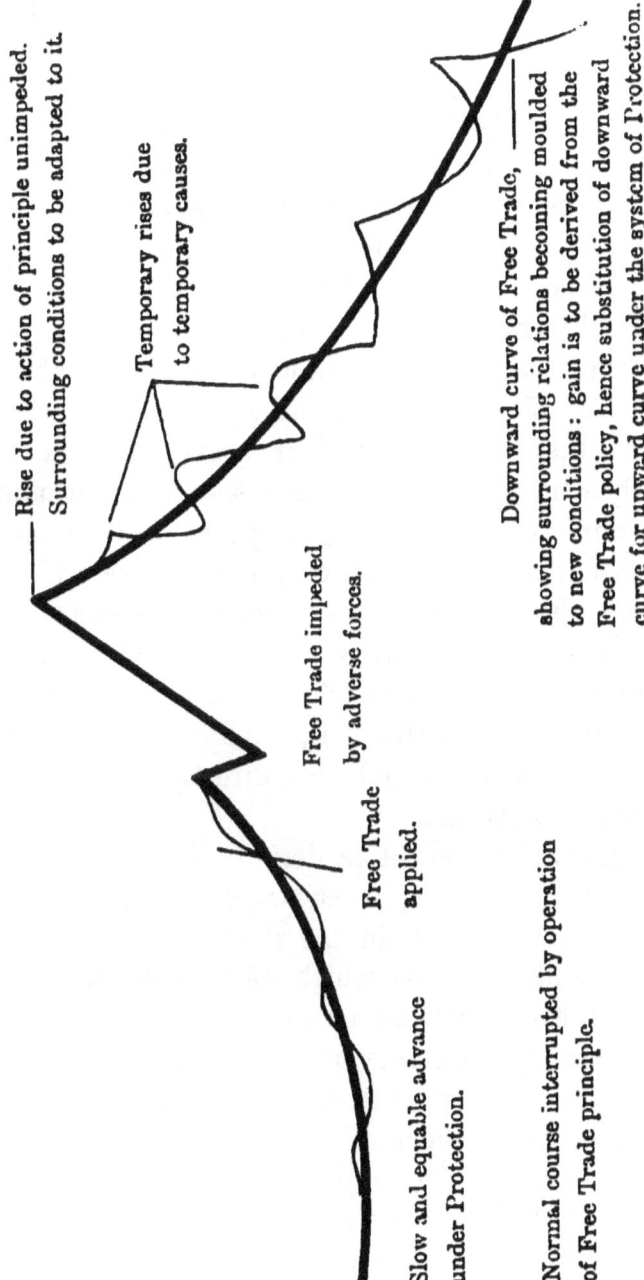

41. What has actually happened to the course of our commerce from the application of the free-trade principle.

42. *The outlook.*—It is to no purpose that the Liberals continually refer to the past trade-prosperity enjoyed by this country under the influence of a principle which was for a short time benign; and if by far the largest part of the present distress can be directly traced to the constant action of this principle, which has now become pernicious, the interests of the country, which seem to have been sacrificed, but sacrificed unintentionally, by the Liberal party, and the spirit of true patriotism, demand that the principle be forthwith abandoned.

The Liberals gain nothing by the prosperity which was first effected by their great economic principle, when it is compared with the constant and steady decline which has of late years been so disastrously evident in all branches of our commerce, and has spread from the country to the town, and become responsible for the unremunerative profits, of which the manufacturers now, as well as the farmers, complain. The decline of agriculture is, equally with the decline in other branches of industry, directly dependent upon an unfair competition.

And what benefit is derived from cheapening bread in one generation, when wages are reduced, through these very means, in the next?

The observations which have been made respecting the present distress are:—

First, Its constancy and increase; and,

Secondly, The large dimensions it has assumed.

It is quite evident that the accuracy of these observations is of the first importance. For, once admit them, and let the state of the markets speak for themselves, is not the next step to look for the cause? And it is due from the Liberal party, in favour of their economic principle, to advance some cause which shall be sufficient to account for the present constant and increasing depression in trade, and the distress associated therewith, which shall be of a *magnitude* that is *capable of bringing it about*, and which shall be *constant*.

It is obvious that the temporary influences of collateral and contingent events are not sufficient to account for the present intense depression; for they bear only partially upon the advancement of trade, their effect is not general, nor do they reach a sufficient degree of strength to become *permanent*.

The causes, therefore, of former temporary and slight depressions, affecting but one branch of trade in the constant and downward course our commerce has taken, are not available to explain the present large depression, which is general over the country. Only one, inordinate speculation, is possible: but there is no evidence of this.

The only other constant element that might be able to bring about a constant depression is the land, the source of all wealth. But it is evident that this element does not reach sufficient dimensions to be capable of effecting the large amount of distress existing at present. The relation of agriculture to trade in this country is expressed by stating that the amount of home-grown wheat is insufficient to satisfy, at the lowest computation, one-thirtieth part of the population. Hence the necessity of depending so largely upon a foreign supply, and placing ourselves in a condition relatively independent of inclement seasons and the "increasing unproductivity" of the soil of political economists. The number of bushels of wheat which were imported during the year 1884 reached beyond fifty millions, the number of bushels yielded by the last favourable crop less than one million and a half, and the amount which overstocked the markets in 1884 was more than the next year's produce of the country.

Thus the people of to-day almost entirely depend for their livelihood on the flourishing condition of trade; and hence the judgment and wisdom shown by the Tory party in thoroughly investigating the causes of its present decline. But the mistaking the collateral effects of the same cause for cause and effect has led the Liberals into their mischievous error; the decline of agriculture was the immediate effect of free trade, the decline of our manufacture the more remote. Thus the decline in both agriculture and manufacture is the result of free trade; for if the rapid decline of agriculture is the primary cause of the depression which is sweeping over the country, they must prove that the tendency to this rapid decline first appeared as the result of inherent weakness in agriculture, and thence spread to the towns and influenced their trades. And have they done this? Can the Liberals deny the truth of the observation that agriculture, though gradually declining before, has declined more rapidly since the free admission of corn into this country?

But it is not difficult to see that, from the slight relationship between the larger towns in the matter of corn, no such disturbance as the effect just described can possibly be created. The first effect of free trade upon the agricultural prospects of the country, by sending down the price of corn, was to add to the benefit of manufacturers, not only by its influence upon manufacture itself, but also by tending towards a relative increase of wages. It is clear that the original depression of agriculture had no influence upon trade itself; for if it had, there must be some evidence, and where is it to be found, during the early period of prosperity which our manufacture experienced under free trade? No; the evil source flows not from agriculture: it comes from without. Nor is there any need to fear about the future of agriculture in those parts of the country remote from towns, and more or less in the state of supplying their own wants in the matter of corn, except from the inclemency of the seasons and the diminishing productivity of the soil; for wherever there is a demand for corn, there it will be met by a proper supply; and so in other districts, which might be independent of the country's bounty, provided that the disabilities under which the farmers work are removed. Agriculture, as well as trade, should be allowed a proper protection. It depends upon the disposition to cultivate the soil; and whenever this disposition can be exerted with advantage, it will be carried into effect.

As regards the question of agriculture, therefore, the Liberal legislation labours under the extraordinary defect of not accounting, with a sufficiently powerful cause, for the dimensions of the present distress. Their mistake lies, not in the constancy of their cause, but in the deficiency of its strength. Their legislation presents some of the appearances of a compromise; for while now, in the ordinary trade difficulties, the labourer is unable to maintain himself, by becoming the owner of a plot of ground he can succeed in doing so. But is there any foresight in this measure? Has trade already reached its lowest level, and is agriculture in unknown hands at once to become profitable? It is impossible, under the existing disabilities which are felt all over the country, that this Liberal legislation will have any, even the slightest, influence for good. For the decline of trade must be arrested, else the labourer will have to depend entirely on the soil. And how unremunerative farming has become, even when carried on extensively, the experience of to-day declares. If unprofitable when conducted over a large area, it is impossible to suppose that the cultivation of the soil will become less so when carried out on a smaller scale. And when agriculture is still groaning beneath its present burdens, what are the chances of the proposed class of small farmers, with a relatively higher expenditure than the larger ones, and left to the mercy of the inclement seasons, and the well-known gradually increasing unproductivity of the soil? which, if to be arrested for a time, can only be attained by an expensive means.

The scheme on page 315 will explain, more distinctly than a mere verbal description, the relation which agriculture has to the trade of this country, and the exact limitation of the proposed Liberal legislation.

In this way the Liberal reform is referred to its strictest limits. It is supposed that by virtue of this species of legislation the trade-prosperity of the towns will be restored. But how?

Nor need there be any further remarks upon this second instance of an experimental method, the introduction of which, in the politics of this country, has already been to the disadvantage of the welfare, the prestige, and the wellbeing of this country — there

FREE TRADE.

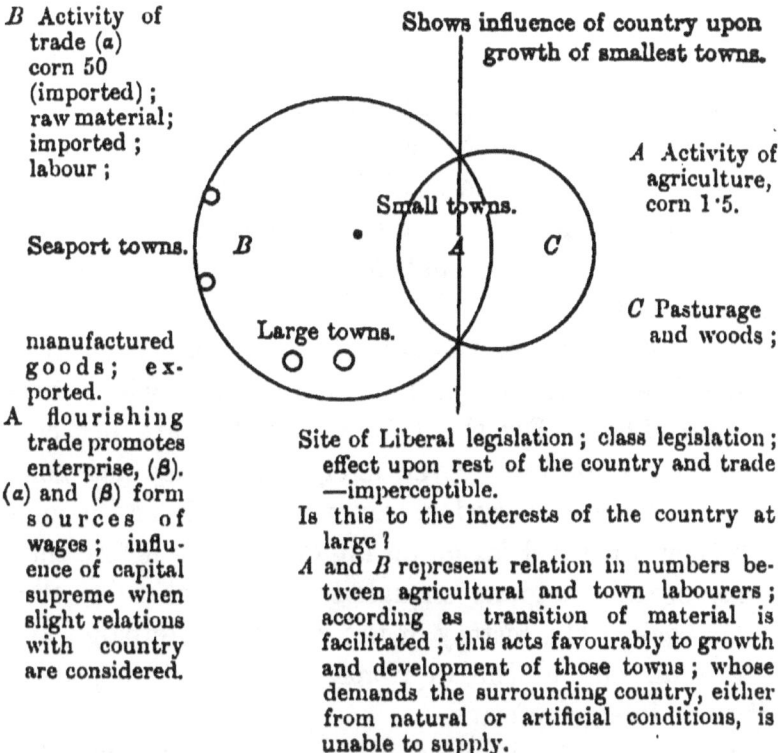

B Activity of trade (a) corn 50 (imported); raw material; imported; labour;

Seaport towns.

manufactured goods; exported.

A flourishing trade promotes enterprise, (β).
(a) and (β) form sources of wages; influence of capital supreme when slight relations with country are considered.

Shows influence of country upon growth of smallest towns.

A Activity of agriculture, corn 1·5.

C Pasturage and woods;

Site of Liberal legislation; class legislation; effect upon rest of the country and trade —imperceptible.
Is this to the interests of the country at large?
A and B represent relation in numbers between agricultural and town labourers; according as transition of material is facilitated; this acts favourably to growth and development of those towns; whose demands the surrounding country, either from natural or artificial conditions, is unable to supply.

have been lately some sort of experiments in foreign policy, and some are now being considered respecting the relations between Church and State—were it not to point out a few of the dangers which are entangled in its procedure. For the independence of our countrymen is engaged to the means whereby this legislation is proposed to be rendered effective. There is to be a State aid; and man no longer remains dependent on his own powers. Besides, all cannot be satisfied, and who are to be the first to taste the insidious benefits of legislative happiness? It is certain that there is, in this proposal of allotment, a source of greater political corruption than has ever yet been felt in this country! Yet the Liberal party, by means of its Reform Bill, pride themselves on having diminished political corruption, and on giving to each the power to vote as he likes. As if this were possible? For every one is impelled by self-interest to protect himself, *unless the dispositions of men are going to be reformed* by a subsequent Liberal bill.

To open up, then, a source of corruption, is an act of inconsistency on the part of the Liberals which they should abhor. For the Liberals, if they are not consistent, are nothing. Even lately, when they had commenced a most hazardous enterprise, their consistency led them to travel far on an inglorious path before their error became flagrant enough to compel them to turn their back. The history of the Egyptian campaign, and the affair on our Indian frontier, show the ineptitude of their foreign reforms.

It may now be inquired of the Liberal party whether they admit that the distress at present is of large dimensions, and general in all branches of industry; and whether they have recognised the constant and steady decline in our trade during many years past, and which has already reached to so low an ebb.

43. *Pointing to the remedy.*—There are many reasons why Liberals exonerate from all responsibility the operation of the free-trade principle, which is fixed and constant. But they must grasp at something, and therefore they fasten upon the land, which is also constant but fluctuating; and refer to the decline in agri-

culture as the source of their present distress, which, as we have already seen, is obviously a false cause. For, first, this cause is not of sufficient dimensions to account for the large effect. And secondly, decline in agriculture proceeded, and proceeds still, equally with decline in other branches of industry. If, therefore, after the introduction of a new principle, its effect upon trade is beneficial, while it is unfavourable upon agriculture, the measure of the depression in one must be the measure of the prosperity of the other, if these phenomena are to stand in the relation of cause and effect.

But this is not so: agriculture has been steadily declining. Trade has had an upward and now it has a downward curve. What in agriculture is to explain the opposite states in trade? They do not, therefore, bear the relation of cause and effect, but are obviously both collateral effects of the same cause; and that cause, the disability under which all branches of our industry are placed by the continued and now pernicious, as we have abundantly proved, action of a principle, which has become historical, and the introduction of which formed an epoch in the progress of our commerce—the principle of free trade.

But still, that the Liberals may hang upon the last straw, the trade depressions in surrounding countries are adduced to bolster up the efficacy of their economic principle. The argument is delivered thus: There is depression in several countries; their trade-systems vary—one is a free-trader, the others protectionists: therefore the depression is to be referred to some other cause or causes than those which govern their respective trades. But they do not tell what other cause or causes, because they know that other cause and causes, except the land, are not constant, and not equivalent to the effect produced.

Their error follows from inaccurate or incomplete observations. They start with the assumption that it is the trade-system which is at fault, and prove in the easiest manner possible that it cannot be. The accurate method of pursuing the problem is to ascertain the times at which the depressions of various countries first made their appearance, and the *order of their succession*, if they appear at different times; and secondly, their relative intensities. And the results of such a study show that this constant trade-depression first appeared in England, and has spread to all those countries with whom she trades, and that the greater her trade with the foreigner, the more, relatively, for a certain period, is his depression.

Thus the depression in England is the source of depression throughout her trade relations, and thus the mistake in the Liberal reasoning is manifested—for the trade-depression at home stands in relation to the depression existing in foreign countries, not as a collateral effect, but as cause and effect. And what can be more evident than that our general trade-depression must make itself felt wherever our commercial activity is sufficiently high enough to be influenced by the change? But this reflected depression is not permanent, and the affected nations find other sources to supply their demands, and thus are relieved in the course of time from the temporary burden the remote consequence of the principle of commercial reform has placed upon them.

But it is not sufficient to demonstrate the falsity of the Liberal cause of the present distress, and it remains to inquire into the erroneous grounds upon which it is based. This will be accomplished soon. It forms one of the chief means which points to the true remedy for distress.

44. *Removal of misconception.*—The Liberals have nourished their consistency in the maintenance of a principle which is thus surrounded with the greatest danger to the country. For the continued operation of the free-trade principle increases the distress of the country, and to remove this distress false measures are introduced, which involve the greatest disasters.

The Liberal party does not attempt to trace the true source of the prevailing misery of the country, otherwise it would reflect discredit upon itself. But this is only one of the methods by which the Liberals sacrifice the prosperity of their country to the interests of their party.

To retain the popularity which they so falsely acquired, they either affect to ignore the present trade difficulties, or else refer them, as is fully shown above, to a false cause. For in the new legislation which they have introduced concerning property in land, which is evidently proposed to benefit a class, and that a very small one, what influence can be traced to have an immediate or subsequent bearing upon the prosperity of the towns? Will this influence be at once felt? And if not, how is the present distress there going on to be met? The influence of this newly made class, which it is presumed will be created by Act of Parliament, for its birth is yet a thing of the future, can only be very slight, if it is appreciated at all, upon the development and welfare of the towns. For it will be admitted that this influence must be caused by a rise in agricultural activity. But how can even a large rise in this direction make itself felt to any extent in the towns, which are in a very large degree dependent upon foreign sources for their supply of corn, and can easily derive all of it from outside? Is it not a fact that when all the agricultural land of this country is brought into requisition, the most favourable crop is insufficient to supply even the thirtieth part of its inhabitants? And what assurance is there that the yield of corn is going to be greater; and if greater, great enough to have such an influence on the amount of corn imported into this country as shall be perceptible upon the price of corn, so as to warrant the introduction of the proposed legislation with reference to the land? What does the history of the seasons and the gradually increasing unproductivity of the soil tell us? And when, as in the present stage of our civilisation, as it must occur in all progressive civilisations, the produce of the country is unequal to the demands of its inhabitants, what an important influence has the foreign supply upon the cultivation of wheat at home? For according as this is less or greater, so are the markets high or low. And how unfavourable to the remunerative cultivation of the soil, when the corn-markets are overstocked, as they were during 1885! And when an additional burden is yet added to the unhappy lot of the farmer, in spite of the cheap prices which foreign supplies tend to bring about, when his competition with the foreigner is unequal, how can it be thought, when all his capital has been expended in an unsuccessful struggle against unfavourable circumstances, that the farmer shall derive such beneficial profits from his occupation as to enable him to proceed in its continuance? But this has been done! And better times have been waited for! and with what result? That the farmer's condition has fallen from bad to worse. And can it possibly improve under the existing state of things? And under the same condition of things, is it likely the allotment system, even if it opens up a larger area of the soil to cultivation, will prove successful, either for a time or in the long-run? In the meanwhile the sorry state of the farmer leads to the distressful condition of the agricultural labourer! It is impossible this can be improved, unless the farmer enjoys prosperity. It is impossible this can be brought about, unless the disability under which he labours be removed, —in a word, unless he is *protected*. It is false to assert that the decline of agriculture in this country is the main cause, or any appreciable minor cause at all, of the present distress. The decline in agriculture must have some cause, or causes, but the importance of the subject demands that the Liberal interpretation be exposed, in order that the extent to which false doctrines may be diffused shall be diminished!

There is a school of political economists which asserts that the cause resides in the high rents which are paid for a successful farm. And they strengthen their position by further asserting that rents increase with the productivity of the soil. It is both true that rents become high, and that rents tend to increase; but both these are the results of a well-known law—the law of competition—a law which it is impossible to destroy, but which may, as in the instance of the free-trade principle, be made unfavourable for the farmers. And it is so in this country at the present time, so these economists state, by reason of the diminishing productivity of the soil, and the influence of the inclement seasons and unequal competition. What else explains the low rents of the present day as compared with previous high ones, or these remissions in rents which are so frequently made, but not so frequently recorded? For the landlord must protect himself by keeping up the nominal rent of the farms, and more especially those which yield a fair profit when circumstances are favourable. But it is these very circumstances that are rendered so unfavourable in virtue of the unequal competition of the farmer of this country with the foreigner. To state the fact that has been observed by all economists worthy of notice, that the cultivation of land is never so prosperous as when the farmers can, out of their profits, pay a high rent, and when these profits increase, a still higher one; and to refer to the present actual condition to which farmers have been reduced, when, with even a large reduction in rent, the cultivation of the soil becomes less and less profitable, and when some farms are thrown out of cultivation, because no profits at all are possible even when the rent is at its lowest point, is quite enough to show that rent considered in itself, high or low, has nothing whatever to do with the present decline in agriculture.

And is it not surprising, and the more so when the facts are viewed in the order of their occurrence, to discover a recent political economist making the assertion that when rent is reduced profits are increased, and therefore the agricultural labourer's wages raised? The existence of the present distress in this country directly refutes such an assertion, based upon an erroneous relation between labour, wages, profits, and rent. For now the agricultural labourers are experiencing the severest distress, in spite of the fact that farms may be occupied by paying the lowest rents, or no rent at all. Is anything further required to demonstrate that the fluctuation in rent has nothing whatever to do with the causation of the distress which is so universally prevalent; and therefore, that the present conditions of private property in land, which obtain in this country and most others, is not responsible for the burden which is weighing down the people?

There is a cause far more potent than rent, for rent possesses in itself the property of being adjusted to the variations in the factors which go to form it, and it is impossible to conceive, from motives of self-interest, that rent could be the primary source of the present distress. Besides, would not its fluctuation, if this were so, have some impression on the steady decline? But this continues, and we are left to trace the main cause not to the rent he pays, but to the disabilities surrounding the farmer, and which now prevent him, and have prevented him for a long time back, from cultivating the soil at a profit which shall be remunerative. The farmer's depressed state arises from his not being able to sell his corn at a profit. And this disability results from the unequal competition under which he is placed, and this inequality arises directly from the operation of the free-trade principle.

It should occur to the Liberal or Radical party, so desirous of bringing about the equality of mankind, that they commence by making those conditions equal which relate our farmers to foreign competition. Let but these conditions be made so, and what will result? There will be once more a remunerative cultivation of the soil, rents will be maintained, the labourers' wages raised, and the source of distress removed.

Nor will this blessing be felt in the country alone: by the removal of a principle which has become pernicious, much of the distress that is prevalent throughout the land will disappear.

And then what need for any alteration in the present and wise system of our land-ownership? The distress has been removed, hence legislation for it is unnecessary.

And when this unnecessary legislation becomes *thus* rightly rejected, how will enterprise, which has well-nigh become paralysed by the feeling of insecurity which *it* engenders, be rapidly promoted?

Then will the wealth which is now resting idle in the banks be set in circulation again; and from increase of capital there will be more wages to pay, and labourers out of employment ready to receive them.

And thus a minor source of the present distress will disappear.

How strange that the Liberals, who are so fond of reforming everything, should fail in the instance of their famous economic principle of free trade! But it is their own creation, and is beyond the limits of reform therefore—in other words, it would be dangerous to the prestige and interests of the party to tamper with it—

and what is of *artificial* origin cannot admit of mistake. But *natural* growths are full of evil, *in the hands of the Liberals or Radicals*, and hence are within the sphere of reform—growths which have appeared in the ordinary course of events as the results of wants, and eminently adapted to the requirements of the state of our society; the natural growths of the relations between Church and State, and the House of Lords.

As these are competent to fulfil the special functions for which they were originally intended, there must be a peculiar reason why the Liberals should think them worthy of being reformed, or, as the terms have almost come to be synonymous, destroyed.

And what deeper reason than that the Liberals shall take these measures to excite commotion, introduce a conflict of opinions, and thus retain their popularity, which is likely to be lost owing to their being responsible for the interruption in the even advancement of our trade, for the subsequent depression and the present distress? But is it possible that in the case of the disestablishment and disendowment—*which are sure to come!*—the Liberal party seeks to repair a little of the mischief it has already done, by diminishing the burdens of the country at the expense of the morality of the people? The State will gain by the transaction, and taxation will be decreased, and the Liberals will confer upon their country another treacherous prosperity, of which their descendants will boast. But the evil day must come! And what the Liberals give, there must be something to take away; as their predecessors, who introduced free trade into this country, in exchange for a momentary rise with all its blessings, took away the inestimable advantages of its slow and equable advance. And is the moral grandeur of the nation to be sacrificed for all time, to the advantage of the present generation of the race?

What species of legislation is this? Is it thus we display a generous concern for our posterity?

And how is this concern for their posterity reflected in the isolated action of the older Liberals, when by their means the operation of the free-trade principle was brought to bear upon the commercial system of this country? And how strangely contrasted are the legislations of the older and the present Liberal party! For the former benefited their own age at the expense of a subsequent one; the latter shun the present wants of the people, and apply themselves vigorously towards the advantages of a future age! Is this an instance of Liberal consistency? and is this kind of Liberal consistency the equivalent of true patriotism? Past Liberals erred in anticipating that surrounding nations would become in course of time free-traders; and present ones err in the peculiar way in which they read the immediate future! For the disestablishment has been finally pronounced to be still *dim on the political horizon!*

And the reason for this usage of speculation in politics, which is carried at the present day to a height which has never been exceeded, and tends to strike at the morality of our age, is not far to seek.

Attention must be diverted from the mistakes, old and recent, of the Liberal party, and, therefore, from the present distress. Instead of "How and when will wages be raised and trade prosper?" there is much fascinating opinion on the future of the Established Church and the House of Lords. And thus an opportunity is provided an expectant people to drown past Liberal errors in a happy state of forgetfulness!

45. *Refutation of the hypothesis that distress is due to the nature of private property in land.*—We have shown how false it is to ascribe the present distress to the decline in agriculture, which has been steadily increasing for many years, and also to the nature of private property in land, as bearing upon the question of rent; and it is of importance to determine how the present distress undergoes a still further increase by that arrest of enterprise which follows a condition of insecurity, for which an injudicious Liberal legislation, based upon false grounds, is directly responsible.

We proceed to examine the grounds which lead to the conclusion that trade-depressions are dependent upon private property in land; to show their inadequacy, and to expose the hollow pretensions of the Liberal or Radical party to cope with the present distress.

But, at the outset, it must be remembered that the present decline is not merely paroxysmal or recurrent; it is constantly and steadily increasing.

And as, in deference to a great economic principle, it will be convenient to omit this latter element for a while, we pass on to consider, according to the Liberal view,—which denies the constant element of exhaustion induced by their free-trade principle—the recurrent nature of the present depression in trade, which is characterised by far larger dimensions than those of any other paroxysms known before. But we display, for the purpose of clearness, the difference between the Liberal and the true explanation of the progress of our trade, with the operation of the free-trade principle in full action :—

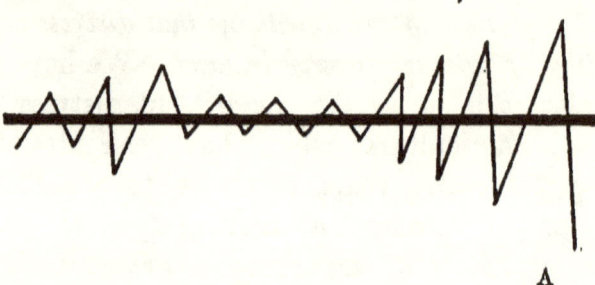

The Liberal explanation, showing fluctuations about a normal level. A, The present depression? to be followed by an equal rise.

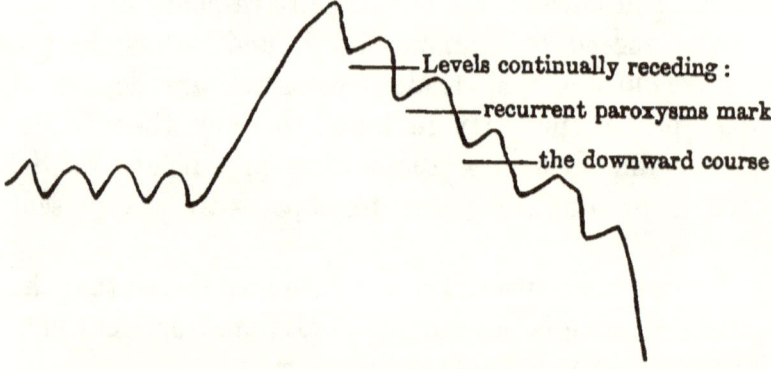

The true explanation of the progress and depression of our trade, as resulting from the action of the free-trade principle. The problem is enunciated thus: recurrent paroxysms in trade-depression are dependent on private property in land.

The relation between recurrent paroxysms in trade and private property in land, that has been thought sufficient to establish the truth of the above generalisation, is easily seen, for these phenomena have but one property in common, and that is periodicity. But the nature of their periodicity is very different; for while the one tends to increase in a *regular* manner, *the result of a law*, with the increased productivity of the soil where this is possible, the other happens *irregularly*, is due to the combined action of a few individuals, and is of such a character that it cannot be predicted by all, while increased rent under favourable conditions is a well-known phenomenon, and is universally expected.

High rent, diminished profits, and small wages, are associated only when enterprise has been unsuccessful, the causes of which may be enumerated under the two heads of—

1. Faults in the individual; and
2. Unequal conditions, permanent or temporary, which surround the conduct of his trade.

With increase in rent, periodically arising from the action of a well-known law, the alterations in surrounding circumstances are *slowly* adjusted to it. This law is the law of competition, and it becomes responsible for the increase in rent, when the occupation of land becomes more profitable; for thus the advantages of the owner are recognised, while the interests of the present tenant are maintained, in opposition to those who would compete against him, did the rent remain fixed, and increase the rent of themselves, in the hopes of greater profits accruing. Nor does this increase in rent take place equally throughout all the town or country, but only when position is accidentally favourable to success or the soil to a higher produce.

In the slow adjustment of mutual relations to a change in any one of the related factors, how can increased rent affect suddenly the prosperity of a trade? For the increase in rent is not limited to any one particular branch of industry, with the exception of agriculture; and we have seen how variation in rent is insufficient to explain the present decline in it; but is spread over many, any one of which cannot become so seriously affected, if affected for the worse at all, as to lead to depression—the supposed cause of depression, increased rent, being not sufficiently concentrated to produce any perceptibly large effect. Besides, an increase in rent operates over a length of time; for there must be the evidence of experience that it will not act adversely to the interests of the tenant. When this results, the property, now no longer profitable in his hands, and perhaps because all its resources are not explored, is quitted for one of a lower rent. Compare the results of increased rent following the law of competition with what occurs in trade-depressions. These are nothing, if they are not sudden; and it is well to remark the accurate observation that has been made of their paroxysmal character, even though their cause has been wrongly deduced.

What is there to account for this suddenness or paroxysm, but the influence of speculation, the combined action of a few men to create a rise or fall in the markets? For the prosperity of a trade depends on the steadiness of the markets, and when these fall suddenly, as by a panic, the result of an adverse information, the labour concerned in them becomes reduced, and thus wages suffer, and depression reigns. But the cause of the depression being temporary, the limited distress is removed by a rise in the markets.

Thus a paroxysmal depression, generally speaking, excepting those instances where the conditions are favourable to universal speculation, is concentrated upon one branch of industry, and according to its relative importance, will affect collaterally, and in different degrees, these other branches which are nearest related to it. But while recurrent or paroxysmal depressions bring about successive rises and falls in the markets, it must be observed that the tendency of rent is steadily to increase up to a certain point, when it begins to descend.

Paroxysms in trade and increased rent are both periodical; but it is shown above that the former results from the operation of the law of speculation—the latter is due directly to the law of competition, which is significant of progress, when equally effected. But the law of speculation enters into the land question, and obviously occupies but a minor position in it, when the small amount of land, the object of speculation, is referred to the whole.

For speculation in land is limited to those parts of the town which are extending, and which, having advantages not present in others, become the means of promoting anticipation and foresight, or a plot of land may be purchased with a view to its becoming useful at some future time, or because it may be required in the promotion of some projected enterprise. But it is obvious that the influence of these cannot impress the value, to any perceptible degree, of the large amount of town and country property which pays a certain, and, under favourable circumstances, an increasing rent.

Hence speculation in land, being of a minor importance, can have no such influence on by far the larger amount of private property generally as would lead to a fluctuation in its rents, and therefore, to a possible depression in trade.

But where does this element of speculation in land, being associated with depression, obviously err? Obviously in mistaking "what is the exception" to be the rule.

And as it is impossible to suppose that a cause which acts slowly and extends through many branches of industry, can have sufficient intensity to create a sudden depression in any one of them, it follows that the necessary relation between private property in land and paroxysms in trade has not been adjusted to cause and effect: both are coexisting effects, but they depend on very different causes.

And thus is demonstrated the insufficiency of the argument that we are to consider private property in land and trade-depressions as cause and effect, simply because they both of them present the common feature of periodicity. As if this slight foundation were strong enough to support so vast a superstructure! But we proceed to trace the erroneous relations which are supposed to confer on these two phenomena the merit of being cause and effect.

The generalisation is immediately dependent for its truth on these two factors:

1. That wages are derived from the produce of labour;
2. That it is the country which makes the town grow.

It is curious to observe that, if taken absolutely and referable to all time, as regards the development and progress of social relations, both these assertions are false, with the exception of that particular period in which they were in operation.

If limited to this period, they are both true; but it is not difficult to see that at such period their mutual relations were extremely simple, and the error of supposing that such simple relations still exist consists in not recognising the progress of a gradual development of complexity in these relations, which before were simple, in the advance of society. It is as much as if the political economist were to state that the present system is disadvantageous to the interests of the community, and that *in his opinion* the proper relations which ought to exist, but which do not really, are those simple ones which obtained in a past period of our civilisation. It seems to be an instance where the imagination opposes itself to actual fact, of discussing the nature of *what ought to be*, and of not referring to what *actually* is.

The scheme on the next page serves to display distinctly and clearly the changes in the transition from a simple to a complex relation between labour and wages.

Thus the labourers' wages have been driven to capital as their certain source; to meet the requirements of that increase of change which has slowly developed since wages were paid out of labour, and which now has reached so great a height, that labourers have been successful in their endeavours to remove even the slight disability under which certain branches of industry were burdened till quite recently, of being paid partly in kind.

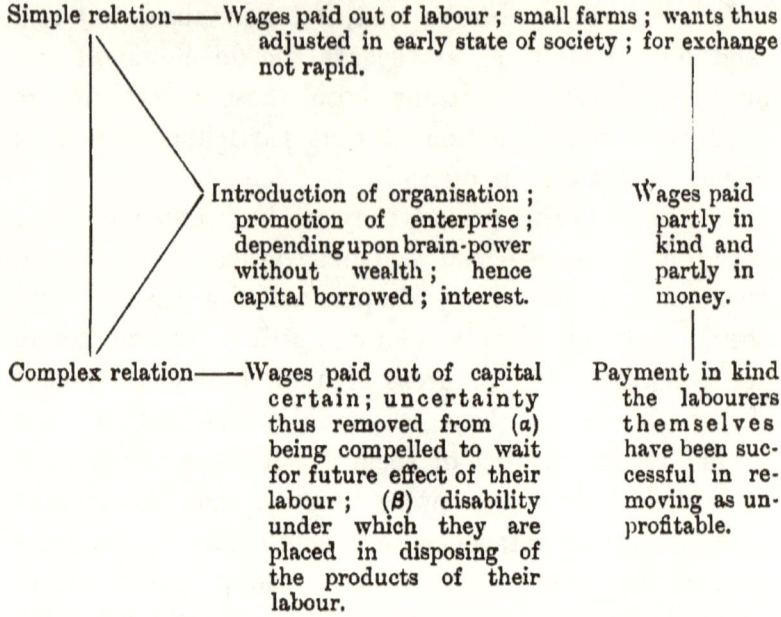

To assert, therefore, that wages are derived from labour's produce is to assume; and the assumption is thus proved to be a false one, and based upon the error of supposing that what has been, always will be.

It is needless to refer to the second assumption that the town depends upon the country for its growth. Of course, in the early phase of the development of the town, it is entirely dependent upon the surrounding country for its supplies, and remains so, till the railways or other means of facilitating transition appear to compete with foreign produce. And this competition commences when the supplies of the country, which is fixed, are unequal to the demand of the town, whose power of extension is practically unlimited. But when the town has reached so large a dimension that all the supplies of the country are too small to satisfy its requirements, and when the produce of a whole island is insufficient to supply the inhabitants of one city, can it in sober earnest be advanced that the town depends upon the country for its growth, when nearly all the wheat it consumes is derived from a foreign source? And all of it might. And such being the case, and the fact being recognised of the inability of this country to supply its inhabitants, is it prudent to legislate for the present distress by ignoring our dependency upon foreign supply? Is it not wiser far to strengthen those bonds which unite us to other countries, and to improve our relations with them, that we may hope to enjoy without interruption in the future, as we have enjoyed successfully in the past, the many advantages accruing from the bounty of their soil?

Thus we have shown that the generalisation, "paroxysms in trade-depression are dependent on the nature of private property in land," is inadequate to account for the present distress, and this without referring to the grounds upon which it is based. And, secondly, we have just examined those grounds and discovered them to be false. Is it probable that a generalisation founded on such extraordinary factors is true in itself? Let us see.

The main grievance of a certain school of economists is that rents are too high; that they increase disproportionately, and that remaining high, when profits begin to diminish, and continue in a downward course, they form a source of depression.

Are those statements more than mere expressions of opinion? And do those who make them inquire into the cause of their grievance, and what it was that produced so great a disturbance in natural relationships, the consequences of which they now deplore? Let us compare them with what has happened and is still happening in our own country.

Here it is evident that an adjustment, and a natural one, has taken place between the former rent which was paid for a property and the continually decreasing profits derived from it. Thus, even when the very cause, of which this school boasts as being the prime factor in the causation of all depression, varies, as rents have varied all over this country, whether regarded from a collective or an individual point of view, the effect still remains. The present distress is not touched even by a diminution in rent.

But the maxim of this school is very definite, and there can be no mistaking its meaning. It is that when rents diminish, profits increase. But it may be observed that this statement depends upon an assumption, and that assumption is that the source of profits remains as proliferous as before. An absolute assertion is founded on a fluctuating phenomenon. An assertion is made absolute when it ought to be "conditional." When such a statement is fabricated, it is quite clear that all the conditions affecting it have not been considered; for what is to account for the present condition of things, when, with rents reduced to the lowest pitch, or to nothing at all, the profits are so low that wages cannot be paid, and thus effect the continuance of the distress, commenced by other causes than those associated with rent? It is true that when the conditions are favourable for trade and the cultivation of the soil, that profits increase when rent is diminished, and thus wages are raised. But in what system of economy, political or otherwise, has such a phenomenon appeared? Is it the rule that the laws governing the relations of rent, profits, and wages, are interrupted? Are not these dependent upon man's disposition? And what is this disposition but that of gain?—that desire of gain which has been characterised by a noble and learned writer as a natural law of society. Where is the inequality in the present law of competition which governs the national affairs of our country? Compare the effects of this law of equal competition operating in our own community with those of the partial action of the free-trade principle, producing such inequalities in our international relations. The root of mischief, which has escaped most of our political economists, and which accounts for the curious phenomenon that when rent is reduced even to nothing at all, yet distress will continue, resides in the adverse influence of the free-trade principle. But it is deeply hidden under the barren soil which the Liberals have heaped around it. Nor has the potency of this for evil been properly recognised at the commencement and during the early period of its action, nor its final results deduced and anticipated.

It is to the operation of the free-trade principle that the distress of the present day is mostly due, and it is due to this main consequence of the pernicious principle that it has succeeded, and is still succeeding, in destroying the springs of profit. There are, it is true, some minor influences at work which add to the distress produced by free trade; but it remains alone the chief source. It has the proper qualifications to account for the great distress of the country, for it is constant and adequate to produce the effect.

But against the assumption that private property in land is the cause of the present trade-depression predominant throughout the country, it may be inquired "How a fluctuating cause can have a constant effect?" for while rents have varied with a downward tendency, the distress has continued and increased.

What is the tendency of the generalisation that private property in land is the cause of paroxysmal trade-depression?

There must be some ultimate reason why an author labours, with the help of observations which are inaccurate, facts which are untrue, arguments which are erroneous, and means which are unjust, to establish a generalisation that carries falsehood in its very face. Private property in land is the burden under which a recent economist is suffering; it is, with how much truth! advanced to the chief place as the source of all depression, temporary or continued. Private property in land being thus iniquitous, the present civilisations are warned of a near decay and ruin, unless an assumed ancient system, described arbitrarily as having been general throughout all society, is again practised, of common property in land.

Then, when land is common property, will wealth be more evenly distributed, poverty wiped away from the face of the earth, and all taxation abolished? besides, the source of trade-depressions will be for ever removed!

But the author who exercises his imagination so wildly must first of all be assured of the phenomenon that the nature of man, which has continued nearly the same for more than a thousand years, is going to experience a gigantic reform! It is easy to see that the so-called reforms of such writers only remove some evils by producing others to take their place.

But we must stay to examine into the nature of these assumptions, for they are only assumptions after all! It is asserted by Rousseau and others that men are born equal (it is supposed, so far as political rights are concerned), that land is common property, and that man has natural rights. But it is hardly necessary, in justice to the wisdom and judgment of our early ancestors, and to their mental equilibrium, to deny that these statements have no historical basis whatsoever; that they are opinions merely, which struggle to rise to the heights of truth, and that they can easily be run to earth in the powerful imagination of a disordered mind.

For what does Cæsar tell us of the early social relations of the Germanic tribes, from whom we are in large part descended, and Tacitus after him? The Nobiles, the Ingenui, the Servi correspond with the levels of society of the present day; and that that inequality was recognised among the early Germans as being in the nature of things is proved in a passage from Cæsar, where it is stated that the land was not equally divided, but that partition was proportioned to rank in society. And in another passage it is asserted that those who laboured most, acquired more land to till. And further, that there was a tendency to intemperance, which is strongly remarked by Tacitus, who says that idleness led to their intemperate and slothful habits. What the relations between land and tiller were in a later phase of society, when the wandering tribes finally became settled, it is impossible to say, for there are no data. And as the stable growth of the elements of society depends entirely upon antecedent facts, and not upon the visionary ideas of enthusiasts, whose opinions must be regarded as assumption till they are proved to be true, we leave the wild ocean of hypothesis to troubled and restless minds, and concern ourselves with the circumscribed area of historic truth.

And this is certain, that when the several kingdoms into which this island was divided, by reason of the influx of German tribes into different parts, were amalgamated into one, that no grant of land was made without the consent of the Witenagemot. And as this was the only representative assembly of these early times (representative *then*, but not considered to be so now, to serve the purpose of tracing the representative assembly of the people), it follows that such grants were made with the full consent of the people. For if there were any objections to such grants, some one, or a few of them, must have found an entry into the early chronicles which note the events of those times.

But what reason is there that land should become common property? on what ground is the assumption based?

Upon the assertion that the present distribution of wealth is adverse to the progress of civilisation, and upon the *assumed* fact that poverty is increasing, not relatively merely but absolutely.

Does not the present distribution of wealth act as a check to the accumulation of still larger fortunes and estates? And when, suppose, the allotment system becomes general (may the wisdom of our country avert it!), how are such checks diminished, to the detriment of the country? Will there not then be far larger accumulations of wealth than any we know of at present, and what will be the tendencies of such further increase?—dependence, enervation, and degradation of the intellect. For all these inequalities in social levels, which characterise our present system, are there for a good purpose. They supply talent with spurs, and stimulate the lazy genius to pursue the arduous path to the goal of his ambition!

This is the grand opening which our system of society presents to all, no matter how low his birth may be! It is the opportunity presented for the use of genius. And without genius in all its degrees, what would become of civilisation? Must not genius, therefore, have its proper cradle?

It is the intention of such reforms as those of making land common property, and of introducing allotment systems, to diminish the evils which form the subject of some pathos to a few who appear to derive a personal satisfaction in their consummation.

They are legislating for the happiness of the people. The end is the object of their legislation; but the means to that end, the adjustment of relations, are ignored, because either they know not how to avoid them, or else they are without their grasp. And it is strange that with the goodness of their intentions they should pursue the very means which will lead to results exactly opposite to those that are expected of them.

But the influence of sentimentalism is at work, and philanthropy, when justice ought to guide, diverts their endeavours into a dangerous channel. For their feelings become engaged in the solution of a problem which demands that it shall be based upon rational grounds, and conducted by rational arguments. Hence the source of error which is resident within themselves; and how freely can errors and prejudice distort a fact and turn an argument!

It is to such sources as these to which certain politicians refer when they are discoursing on the extraordinary advantages to be derived from the practice of their hypotheses. A blind support is afforded to those who have not yet learnt to reason without feeling, and remove every source of those prejudices and errors which the latter engenders. For when pathos is expressed in every page, and a false sympathy with poverty guides our conclusions, how can we reach the truth? But Rousseau knew so little of his own mind that he failed to lead the prosperous career which was open to him; but preferred, in accordance with a personal object which he did not control, to exhibit that spirit of antagonism which wrecked his life. How then can a man who knew not how to be happy himself be the source of conveying the means of happiness to others!

Such measures may be discussed, such sympathies aroused, and the attention diverted by the apparent injustice of what are strictly exceptional instances. But with all this designed interference, with all the feelings which may be called forth at the picture of a falling race, if the cause of that decline be a false one, if it is true that our society can continue with trade in a flourishing condition, then neither the means to the happiness nor the welfare of the people will be promoted so long as the operation of a pernicious principle—the real cause of distress—remains at work.

Can anything be more clear than that the main source of the present distress is due to the disabilities under which trade in all its branches is carried on? But there are other minor sources to add to the general distress, and one of these we have mentioned already—the paralysis of enterprise following the state of insecurity engendered by a late proposed legislation. And this is found in the want of confidence and loss of reputation our country underwent during the disastrous foreign policy of a Liberal Administration. The Liberals found it necessary to reform our foreign policy as regards our relation with Egypt and the scientific frontier of India which had been proposed (and its want how truly predicted!) by a late illustrious statesman. What followed this interruption in the natural progress of events? An inglorious campaign in the Soudan and the affair on the Indian frontier.

And how were the Liberal anticipations fulfilled after the commencement of their error? The railway to Quetta had to be reconstructed, and the evacuation of the Soudan accomplished. And how was this effected? At the cost of a hero, who undertook, at a critical juncture, to relieve them from their embarrassment. And so General Gordon set out for Khartoum. What measures were taken for his immediate relief, and to protect those of the native inhabitants who had placed themselves under his care? And did he break that solemn trust? But it was destined that the Liberals should pursue the shadow of events; and when Khartoum was reached, General Gordon was *dead!* So fatal an error was immediately resented by an angry populace, and the national sentiment of justice and right expressed its disgust at this last mistake of the Liberal party. And when the history of those inglorious times comes to be written, the historian will pause at the death of Gordon, and think awhile of a patriot who, in the discharge of his duties to his country and to a Government which ignored his distress, as they ignore still the general distress of the people—of an Englishman who suffered, as he must have suffered cheerfully and contentedly, all the horrors of an approaching starvation!—but no: he proceeds to analyse the Epimethean policy which led to his death. But not even injustice can interrupt the course of a noble and a well-ordered mind. Gordon preferred death in the faithful discharge of his duties to an inglorious escape. And the result of this disastrous foreign policy, in depressing still further our already burdened trade by weakening our relations with surrounding nations, and in the increased expenditure of the country? The result of the reform in Egyptian policy cost this country close upon a hundred millions; the termination of the experiment on the Indian frontier concluded by a vote of credit for fifteen millions. And these lavish and unnecessary proceedings were directly brought about by a party whose motto is Peace, Retrenchment, and Reform! If, therefore, such extraordinary results appear from such apparently simple reforms in foreign policy, what is the probability that the reform in the land will be equally unsuccessful? The Liberals interrupted, or reformed, as they call it, the equable progress of our trade. What results? The present distress.

The Liberals interrupted our peaceful foreign policy. What results? A costly war, with an increased expenditure under an economic (!) Liberal Government.

And now the Liberals, or Radicals, propose to interrupt our relations respecting the ownership of the soil in this country? Is the result of this interruption at all likely to accrue to the wellbeing of the nation? Is not the reference to *interruption* enough to make us shun the very name?

And how has the increased expenditure of the country been borne? By raising the income-tax.

It appears ridiculous, yet is quite true, that the very statesman who proposed the abolition of the income-tax within no distant time, is the one to resort to an increase of it, to meet an increased expenditure which he had not foreseen!

A costly and inglorious campaign, and nothing gained, during a period of distress, which has now marked the results of the downward progress of our trade during many years! How can the increased income-tax be received by an indignant people under the present so unfavourable conditions of distress?

Yet the Liberal party had the confidence of the country, and the country pays for the popularity of the party! It cannot be conceived, seeing the nature of the present general distress, directly dependent as it is on the pernicious action of the Liberal economic principle, intensified by their disastrous foreign policy and aggravated by their projected land reforms, and with a people placed under the unexpected burden of a higher income-tax than is known to our experience, discontented at the unequal competition which surrounds their various trades—it cannot for a moment be supposed that a thoughtful man can continue his confidence in a party which has been at once reckless, extravagant, and weak. And it remains to see whether the people, departing from the ways of their fathers, will be captivated by promises which are as unjustly made as they are unfairly founded!

But if the country, recognising the ability and success of the Tory leaders, continue them in office, then will the Tory party develop its old quality of being the true reformer of the nation, by removing that evil which bears so unequally upon all, while it strikes at the independency and injures the interests of none!

And the Tory party will gain the thanks of the nation, after our trade has once again reached that condition of prosperity which marked its progress before the fatal application of free trade!

Thus have we proved the hollowness of those schemes which are adduced to prevent an anticipated decline in our civilisation—schemes that are characterised more by their extravagance than their novelty; original sometimes, as in the case of the peasant proprietor, but more often obtained at second-hand—the working of which is doubtfully confused, and the success thereof more than obscure.

THE END.

www.ingramcontent.com/pod-product-compliance
Lightning Source LLC
Chambersburg PA
CBHW032353230426
43672CB00007B/689